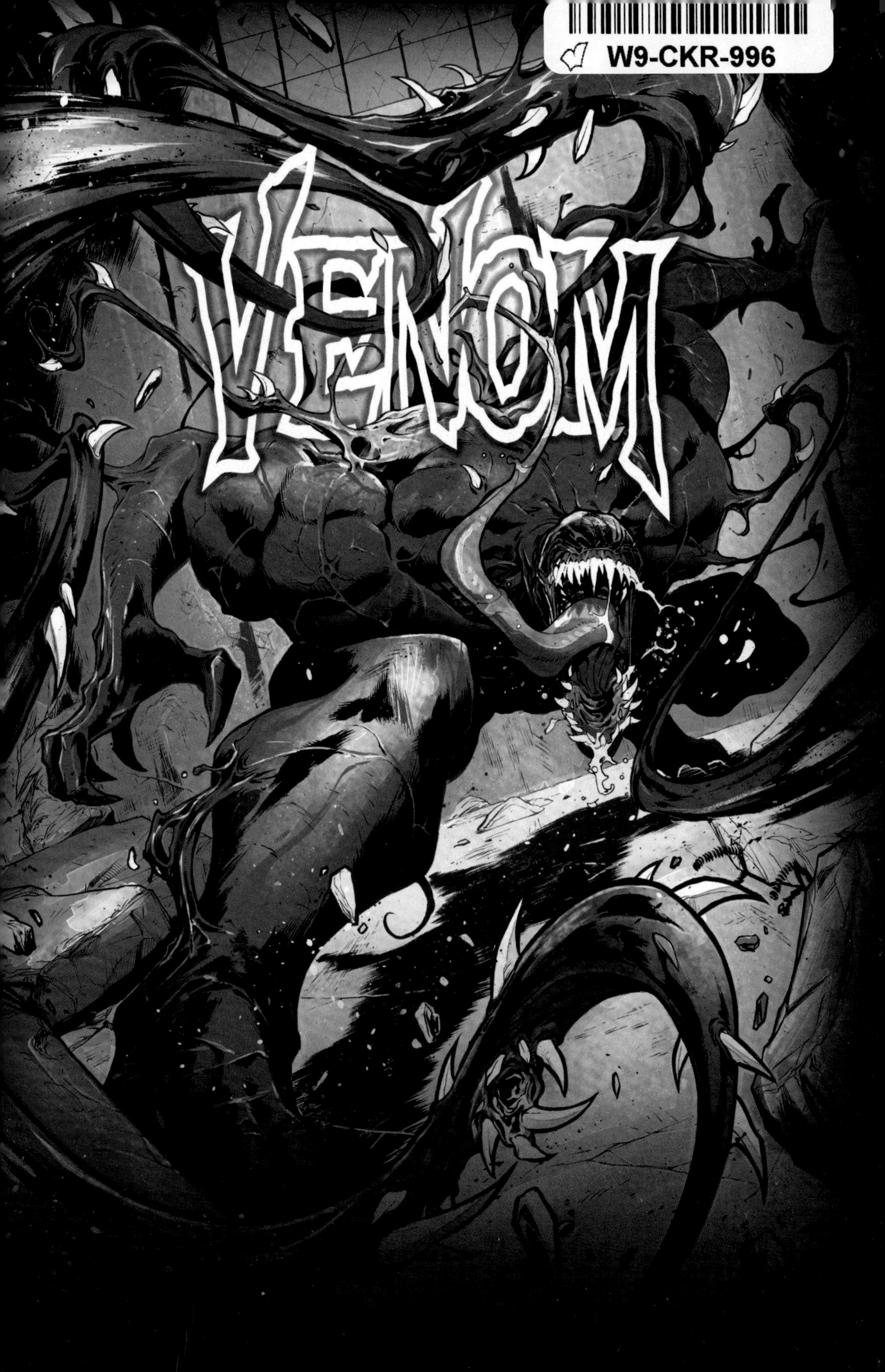
VENOM

THE ABYSS

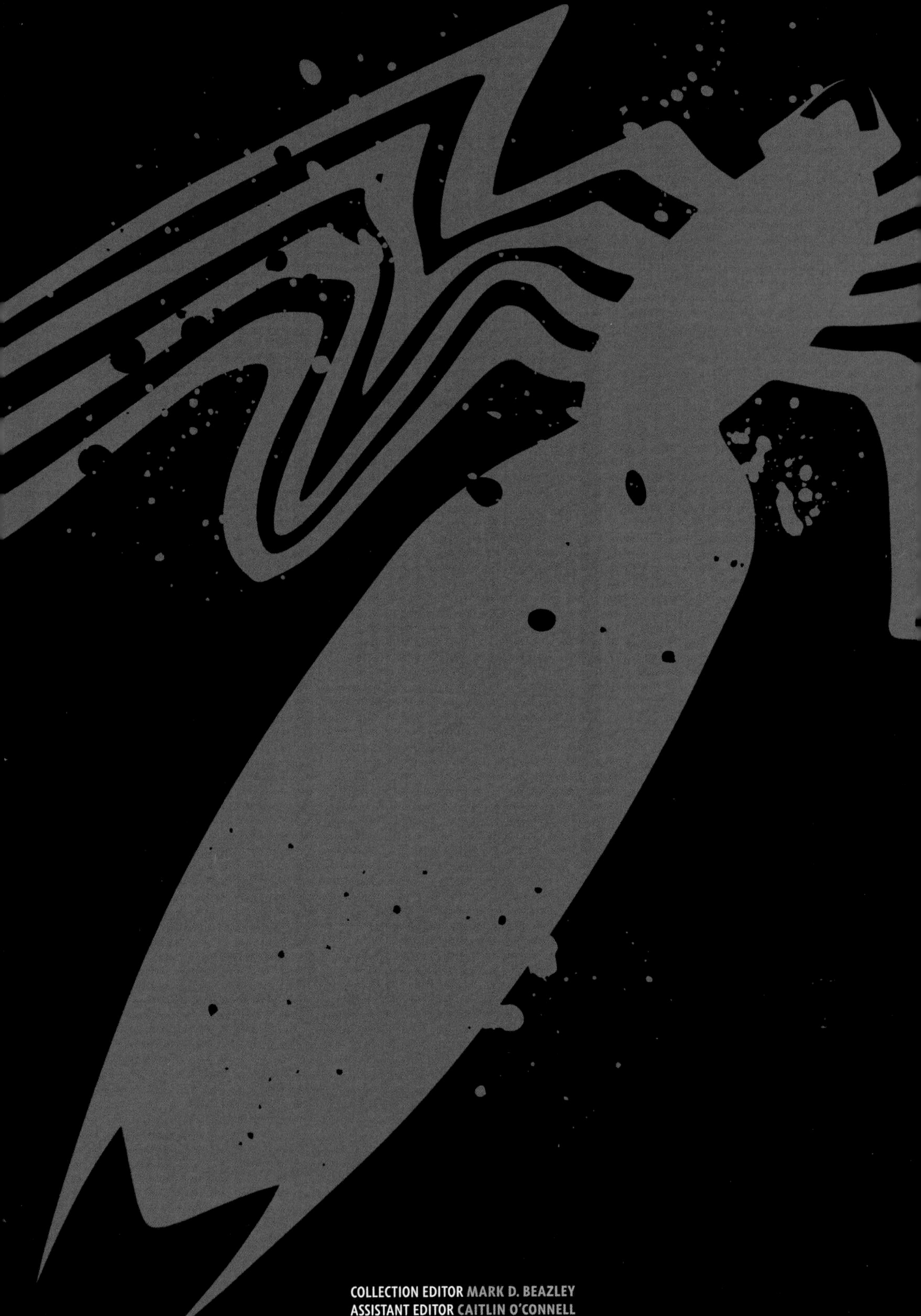

COLLECTION EDITOR MARK D. BEAZLEY
ASSISTANT EDITOR CAITLIN O'CONNELL
ASSOCIATE MANAGING EDITOR KATERI WOODY
SENIOR EDITOR, SPECIAL PROJECTS JENNIFER GRÜNWALD
VP PRODUCTION & SPECIAL PROJECTS JEFF YOUNGQUIST
SVP PRINT, SALES & MARKETING DAVID GABRIEL
BOOK DESIGNER JAY BOWEN WITH STACIE ZUCKER

EDITOR IN CHIEF C.B. CEBULSKI
CHIEF CREATIVE OFFICER JOE QUESADA

YEARS AGO, THE AMAZING SPIDER-MAN ACCIDENTALLY BONDED WITH A UNIQUE ALIEN ORGANISM CALLED A SYMBIOTE. AFTER REALIZING THE COSTUME WAS READING HIS MIND AND TRYING TO MAKE THEIR UNION PERMANENT, SPIDER-MAN REJECTED IT. BETRAYED AND LEFT FOR DEAD, THE SYMBIOTE FOUND A WILLING HOST IN EDDIE BROCK, A REPORTER WHOSE LIFE SPIDER-MAN HAD ALSO RUINED. BROCK WELCOMED THE SYMBIOTE AND THE TWO WERE JOINED, SWEARING VENGEANCE ON SPIDER-MAN AND BECOMING THE SINGULAR ENTITY CALLED...

VENOM

THE ABYSS

WRITER
DONNY CATES

IBAN **COELLO** (#7-8)
RYAN **STEGMAN** (#9-11)
JOSHUA **CASSARA** (#11-12)

PENCILERS

INKERS

IBAN **COELLO** (#7-8)
JP **MAYER** (#9-11)
JOSHUA **CASSARA** (#11-12)

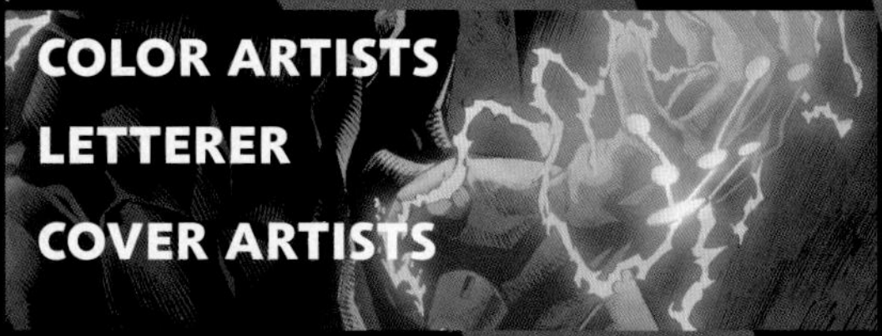

ANDRES **MOSSA** (#7-8) & FRANK **MARTIN** (#9-12)

COLOR ARTISTS

VC's **CLAYTON COWLES**

LETTERER

RYAN **STEGMAN**, JP **MAYER** & FRANK **MARTIN** (#7, 10-11);
RYAN **STEGMAN**, JP **MAYER** & EDGAR **DELGADO** (#8-9)

COVER ARTISTS

ASSISTANT EDITORS
LAUREN **AMARO** & DANNY **KHAZEM**

EDITOR
DEVIN **LEWIS**

EXECUTIVE EDITOR
NICK **LOWE**

VENOM BY DONNY CATES VOL. 2: THE ABYSS. Contains material originally published in magazine form as VENOM #7-12. First printing 2019. ISBN 978-1-302-91307-6. Published by MARVEL WORLDWIDE, INC., a subsidiary of MARVEL ENTERTAINMENT, LLC. OFFICE OF PUBLICATION: 135 West 50th Street, New York, NY 10020. © 2019 MARVEL No similarity between any of the names, characters, persons, and/or institutions in this magazine with those of any living or dead person or institution is intended, and any such similarity which may exist is purely coincidental. **Printed in Canada.** DAN BUCKLEY, President, Marvel Entertainment; JOHN NEE, Publisher; JOE QUESADA, Chief Creative Officer; TOM BREVOORT, SVP of Publishing; DAVID BOGART, Associate Publisher & SVP of Talent Affairs; DAVID GABRIEL, SVP of Sales & Marketing, Publishing; JEFF YOUNGQUIST, VP of Production & Special Projects; DAN CARR, Executive Director of Publishing Technology; ALEX MORALES, Director of Publishing Operations; DAN EDINGTON, Managing Editor; SUSAN CRESPI, Production Manager; STAN LEE, Chairman Emeritus. For information regarding advertising in Marvel Comics or on Marvel.com, please contact Vit DeBellis, Custom Solutions & Integrated Advertising Manager, at vdebellis@marvel.com. For Marvel subscription inquiries, please call 888-511-5480. **Manufactured between 3/1/2019 and 4/2/2019 by SOLISCO PRINTERS, SCOTT, QC, CANADA.**

10 9 8 7 6 5 4 3 2 1

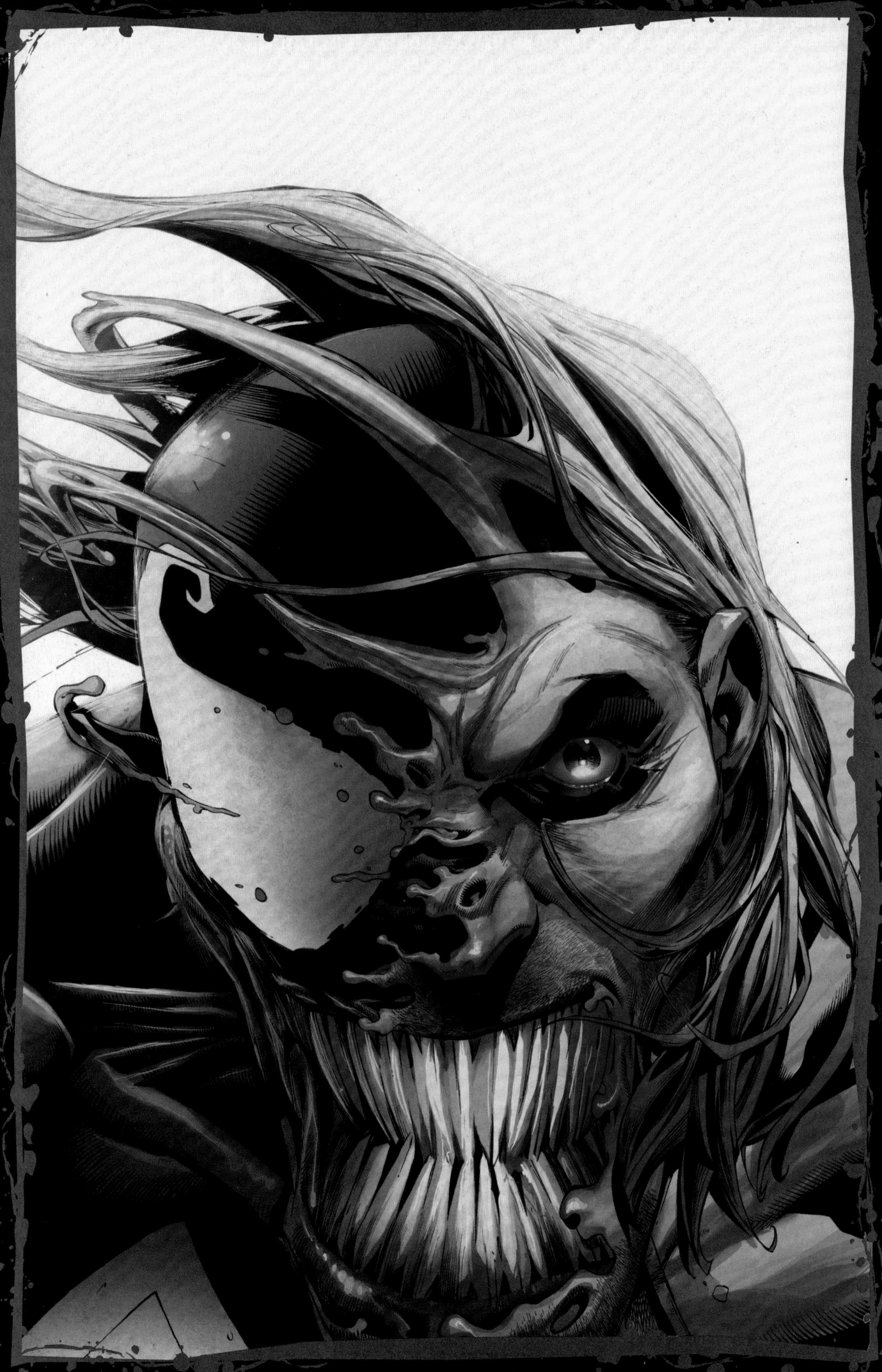

7

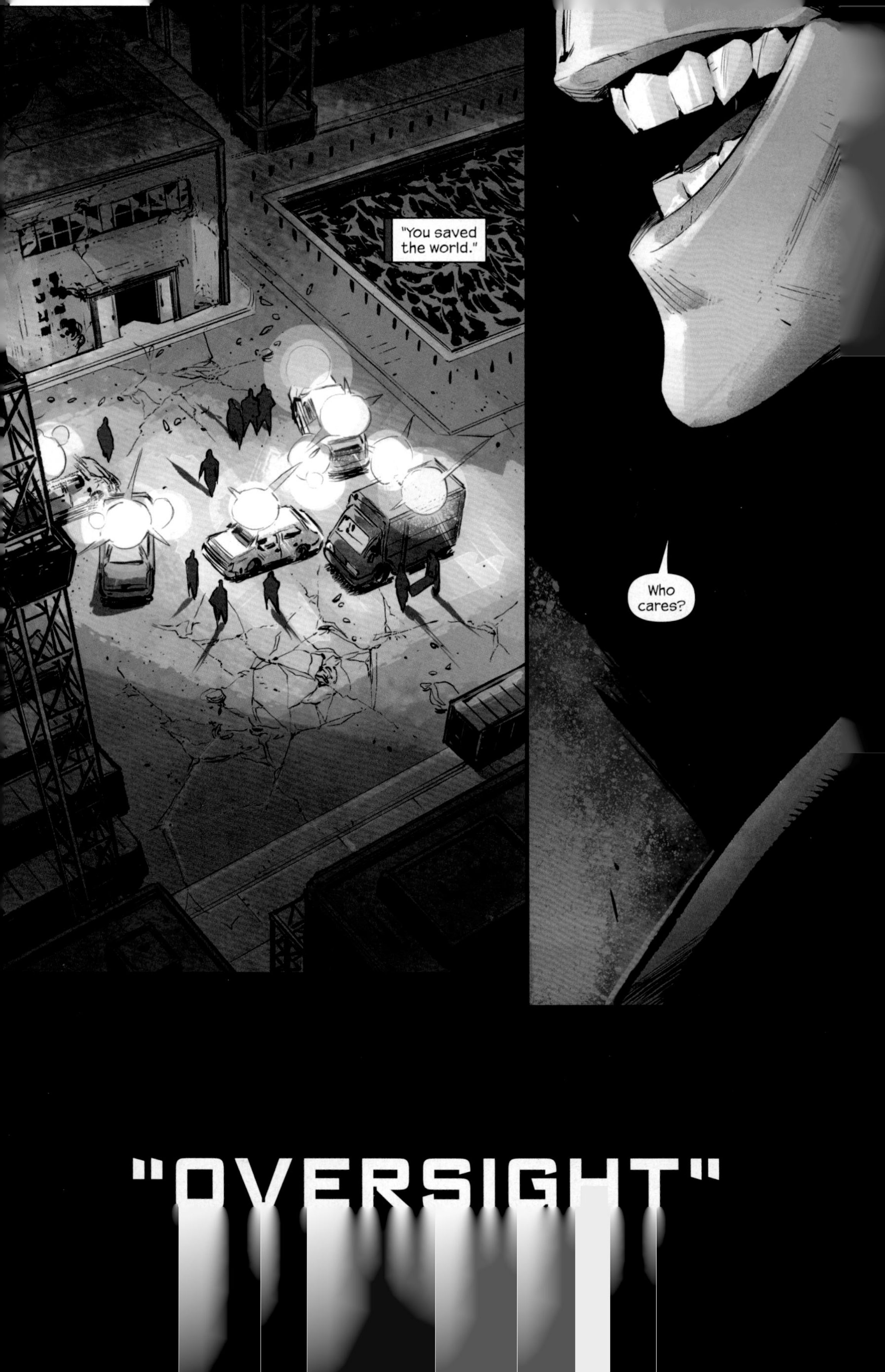
"You saved the world."
Who cares?

"OVERSIGHT"

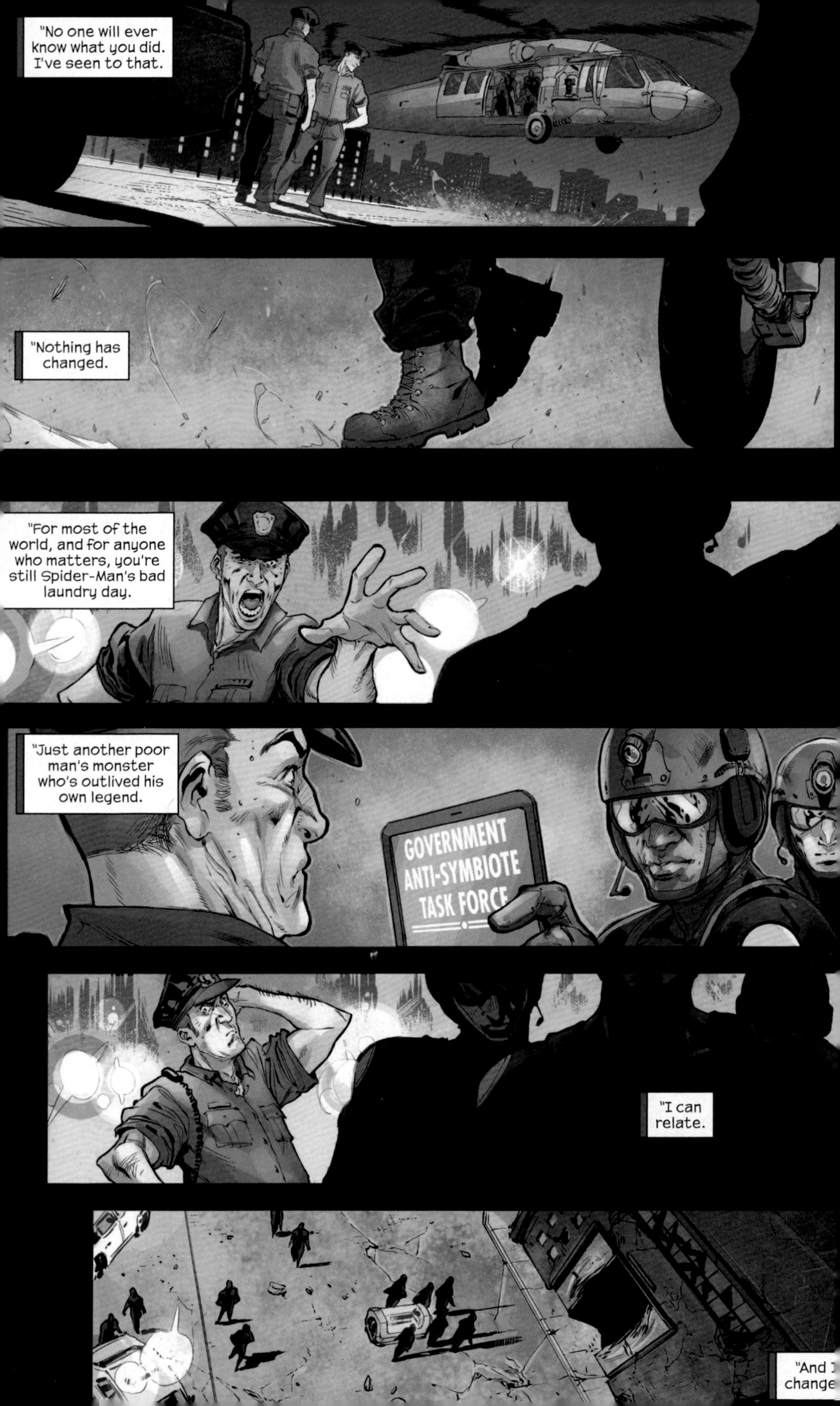
"No one will ever know what you did. I've seen to that.
"Nothing has changed.
"For most of the world, and for anyone who matters, you're still Spider-Man's bad laundry day.
"Just another poor man's monster who's outlived his own legend.
GOVERNMENT ANTI-SYMBIOTE TASK FORCE
"I can relate.
"And I change

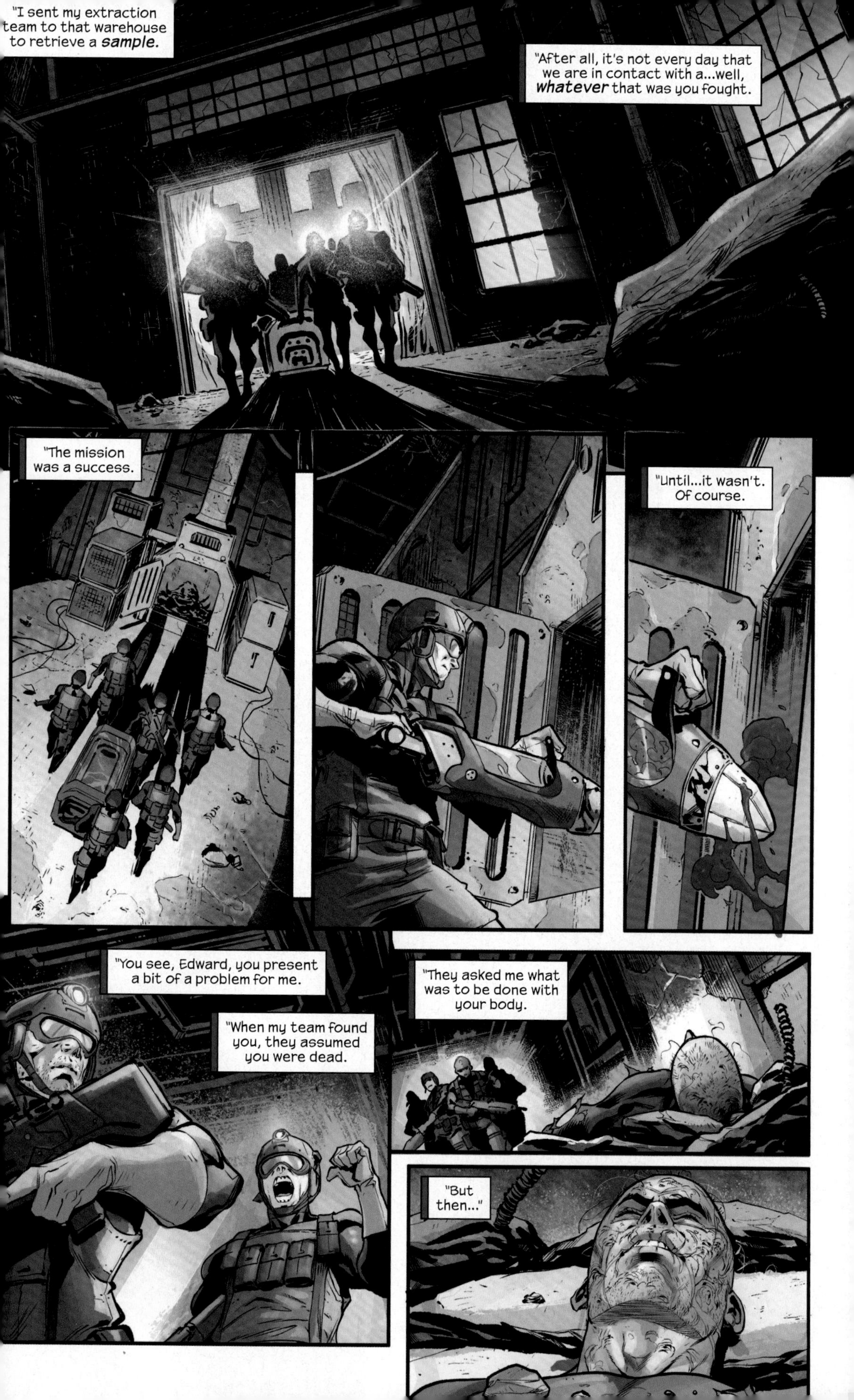
"I sent my extraction team to that warehouse to retrieve a ***sample.***
"After all, it's not every day that we are in contact with a...well, ***whatever*** that was you fought.
"The mission was a success.
"Until...it wasn't. Of course.
"You see, Edward, you present a bit of a problem for me.
"When my team found you, they assumed you were dead.
"They asked me what was to be done with your body.
"But then..."

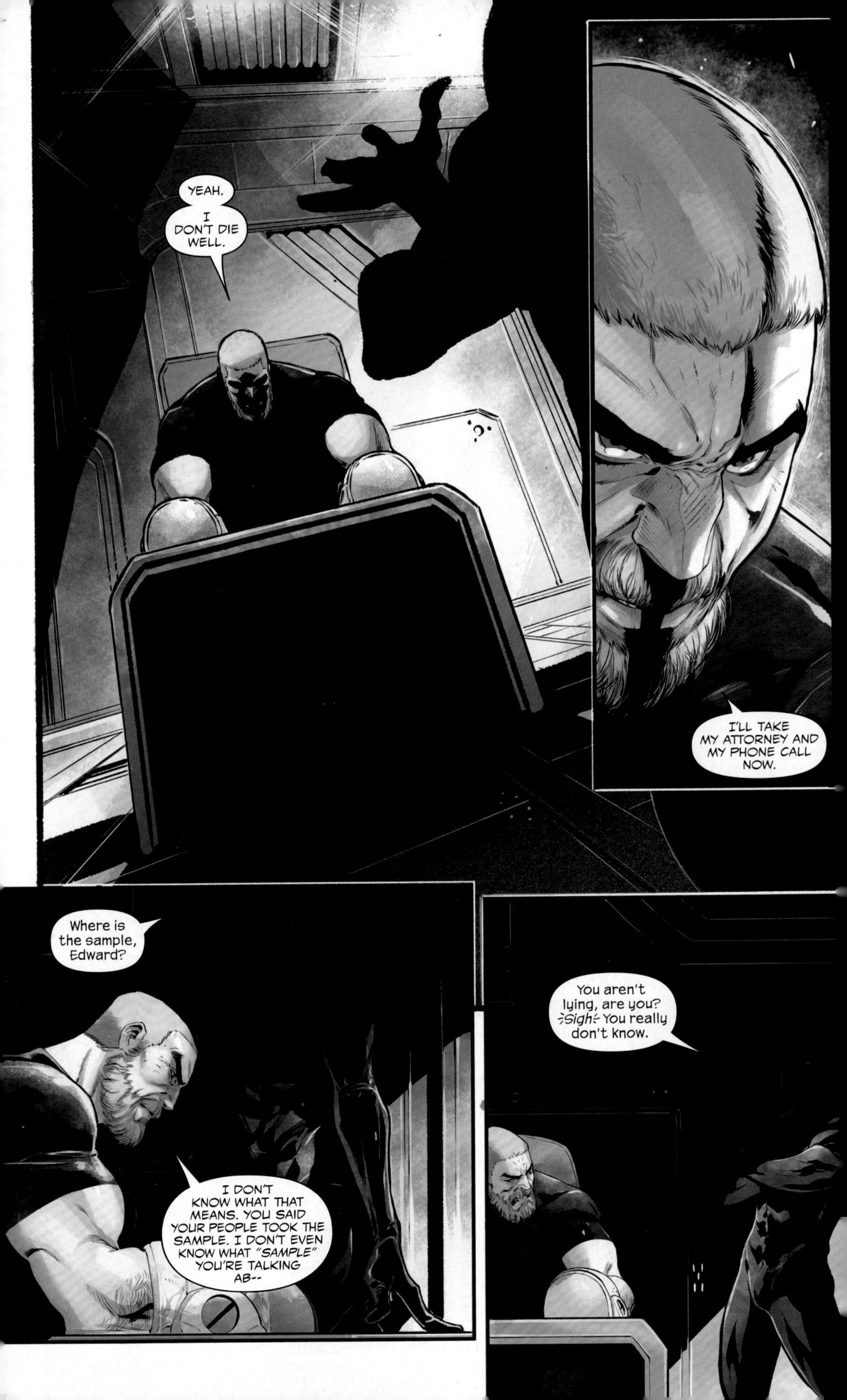
YEAH.
I DON'T DIE WELL.
?
I'LL TAKE MY ATTORNEY AND MY PHONE CALL NOW.
Where is the sample, Edward?
I DON'T KNOW WHAT THAT MEANS. YOU SAID YOUR PEOPLE TOOK THE SAMPLE. I DON'T EVEN KNOW WHAT "SAMPLE" YOU'RE TALKING AB--
You aren't lying, are you? *Sigh* You really don't know.

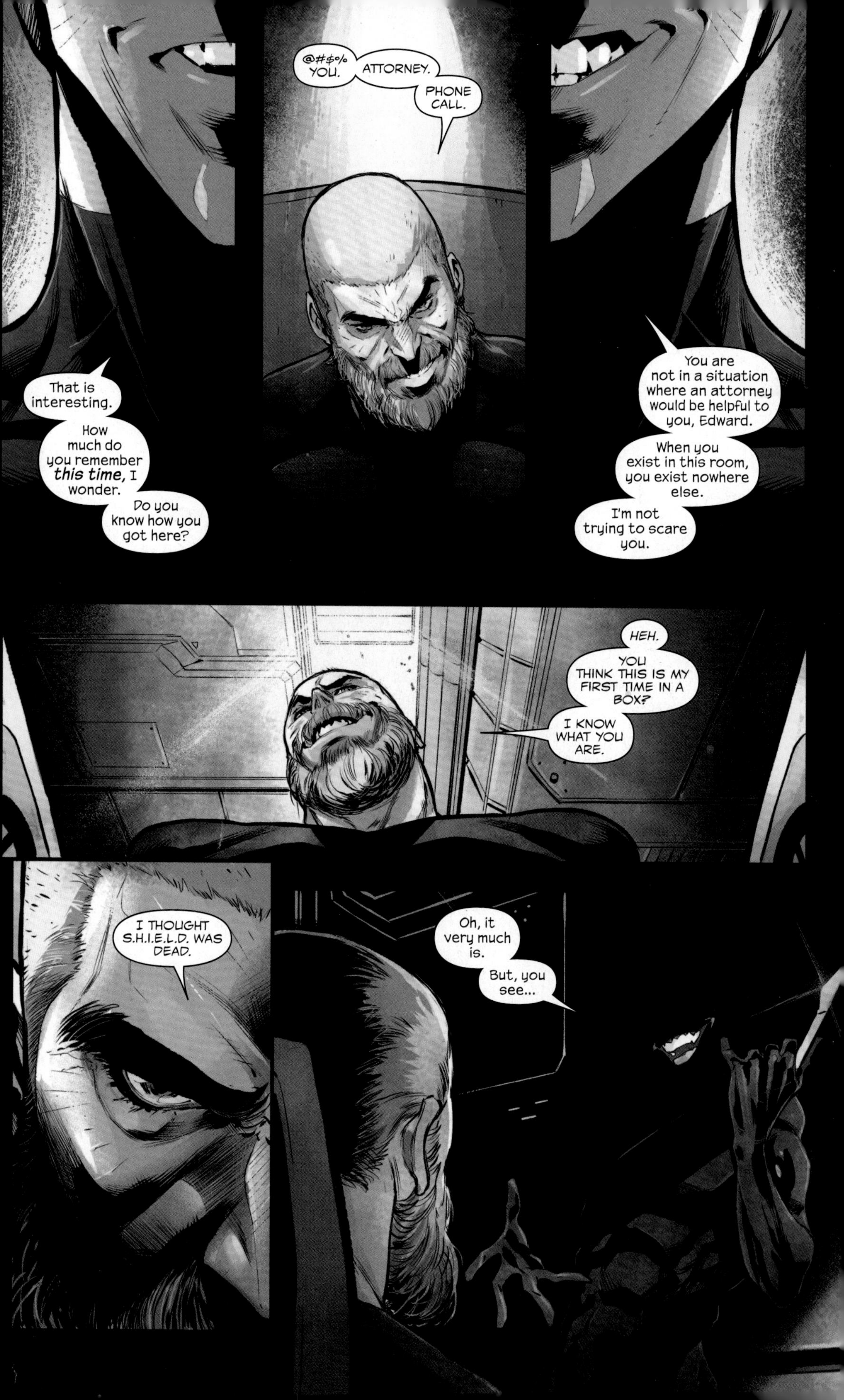

@#$% YOU.
ATTORNEY.
PHONE CALL.
That is interesting.
How much do you remember *this time,* I wonder.
Do you know how you got here?
You are not in a situation where an attorney would be helpful to you, Edward.
When you exist in this room, you exist nowhere else.
I'm not trying to scare you.
HEH.
YOU THINK THIS IS MY FIRST TIME IN A BOX?
I KNOW WHAT YOU ARE.
I THOUGHT S.H.I.E.L.D. WAS DEAD.
Oh, it very much is.
But, you see...

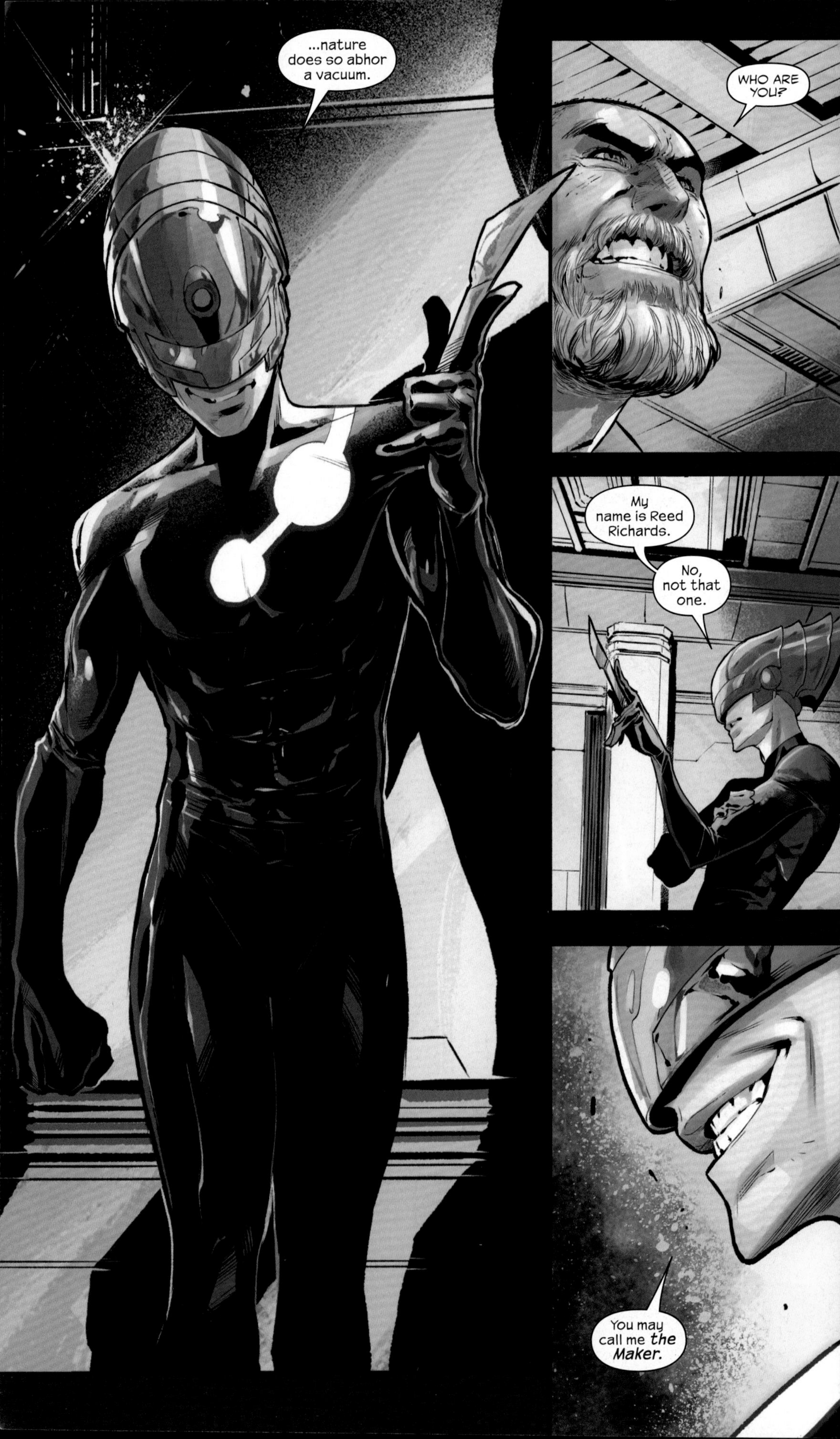
...nature does so abhor a vacuum.
WHO ARE YOU?
My name is Reed Richards.
No, not that one.
You may call me *the Maker.*

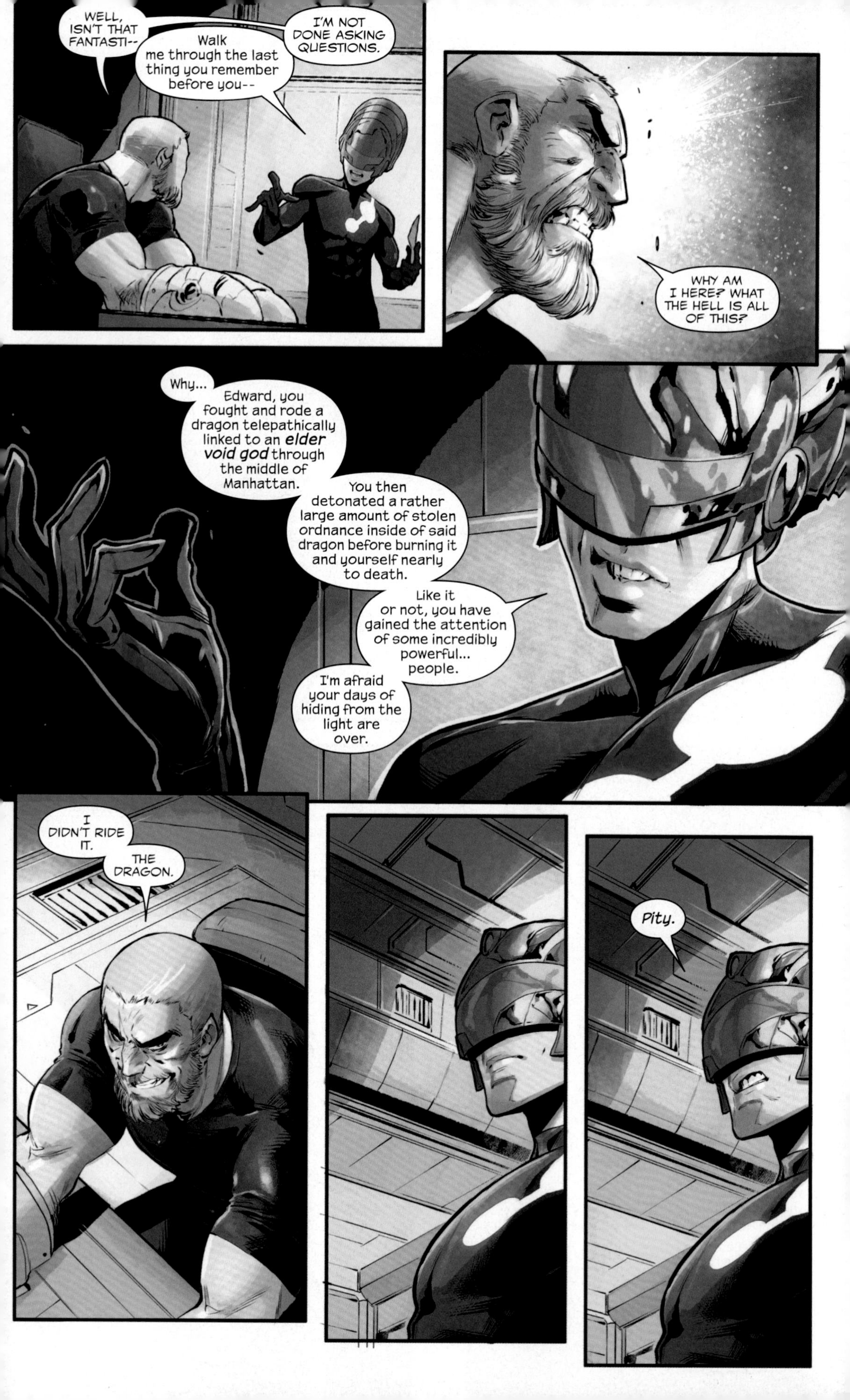
WELL, ISN'T THAT FANTASTI--
I'M NOT DONE ASKING QUESTIONS.
Walk me through the last thing you remember before you--
WHY AM I HERE? WHAT THE HELL IS ALL OF THIS?
Why...
Edward, you fought and rode a dragon telepathically linked to an elder void god through the middle of Manhattan.
You then detonated a rather large amount of stolen ordnance inside of said dragon before burning it and yourself nearly to death.
Like it or not, you have gained the attention of some incredibly powerful... people.
I'm afraid your days of hiding from the light are over.
I DIDN'T RIDE IT.
THE DRAGON.
Pity.

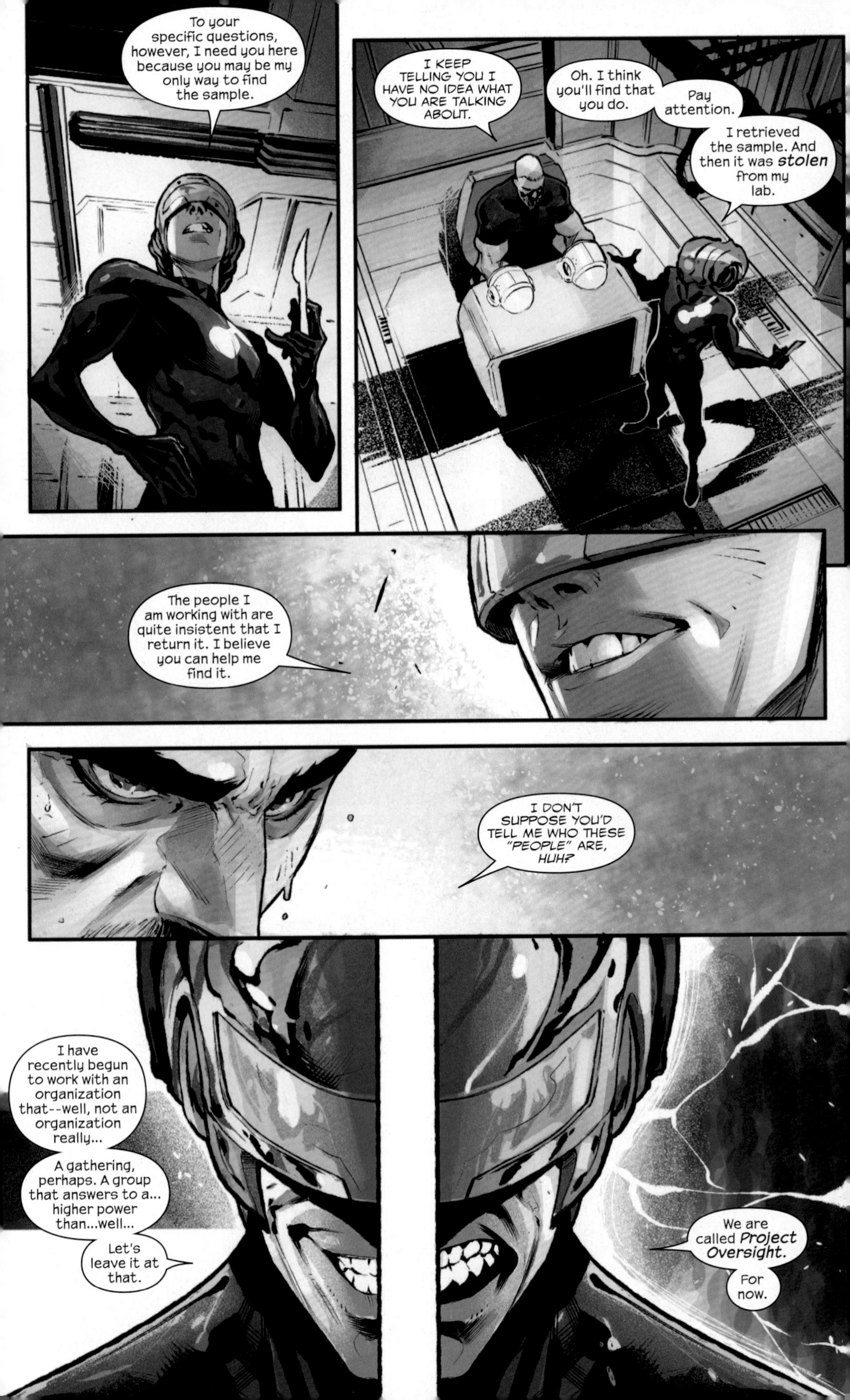
To your specific questions, however, I need you here because you may be my only way to find the sample.
I KEEP TELLING YOU I HAVE NO IDEA WHAT YOU ARE TALKING ABOUT.
Oh. I think you'll find that you do.
Pay attention.
I retrieved the sample. And then it was *stolen* from my lab.
The people I am working with are quite insistent that I return it. I believe you can help me find it.
I DON'T SUPPOSE YOU'D TELL ME WHO THESE "PEOPLE" ARE, *HUH?*
I have recently begun to work with an organization that--well, not an organization really...
A gathering, perhaps. A group that answers to a... higher power than...well...
Let's leave it at that.
We are called *Project Oversight.*
For now.

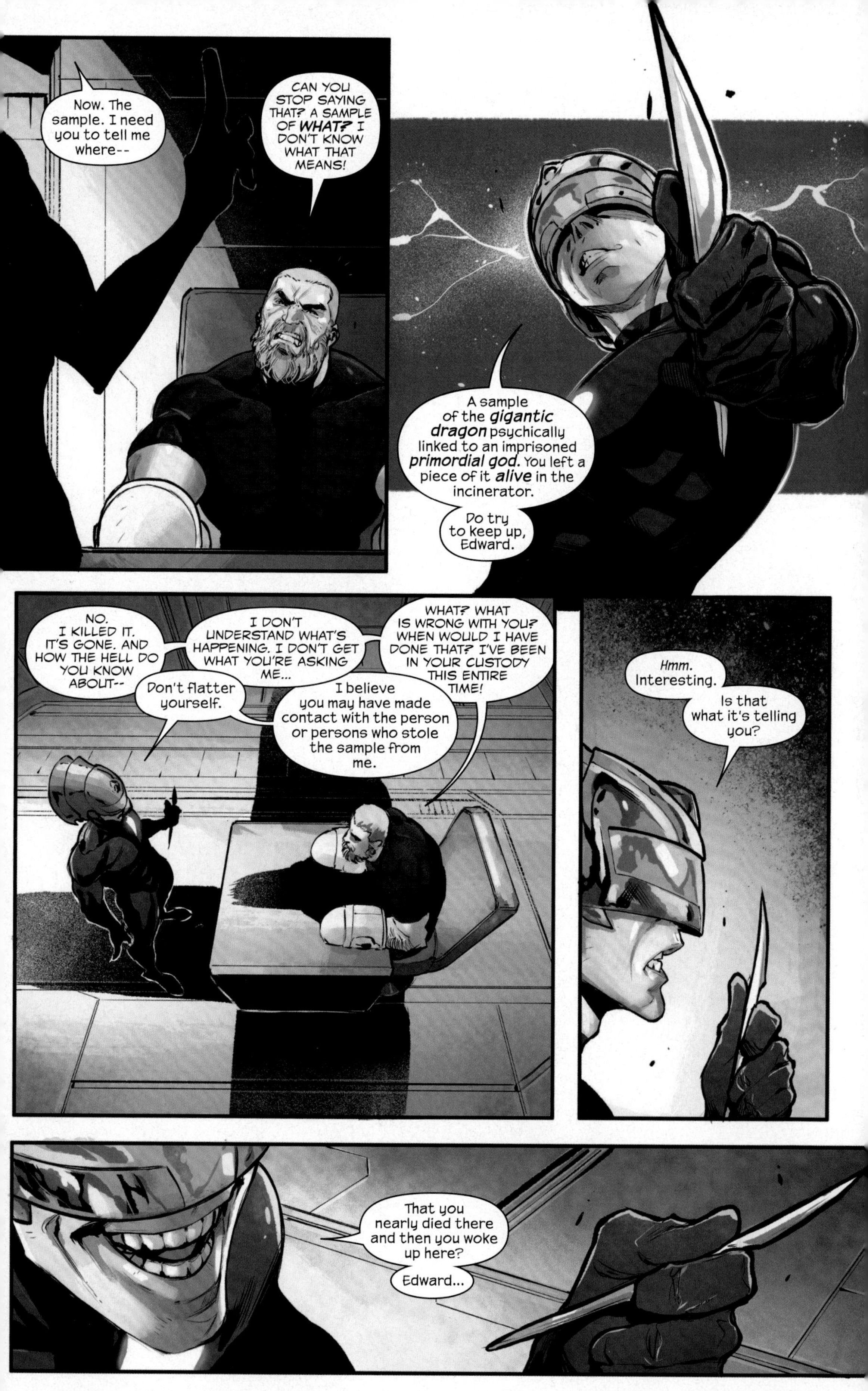
Now. The sample. I need you to tell me where--
CAN YOU STOP SAYING THAT? A SAMPLE OF *WHAT?* I DON'T KNOW WHAT THAT MEANS!
A sample of the ***gigantic dragon*** psychically linked to an imprisoned ***primordial god.*** You left a piece of it ***alive*** in the incinerator.
Do try to keep up, Edward.
NO. I KILLED IT. IT'S GONE. AND HOW THE HELL DO YOU KNOW ABOUT--
Don't flatter yourself.
I DON'T UNDERSTAND WHAT'S HAPPENING. I DON'T GET WHAT YOU'RE ASKING ME...
I believe you may have made contact with the person or persons who stole the sample from me.
WHAT? WHAT IS WRONG WITH YOU? WHEN WOULD I HAVE DONE THAT? I'VE BEEN IN YOUR CUSTODY THIS ENTIRE TIME!
Hmm. Interesting.
Is that what it's telling you?
That you nearly died there and then you woke up here?
Edward...

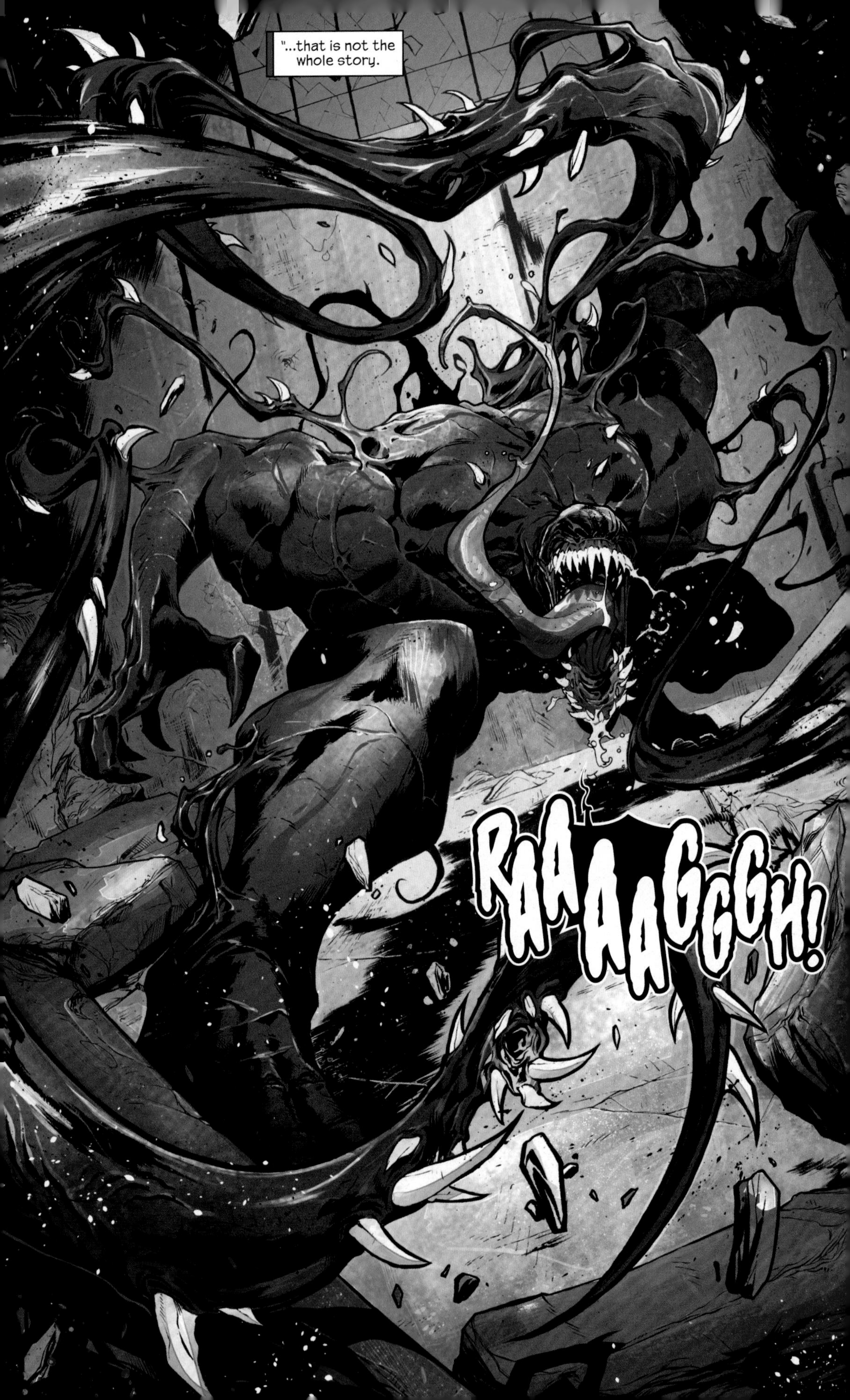
"...that is not the whole story.
RAAAAAGGGH!

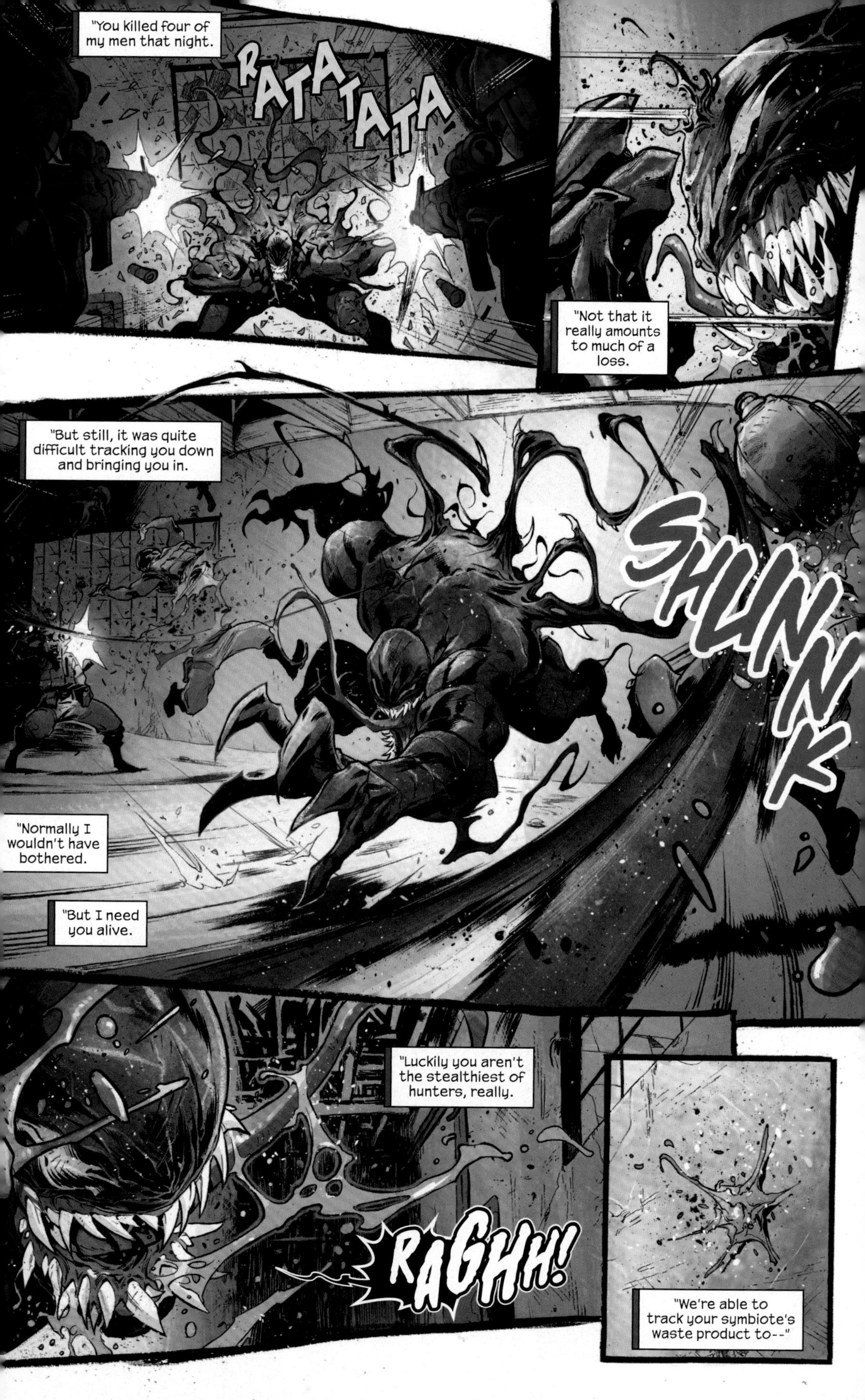
"You killed four of my men that night.
RATATATATA
"Not that it really amounts to much of a loss.
"But still, it was quite difficult tracking you down and bringing you in.
SHUNNNK
"Normally I wouldn't have bothered.
"But I need you alive.
"Luckily you aren't the stealthiest of hunters, really.
RAGHH!
"We're able to track your symbiote's waste product to--"

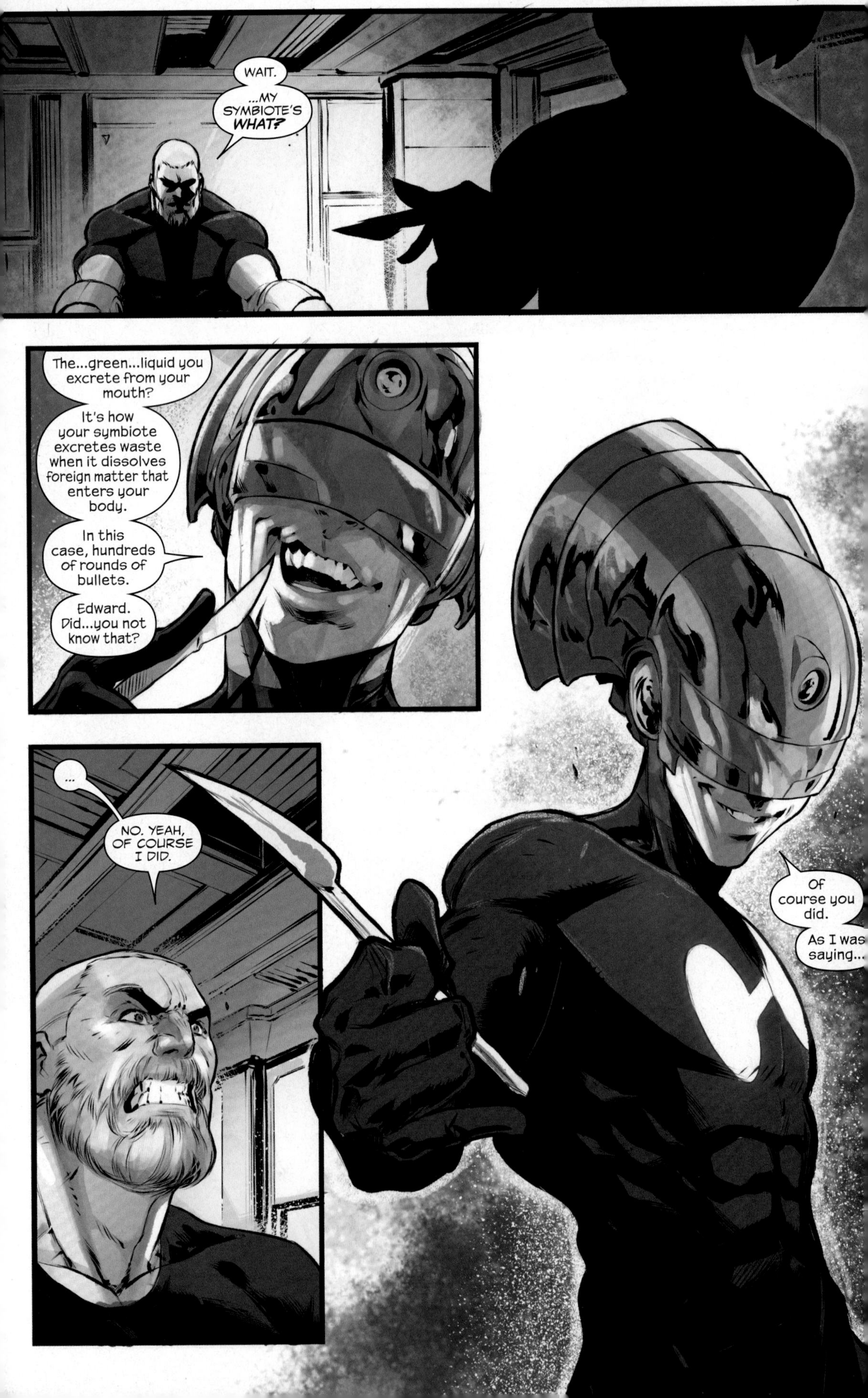
WAIT.
...MY SYMBIOTE'S WHAT?
The...green...liquid you excrete from your mouth?
It's how your symbiote excretes waste when it dissolves foreign matter that enters your body.
In this case, hundreds of rounds of bullets.
Edward. Did...you not know that?
...
NO. YEAH, OF COURSE I DID.
Of course you did.
As I was saying...

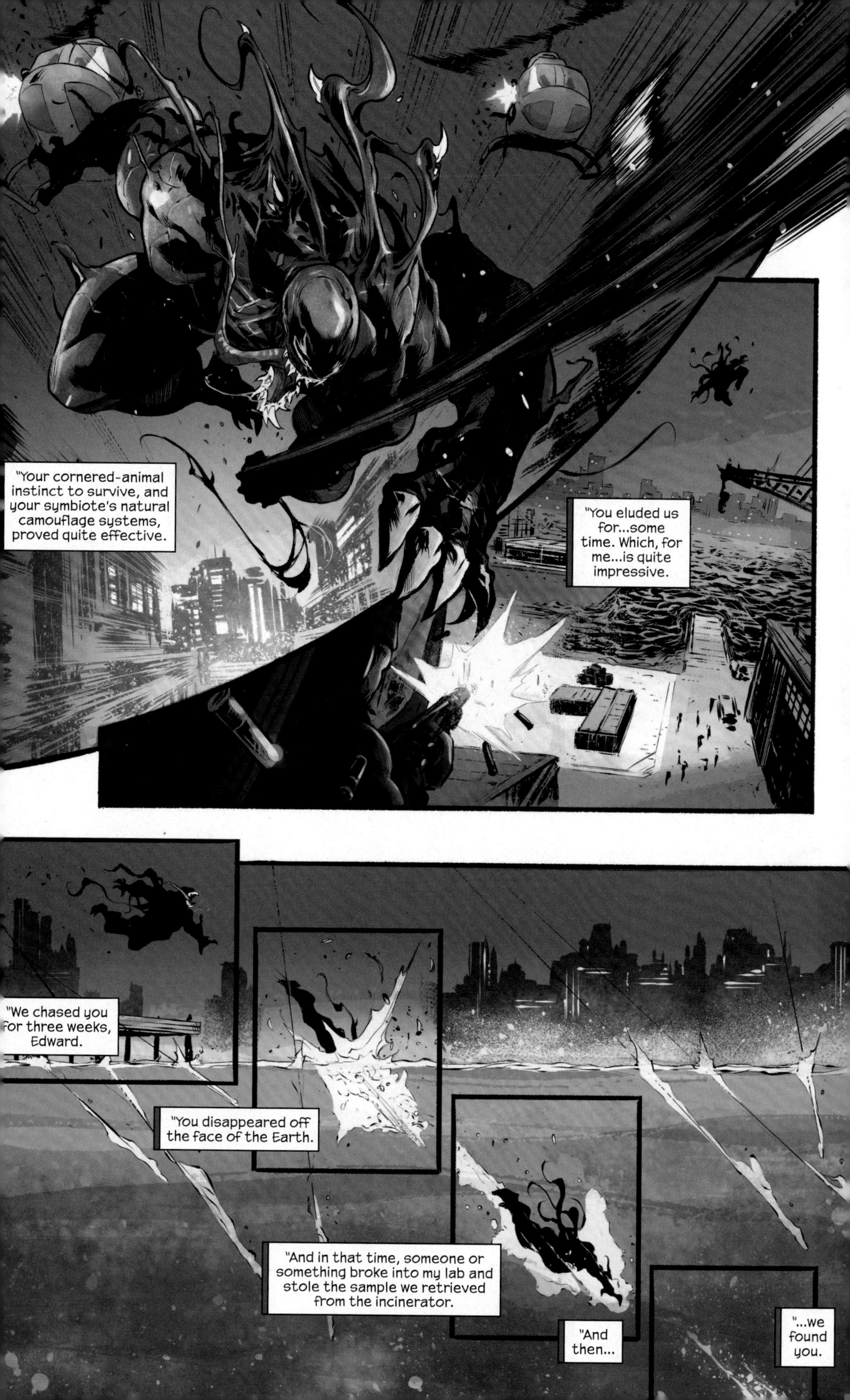
"Your cornered-animal instinct to survive, and your symbiote's natural camouflage systems, proved quite effective.
"You eluded us for...some time. Which, for me...is quite impressive.
"We chased you for three weeks, Edward.
"You disappeared off the face of the Earth.
"And in that time, someone or something broke into my lab and stole the sample we retrieved from the incinerator.
"And then...
"...we found you.

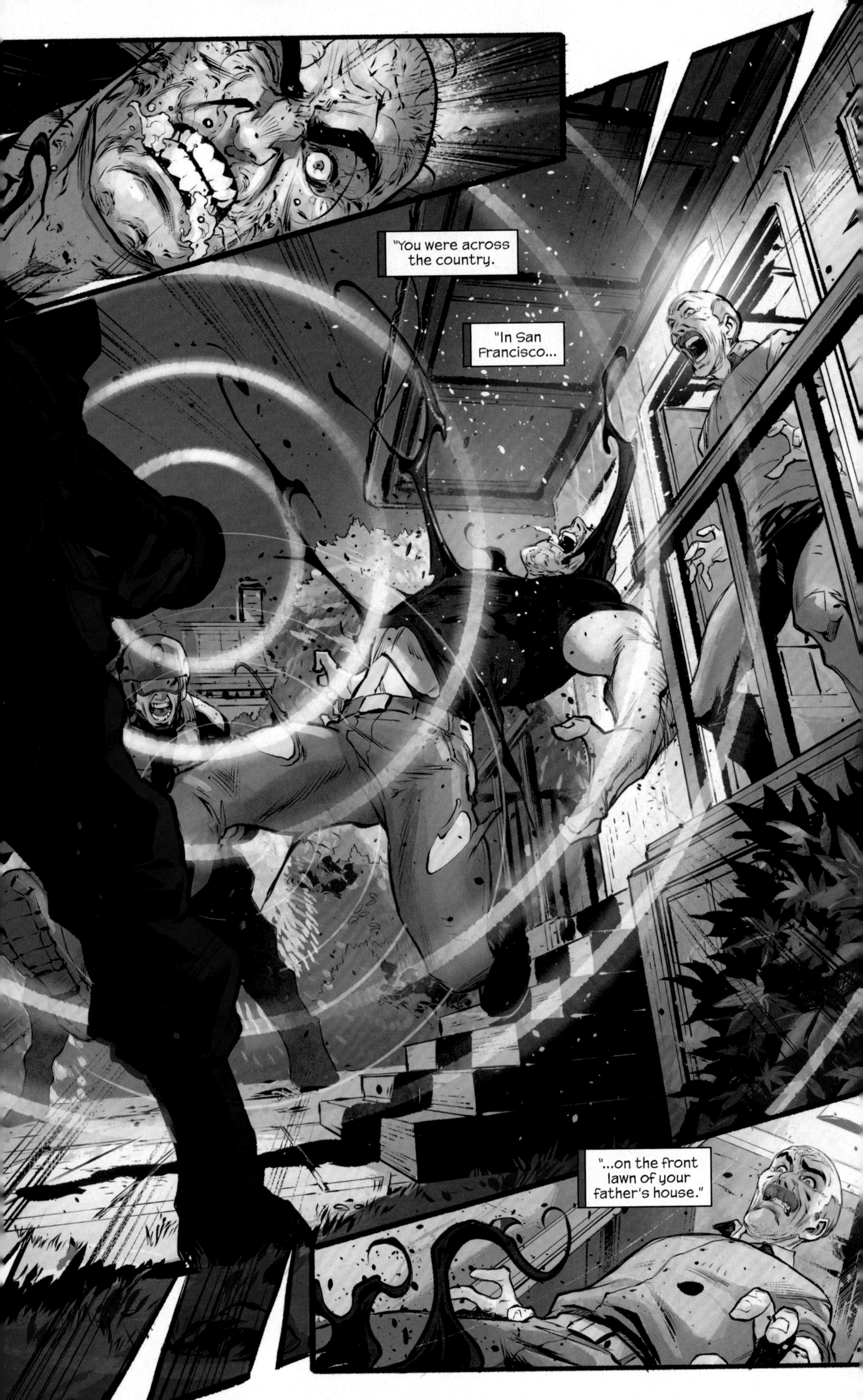
"You were across the country.
"In San Francisco...
"...on the front lawn of your father's house."

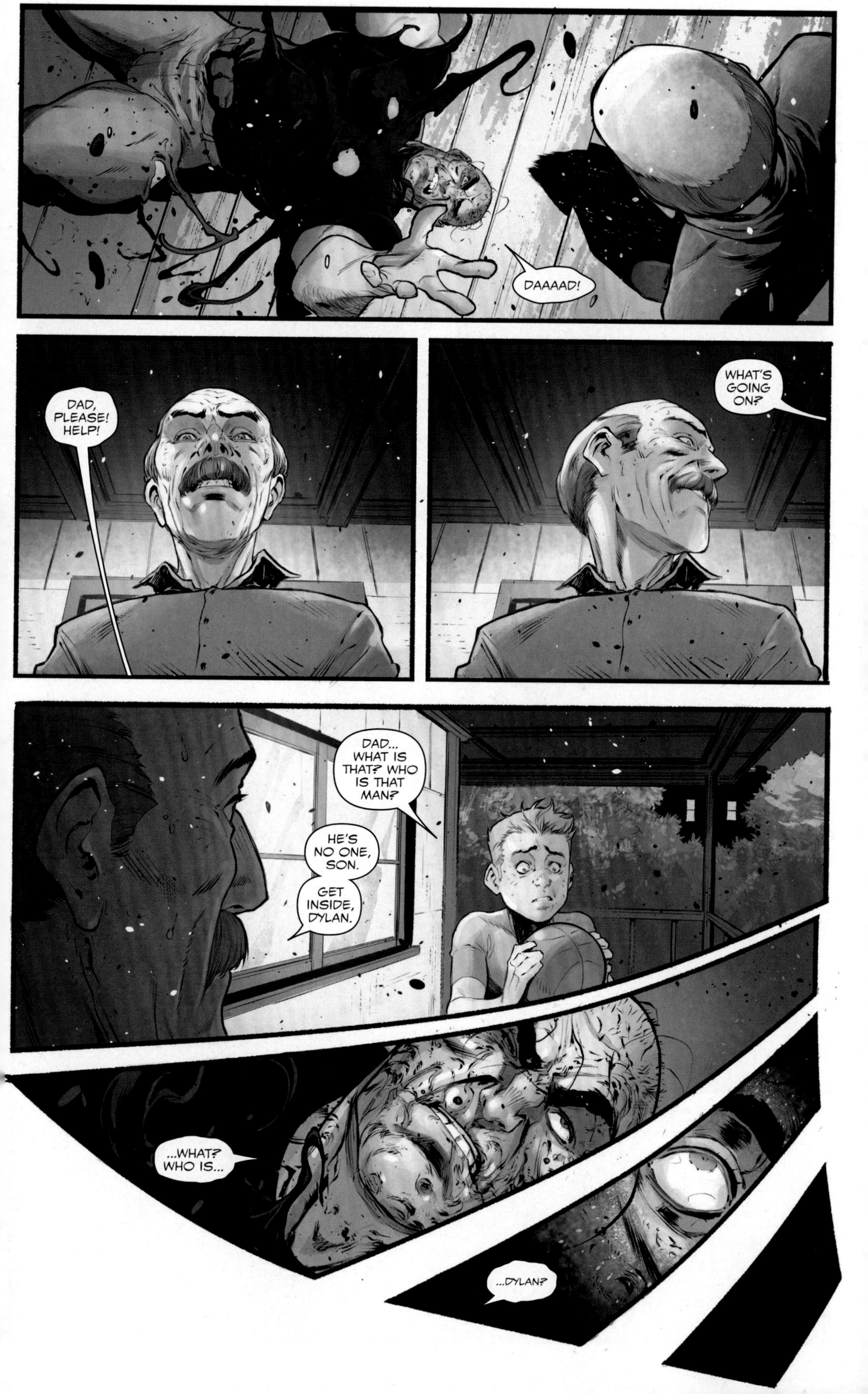
DAAAAD!
DAD, PLEASE! HELP!
WHAT'S GOING ON?
DAD... WHAT IS THAT? WHO IS THAT MAN?
HE'S NO ONE, SON.
GET INSIDE, DYLAN.
...WHAT? WHO IS...
...DYLAN?

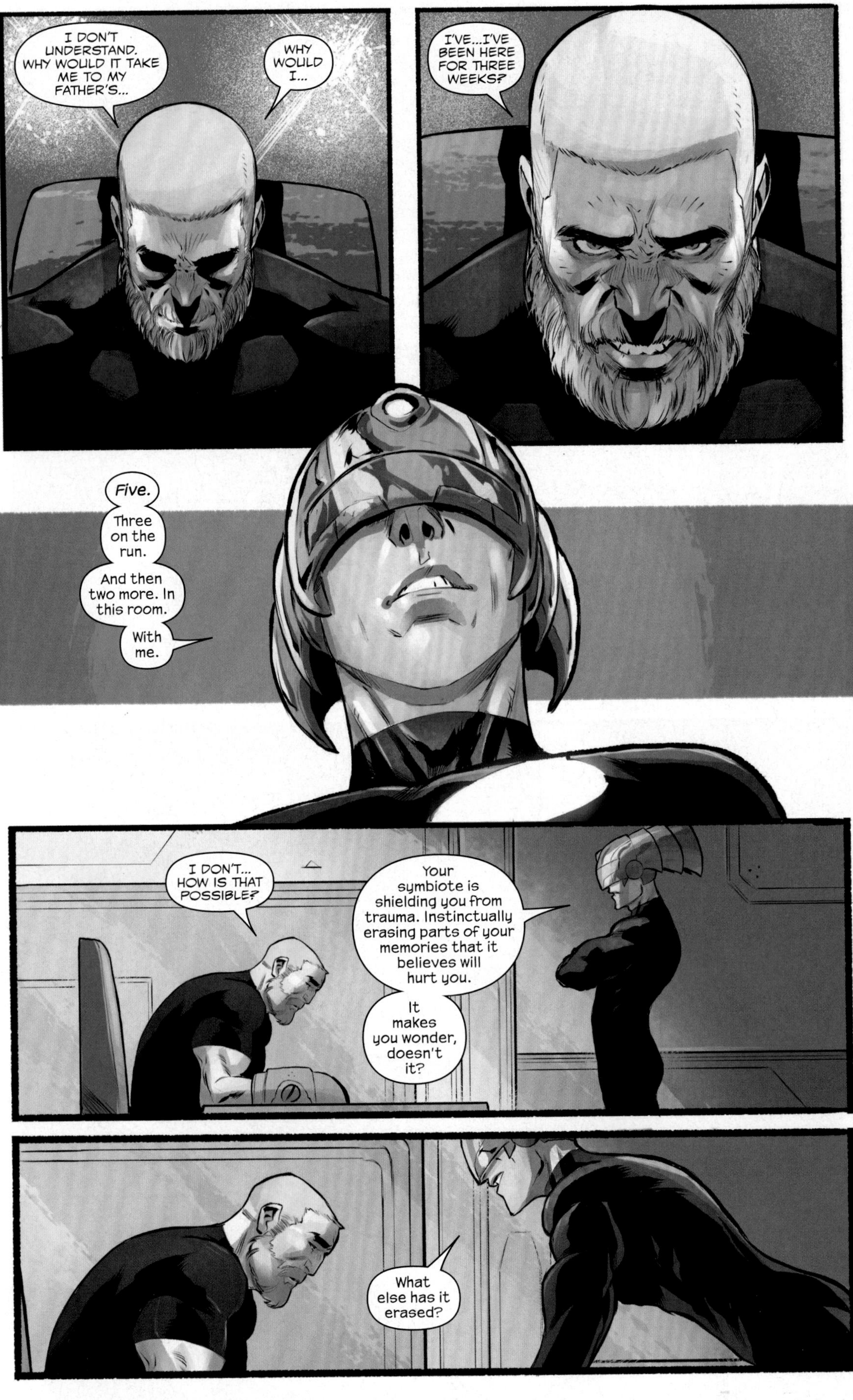
I DON'T UNDERSTAND. WHY WOULD IT TAKE ME TO MY FATHER'S...
WHY WOULD I...
I'VE...I'VE BEEN HERE FOR THREE WEEKS?
Five.
Three on the run.
And then two more. In this room.
With me.
I DON'T... HOW IS THAT POSSIBLE?
Your symbiote is shielding you from trauma. Instinctually erasing parts of your memories that it believes will hurt you.
It makes you wonder, doesn't it?
What else has it erased?

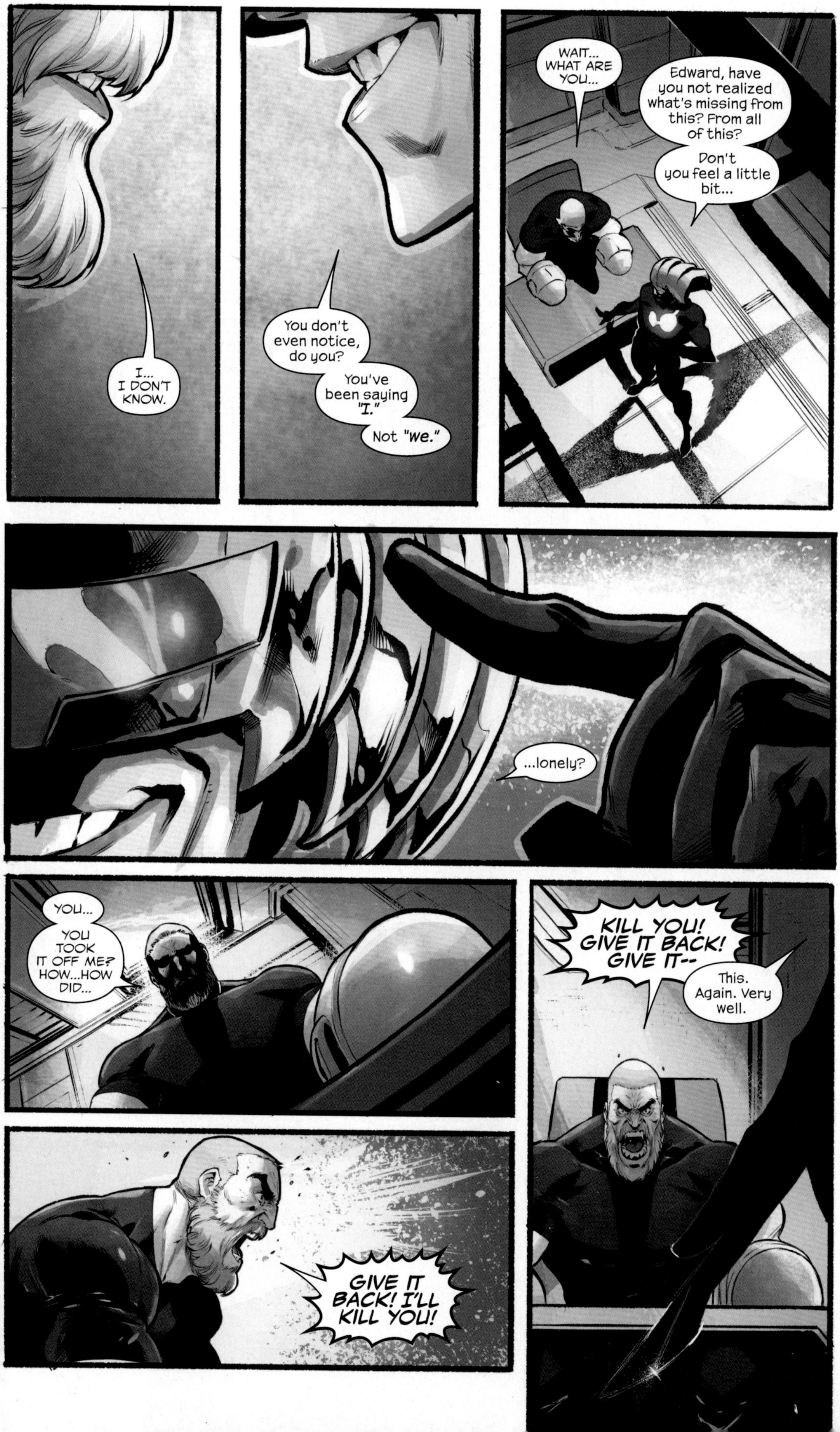
I... I DON'T KNOW.
You don't even notice, do you?
You've been saying "I."
Not "we."
WAIT... WHAT ARE YOU...
Edward, have you not realized what's missing from this? From all of this?
Don't you feel a little bit...
...lonely?
YOU...
YOU TOOK IT OFF ME? HOW...HOW DID...
GIVE IT BACK! I'LL KILL YOU!
KILL YOU! GIVE IT BACK! GIVE IT--
This. Again. Very well.

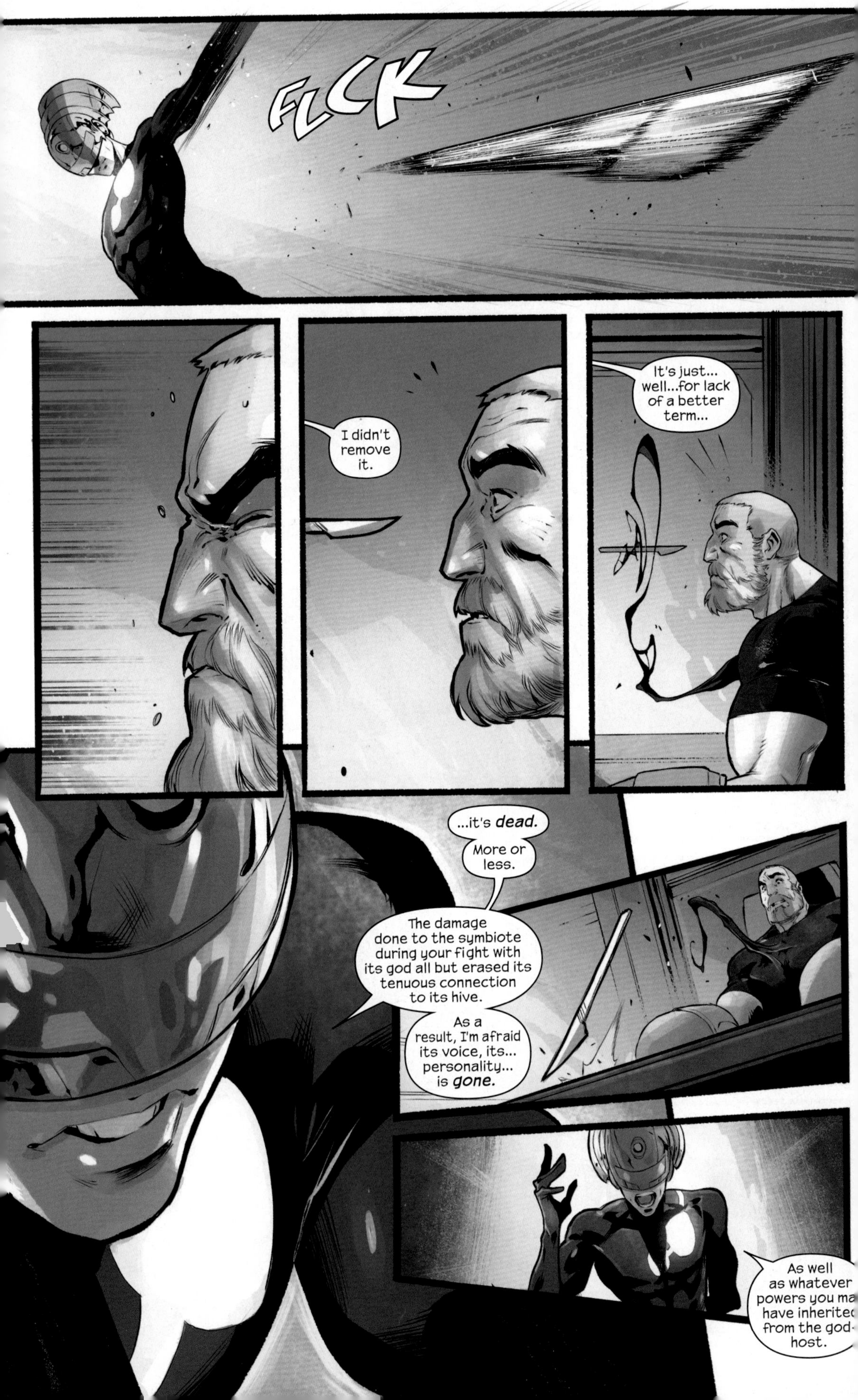
FLCK
I didn't remove it.
It's just... well...for lack of a better term...
...it's dead.
More or less.
The damage done to the symbiote during your fight with its god all but erased its tenuous connection to its hive.
As a result, I'm afraid its voice, its... personality... is gone.
As well as whatever powers you ma have inheritec from the god-host.

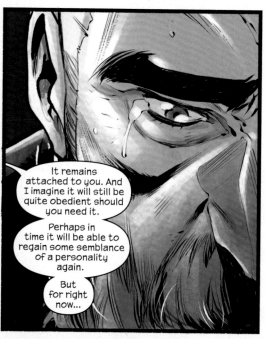

...it's little else but a guard dog.

It remains attached to you. And I imagine it will still be quite obedient should you need it.

Perhaps in time it will be able to regain some semblance of a personality again.

But for right now...

NO...

YOU... YOU HAVE TO HELP...

YOU HAVE TO FIX IT. PLEASE, I NEED--

There's nothing I can do.

The only way to regenerate the symbiote's original makeup would be to reconnect it and restore it from the central hive itself.

And the only person to have ever made contact and survived that experience was *Flash Thompson.*

But I'm afraid with Flash dead, there's little else that can be done.

Now, I have a few ideas as to how we can extract this information, but I'm afraid they are a bit invasive. But I am willing to--

WAIT...

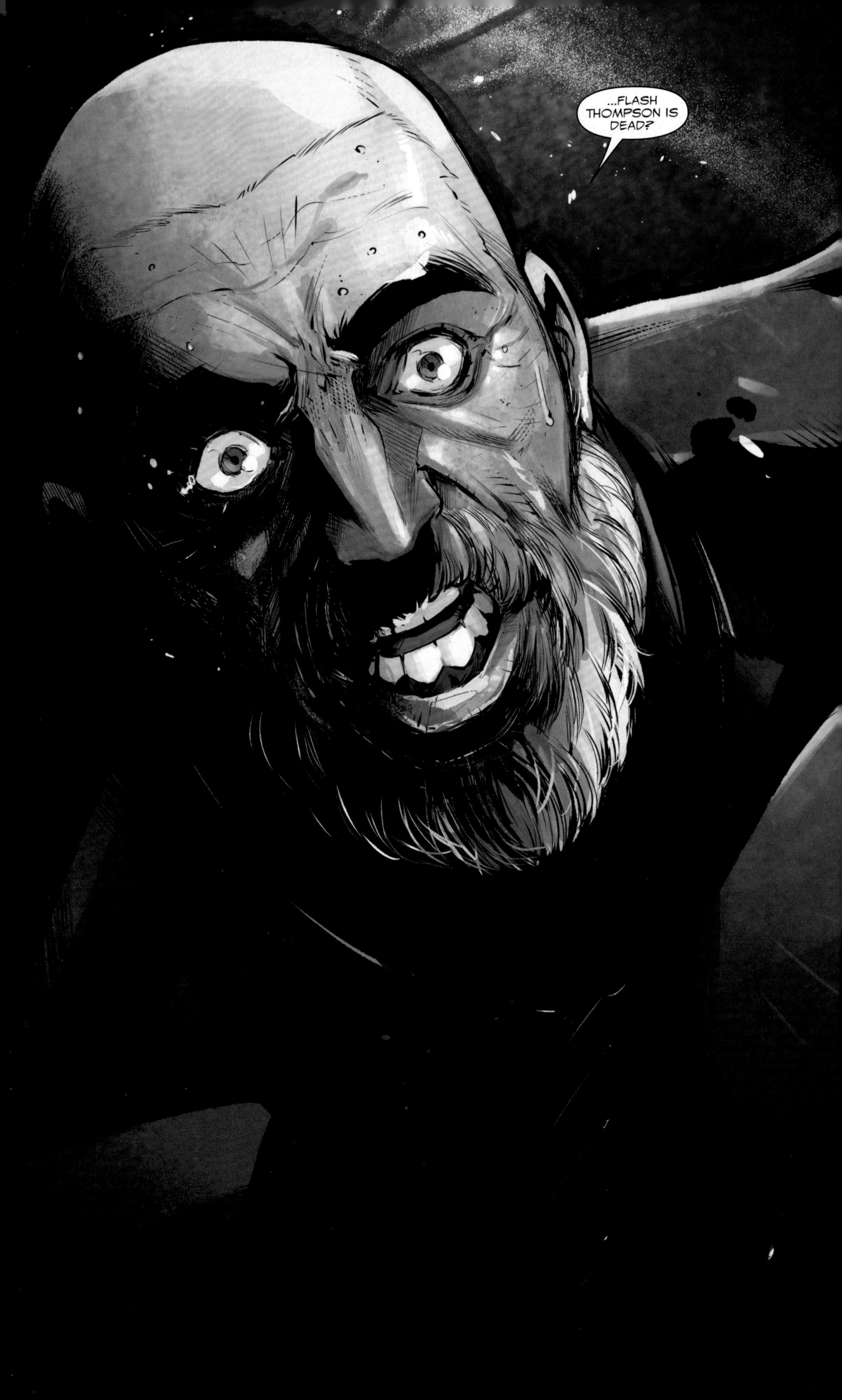
...FLASH
THOMPSON IS
DEAD?

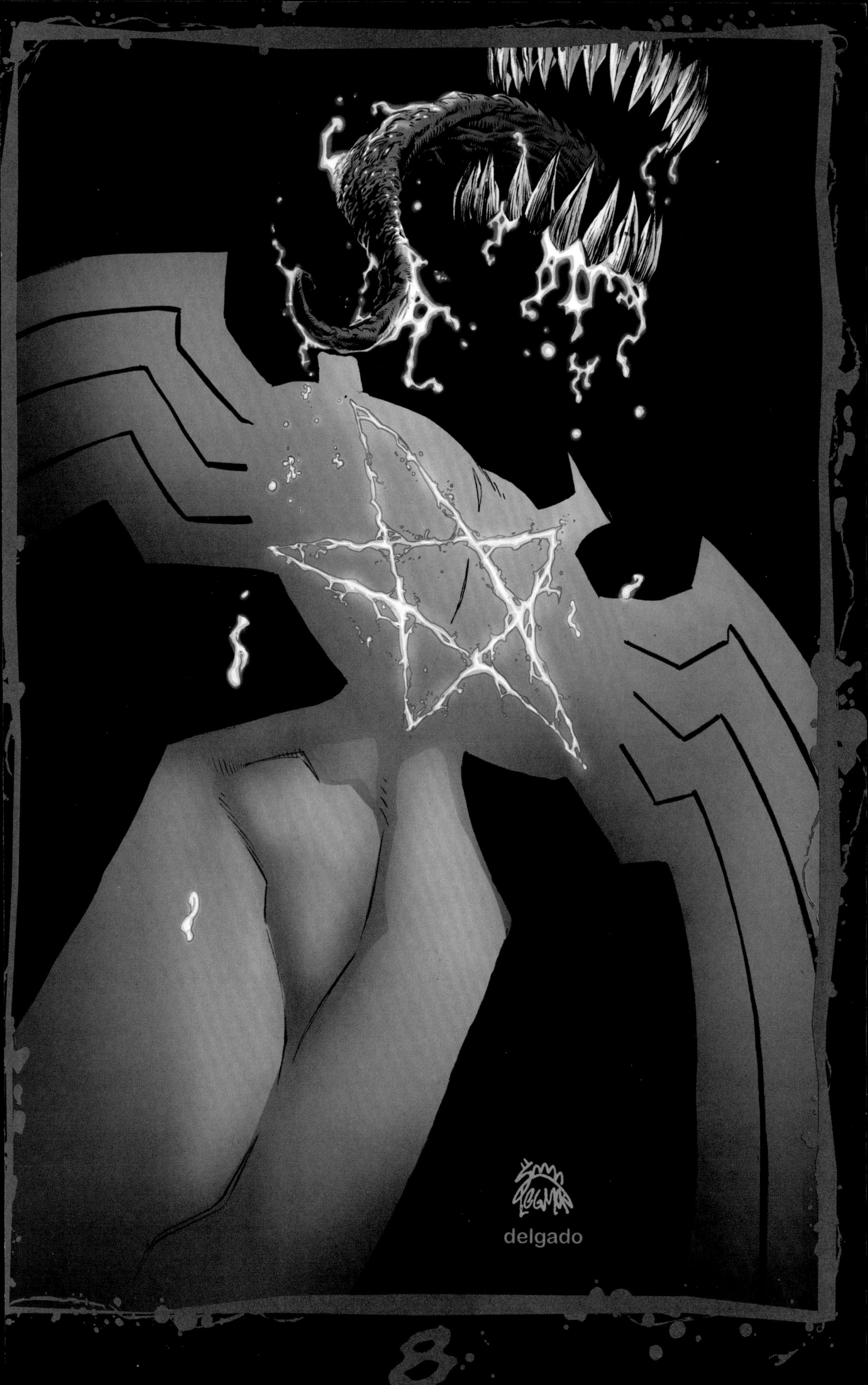
delgado

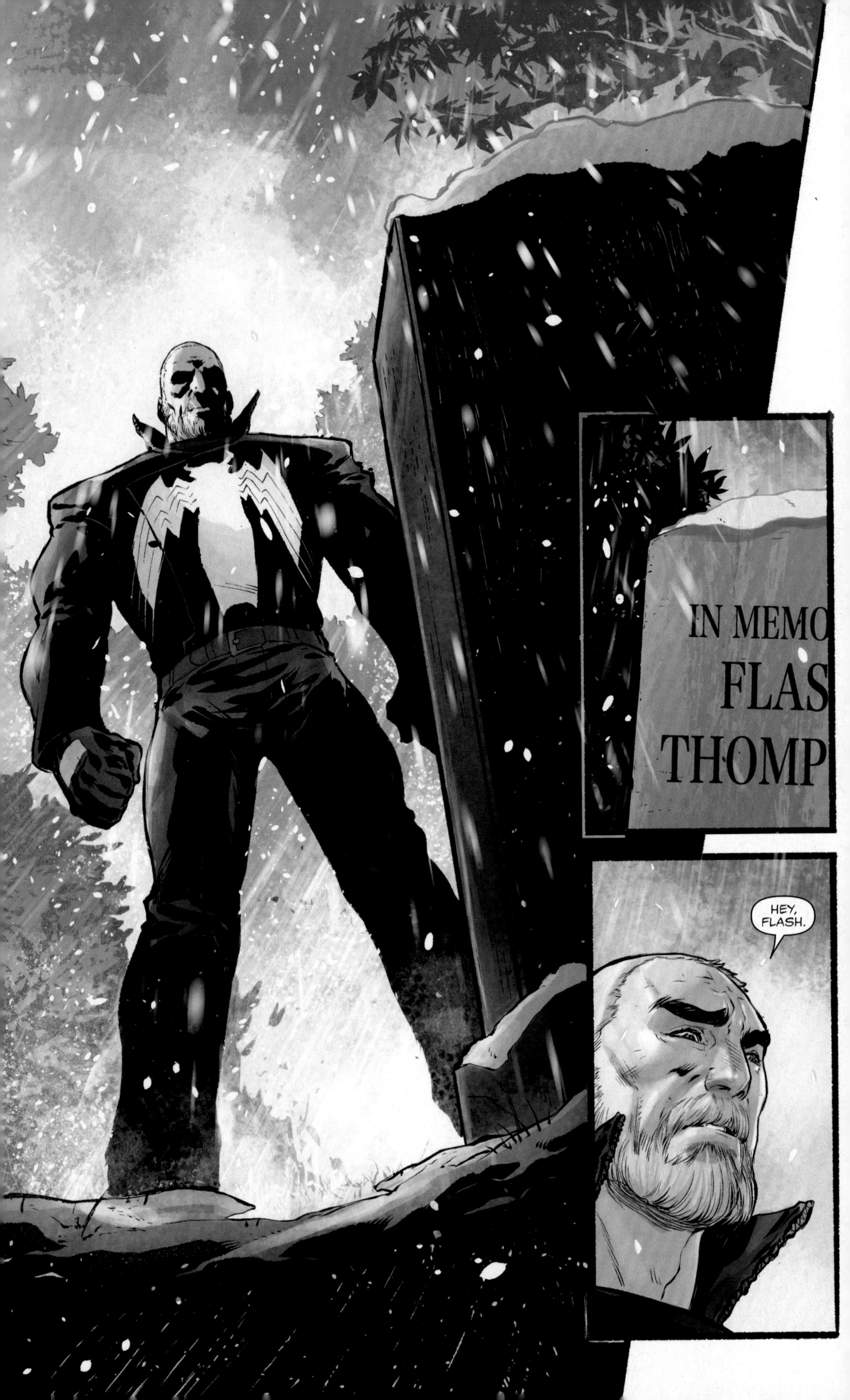
IN MEMO
FLAS
THOMP
HEY, FLASH.

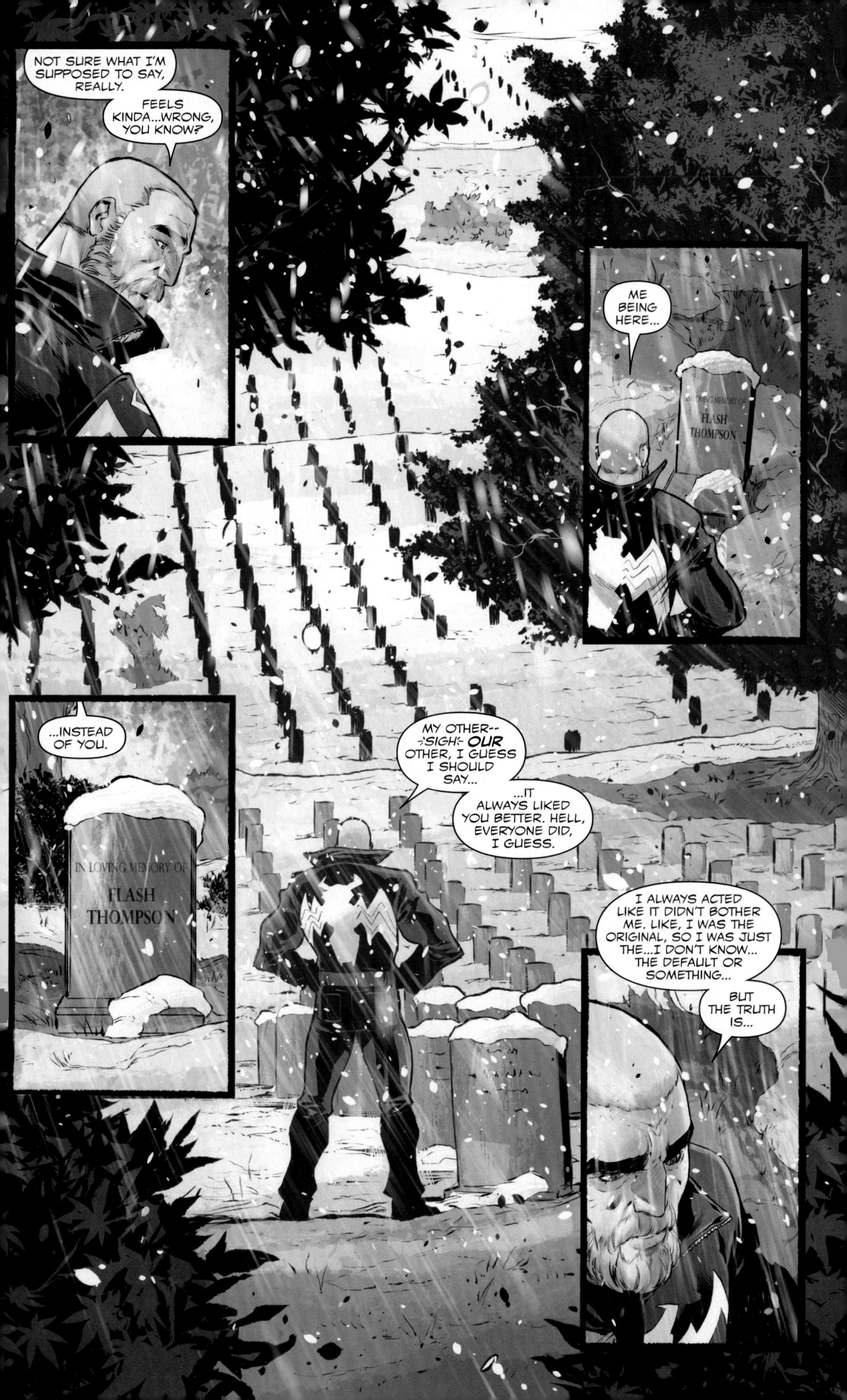
NOT SURE WHAT I'M SUPPOSED TO SAY, REALLY.
FEELS KINDA...WRONG, YOU KNOW?
ME BEING HERE...
...INSTEAD OF YOU.
IN LOVING MEMORY OF FLASH THOMPSON
MY OTHER-- -SIGH- OUR OTHER, I GUESS I SHOULD SAY...
...IT ALWAYS LIKED YOU BETTER. HELL, EVERYONE DID, I GUESS.
I ALWAYS ACTED LIKE IT DIDN'T BOTHER ME. LIKE, I WAS THE ORIGINAL, SO I WAS JUST THE...I DON'T KNOW... THE DEFAULT OR SOMETHING...
BUT THE TRUTH IS...

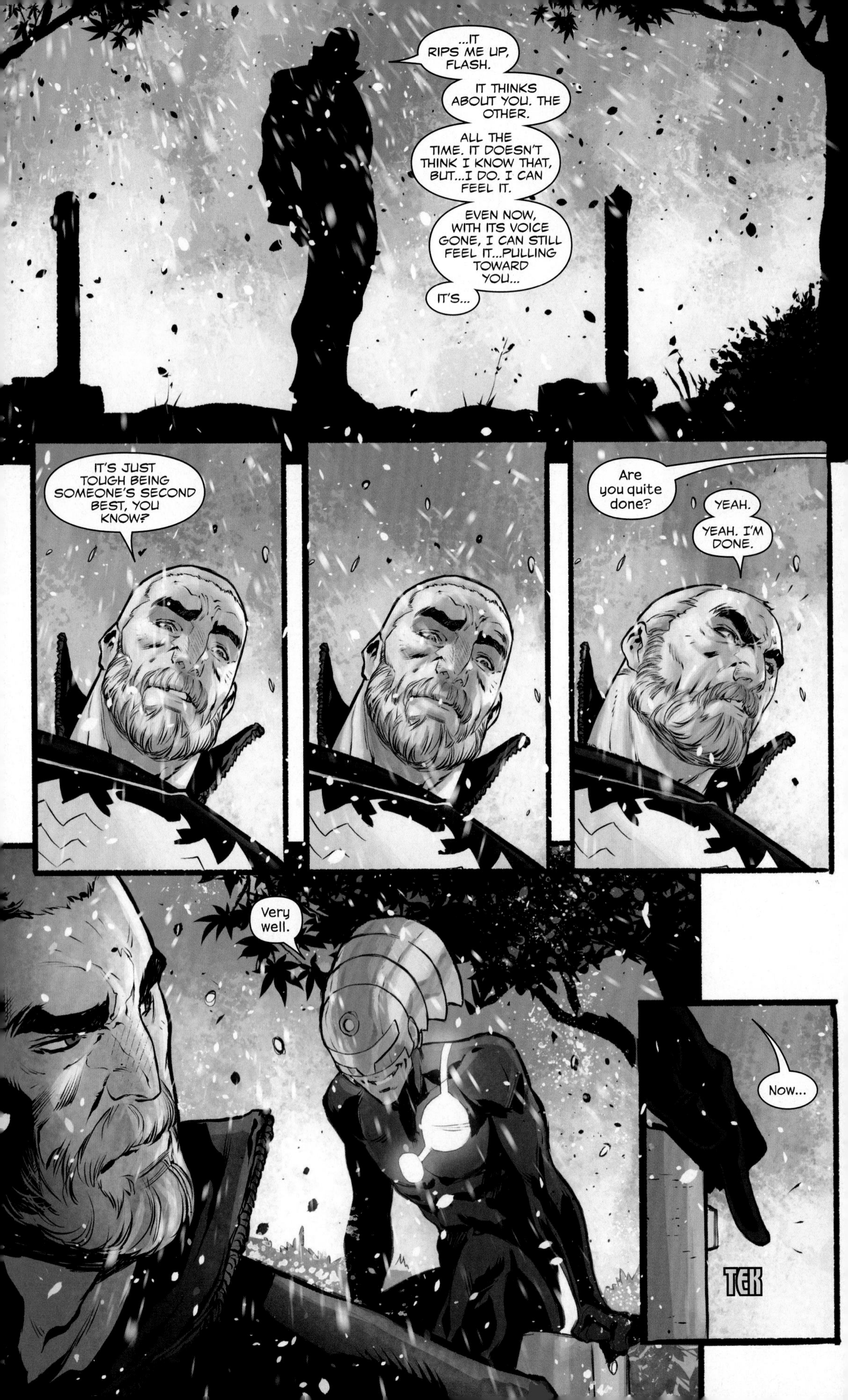
...IT RIPS ME UP, FLASH.
IT THINKS ABOUT YOU. THE OTHER.
ALL THE TIME. IT DOESN'T THINK I KNOW THAT, BUT...I DO. I CAN FEEL IT.
EVEN NOW, WITH ITS VOICE GONE, I CAN STILL FEEL IT...PULLING TOWARD YOU...
IT'S...
IT'S JUST TOUGH BEING SOMEONE'S SECOND BEST, YOU KNOW?
Are you quite done?
YEAH.
YEAH. I'M DONE.
Very well.
Now...
TEK

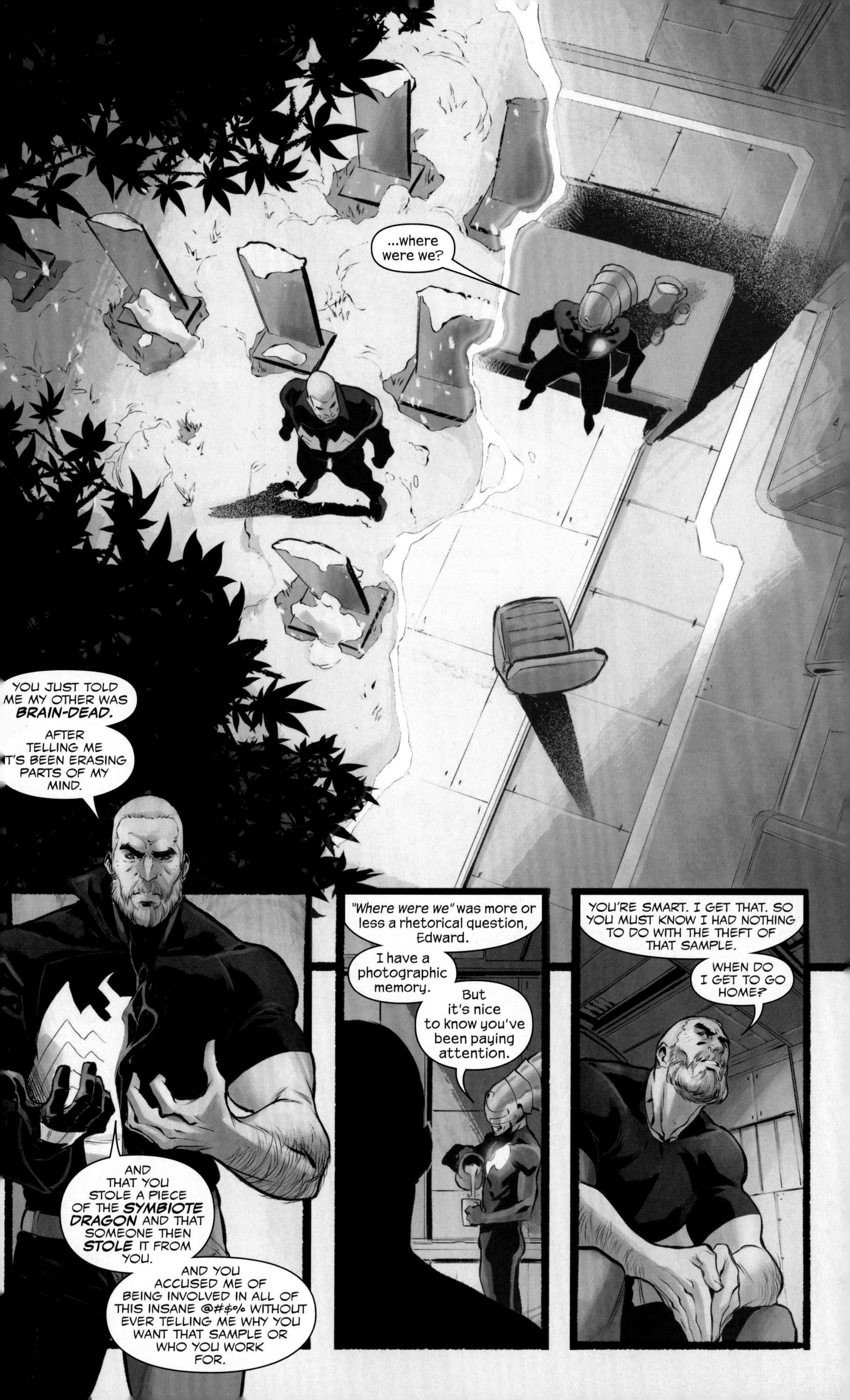

...where were we?
YOU JUST TOLD ME MY OTHER WAS BRAIN-DEAD.
AFTER TELLING ME IT'S BEEN ERASING PARTS OF MY MIND.
AND THAT YOU STOLE A PIECE OF THE SYMBIOTE DRAGON AND THAT SOMEONE THEN STOLE IT FROM YOU.
AND YOU ACCUSED ME OF BEING INVOLVED IN ALL OF THIS INSANE @#$% WITHOUT EVER TELLING ME WHY YOU WANT THAT SAMPLE OR WHO YOU WORK FOR.
"Where were we" was more or less a rhetorical question, Edward.
I have a photographic memory.
But it's nice to know you've been paying attention.
YOU'RE SMART. I GET THAT. SO YOU MUST KNOW I HAD NOTHING TO DO WITH THE THEFT OF THAT SAMPLE.
WHEN DO I GET TO GO HOME?

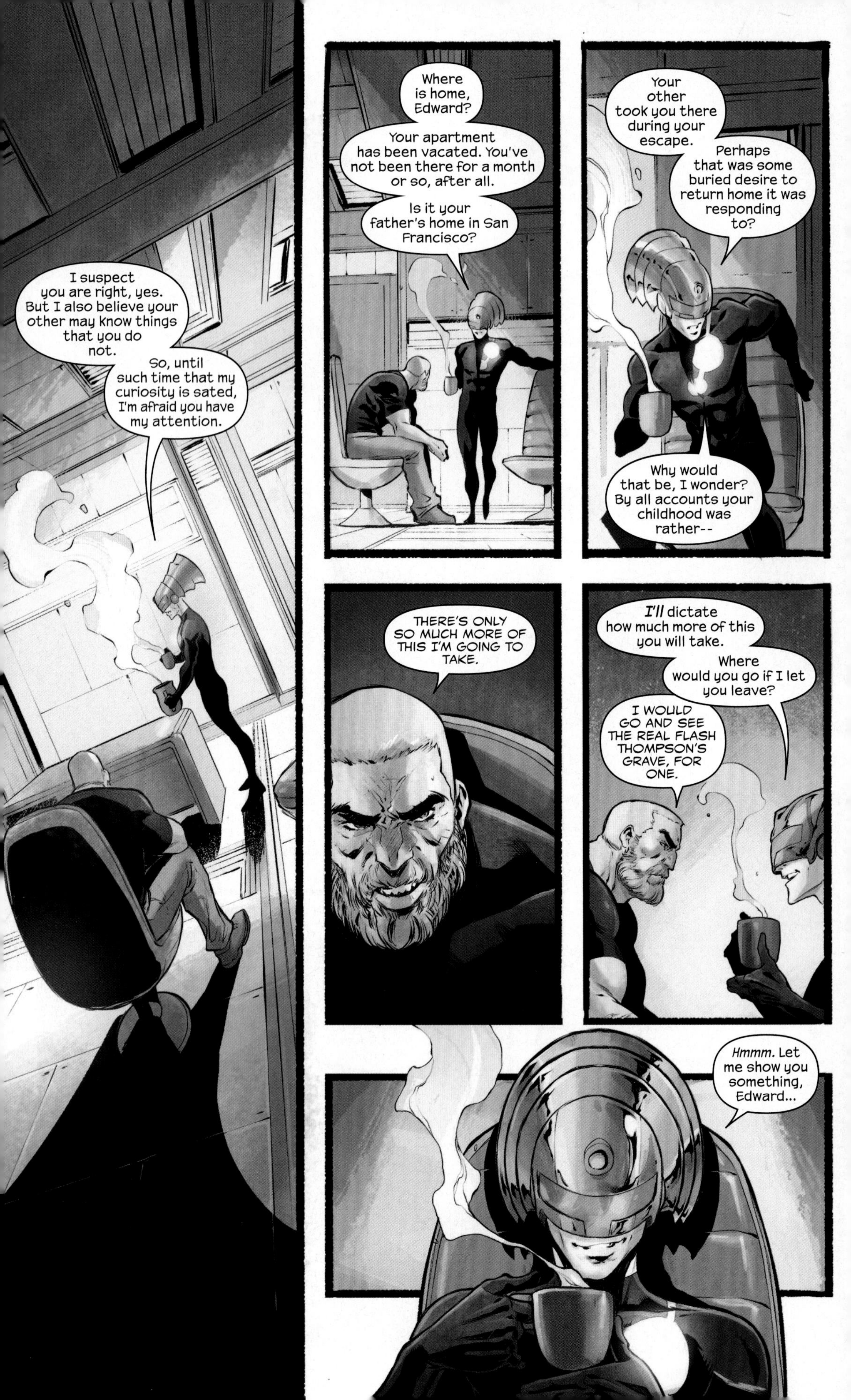
I suspect you are right, yes. But I also believe your other may know things that you do not.
So, until such time that my curiosity is sated, I'm afraid you have my attention.
Where is home, Edward?
Your apartment has been vacated. You've not been there for a month or so, after all.
Is it your father's home in San Francisco?
Your other took you there during your escape.
Perhaps that was some buried desire to return home it was responding to?
Why would that be, I wonder? By all accounts your childhood was rather--
THERE'S ONLY SO MUCH MORE OF THIS I'M GOING TO TAKE.
I'll dictate how much more of this you will take.
Where would you go if I let you leave?
I WOULD GO AND SEE THE REAL FLASH THOMPSON'S GRAVE, FOR ONE.
Hmmm. Let me show you something, Edward...

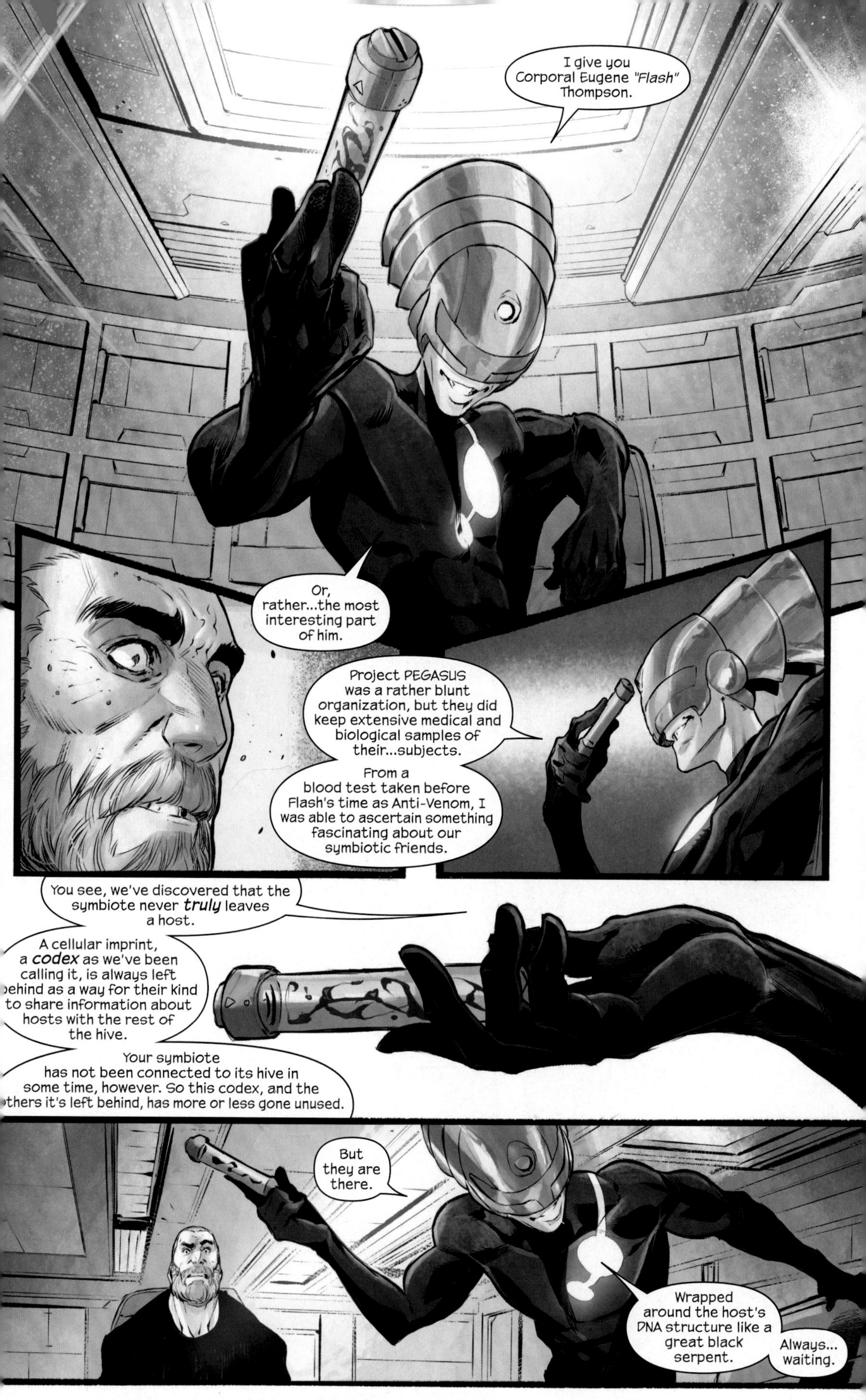
I give you Corporal Eugene "Flash" Thompson.
Or, rather...the most interesting part of him.
Project PEGASUS was a rather blunt organization, but they did keep extensive medical and biological samples of their...subjects.
From a blood test taken before Flash's time as Anti-Venom, I was able to ascertain something fascinating about our symbiotic friends.
You see, we've discovered that the symbiote never *truly* leaves a host.
A cellular imprint, a *codex* as we've been calling it, is always left behind as a way for their kind to share information about hosts with the rest of the hive.
Your symbiote has not been connected to its hive in some time, however. So this codex, and the others it's left behind, has more or less gone unused.
But they are there.
Wrapped around the host's DNA structure like a great black serpent.
Always... waiting.

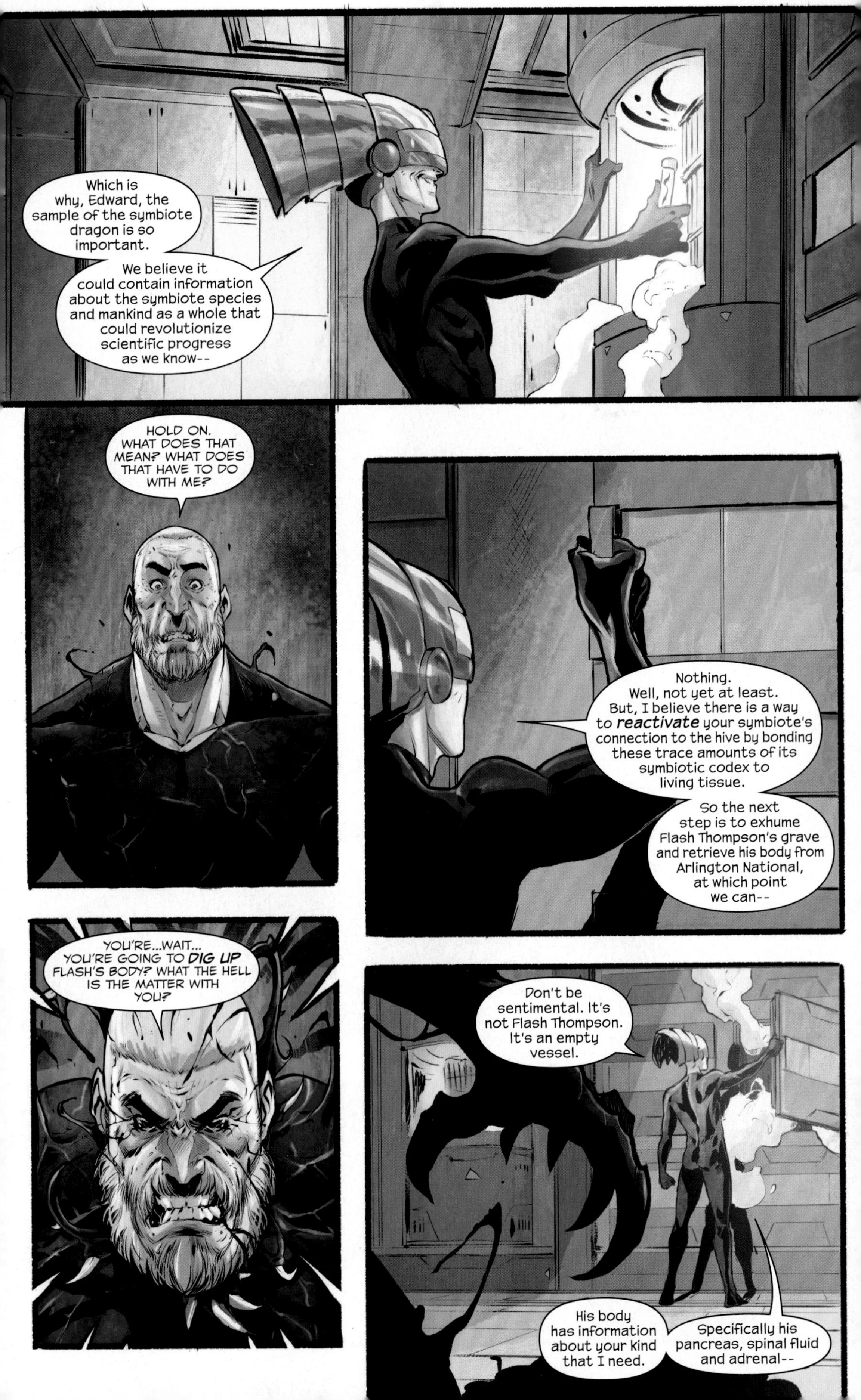
Which is why, Edward, the sample of the symbiote dragon is so important.
We believe it could contain information about the symbiote species and mankind as a whole that could revolutionize scientific progress as we know--
HOLD ON. WHAT DOES THAT MEAN? WHAT DOES THAT HAVE TO DO WITH ME?
Nothing. Well, not yet at least. But, I believe there is a way to *reactivate* your symbiote's connection to the hive by bonding these trace amounts of its symbiotic codex to living tissue.
So the next step is to exhume Flash Thompson's grave and retrieve his body from Arlington National, at which point we can--
YOU'RE...WAIT... YOU'RE GOING TO *DIG UP* FLASH'S BODY? WHAT THE HELL IS THE MATTER WITH YOU?
Don't be sentimental. It's not Flash Thompson. It's an empty vessel.
His body has information about your kind that I need.
Specifically his pancreas, spinal fluid and adrenal--

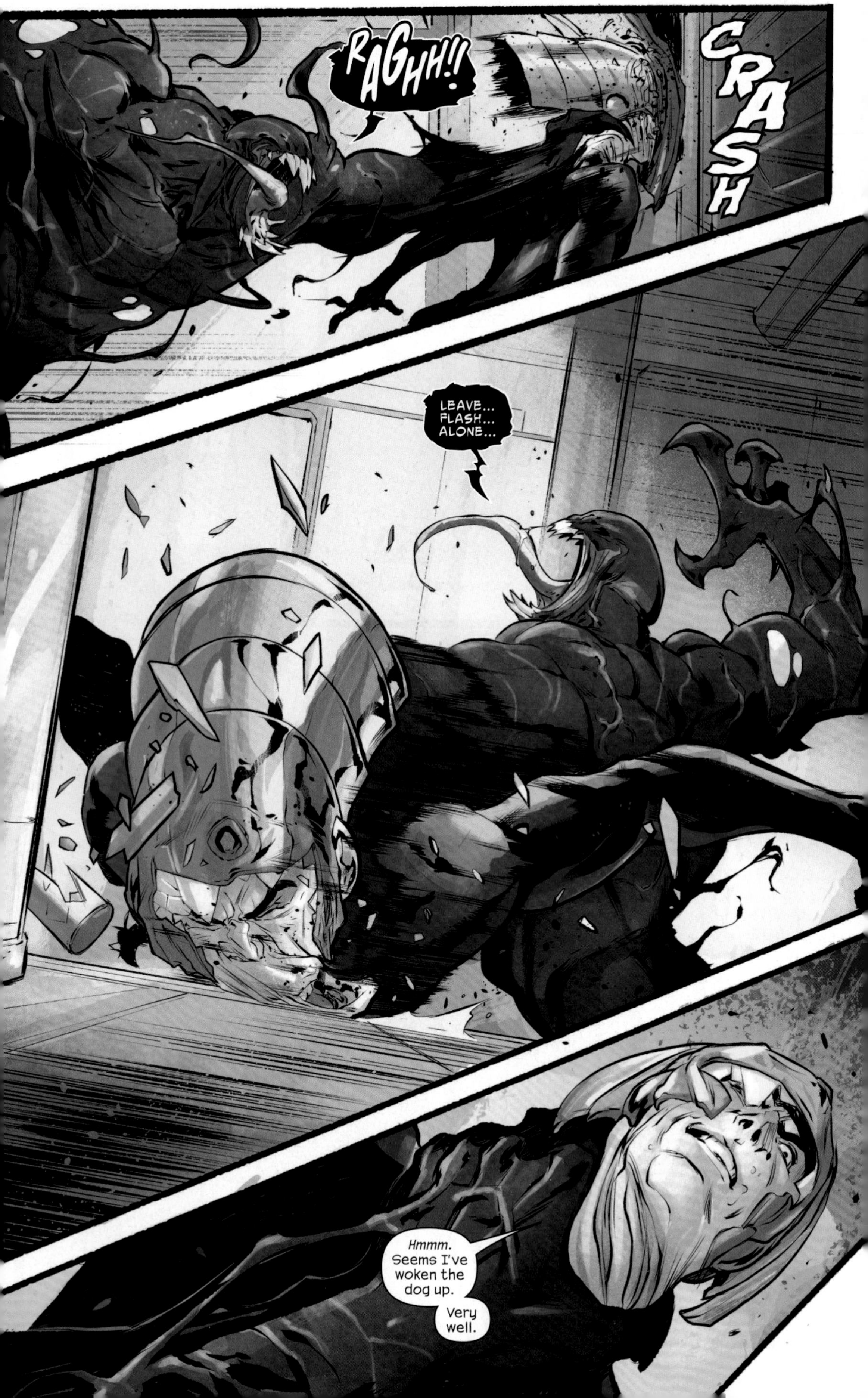
RAGHH!!
CRASH
LEAVE... FLASH... ALONE...
Hmmm. Seems I've woken the dog up.
Very well.

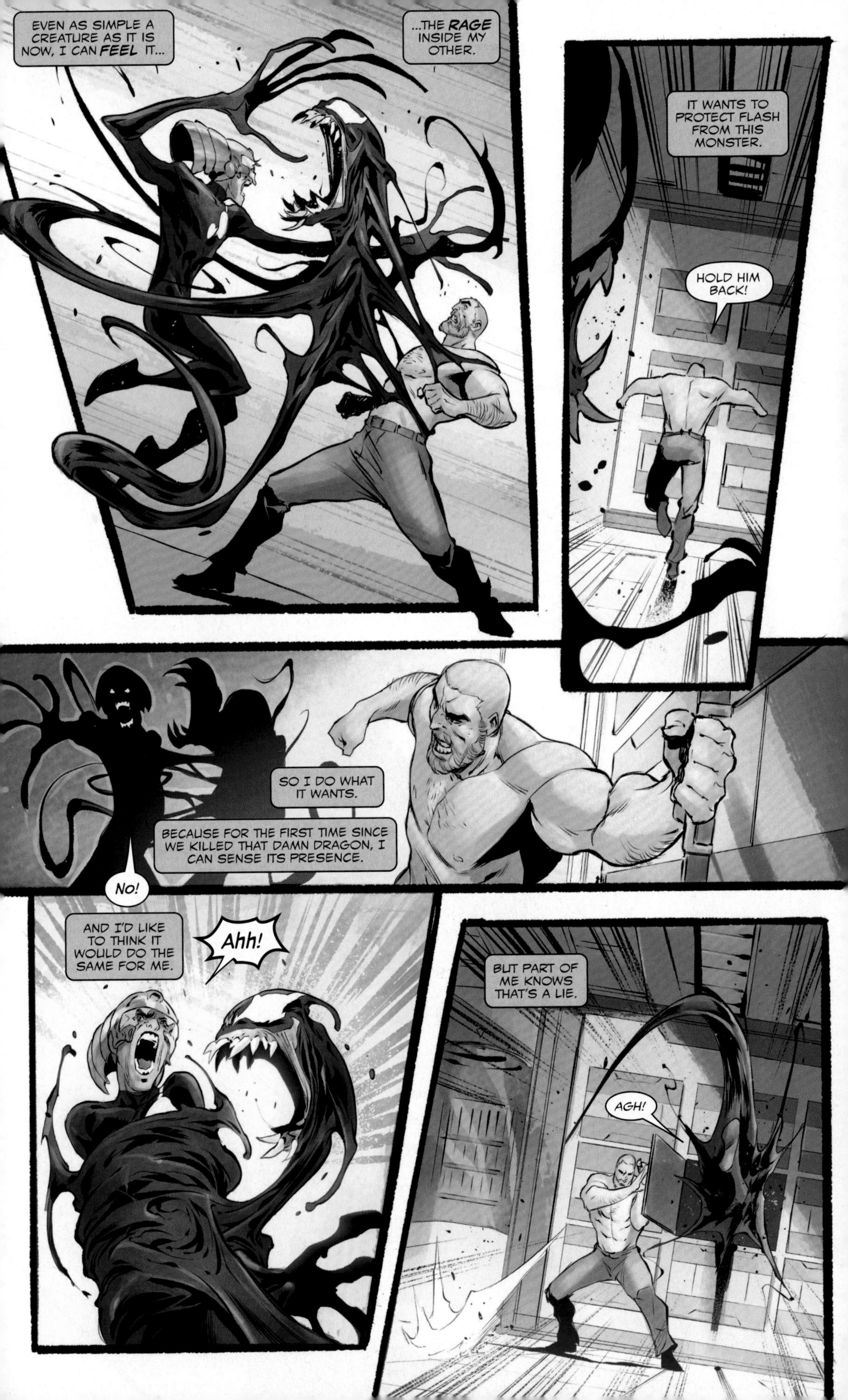
EVEN AS SIMPLE A CREATURE AS IT IS NOW, I CAN FEEL IT...
...THE RAGE INSIDE MY OTHER.
IT WANTS TO PROTECT FLASH FROM THIS MONSTER.
HOLD HIM BACK!
SO I DO WHAT IT WANTS.
BECAUSE FOR THE FIRST TIME SINCE WE KILLED THAT DAMN DRAGON, I CAN SENSE ITS PRESENCE.
No!
AND I'D LIKE TO THINK IT WOULD DO THE SAME FOR ME.
Ahh!
BUT PART OF ME KNOWS THAT'S A LIE.
AGH!

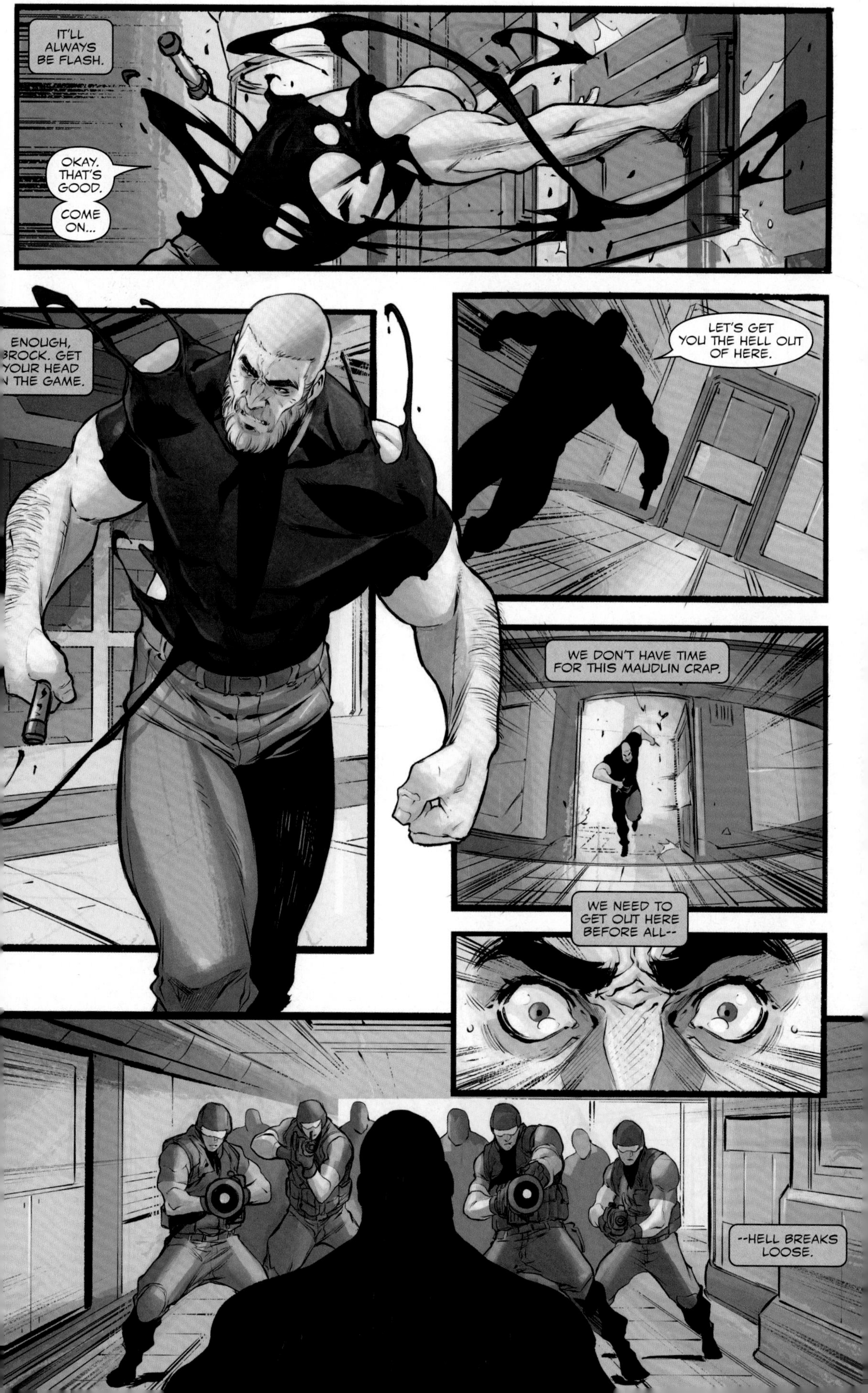
IT'LL ALWAYS BE FLASH.
OKAY. THAT'S GOOD.
COME ON...
ENOUGH, BROCK. GET YOUR HEAD IN THE GAME.
LET'S GET YOU THE HELL OUT OF HERE.
WE DON'T HAVE TIME FOR THIS MAUDLIN CRAP.
WE NEED TO GET OUT HERE BEFORE ALL--
--HELL BREAKS LOOSE.

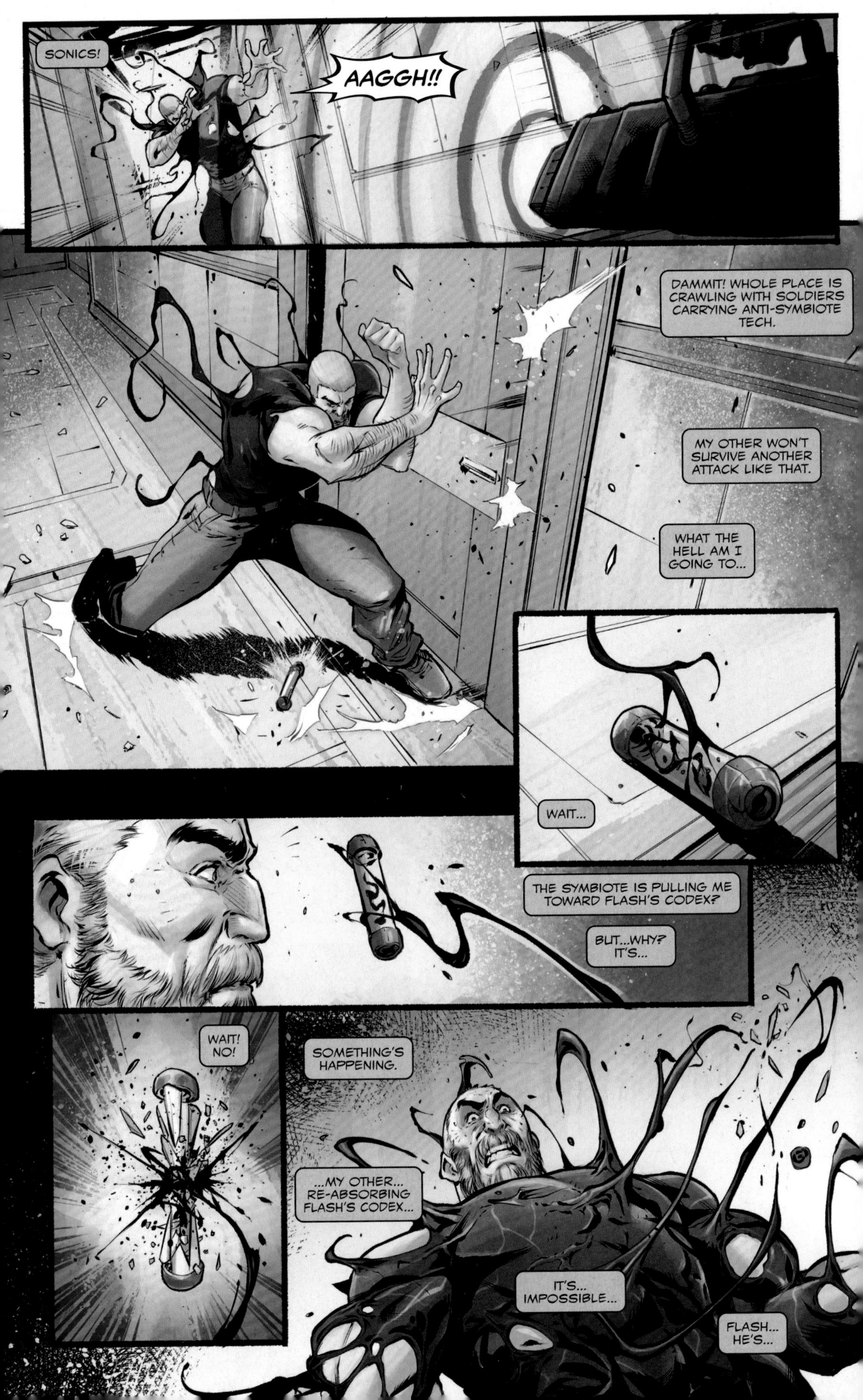
SONICS!
AAGGH!!
DAMMIT! WHOLE PLACE IS CRAWLING WITH SOLDIERS CARRYING ANTI-SYMBIOTE TECH.
MY OTHER WON'T SURVIVE ANOTHER ATTACK LIKE THAT.
WHAT THE HELL AM I GOING TO...
WAIT...
THE SYMBIOTE IS PULLING ME TOWARD FLASH'S CODEX?
BUT...WHY? IT'S...
WAIT! NO!
SOMETHING'S HAPPENING.
...MY OTHER... RE-ABSORBING FLASH'S CODEX...
IT'S... IMPOSSIBLE...
FLASH... HE'S...

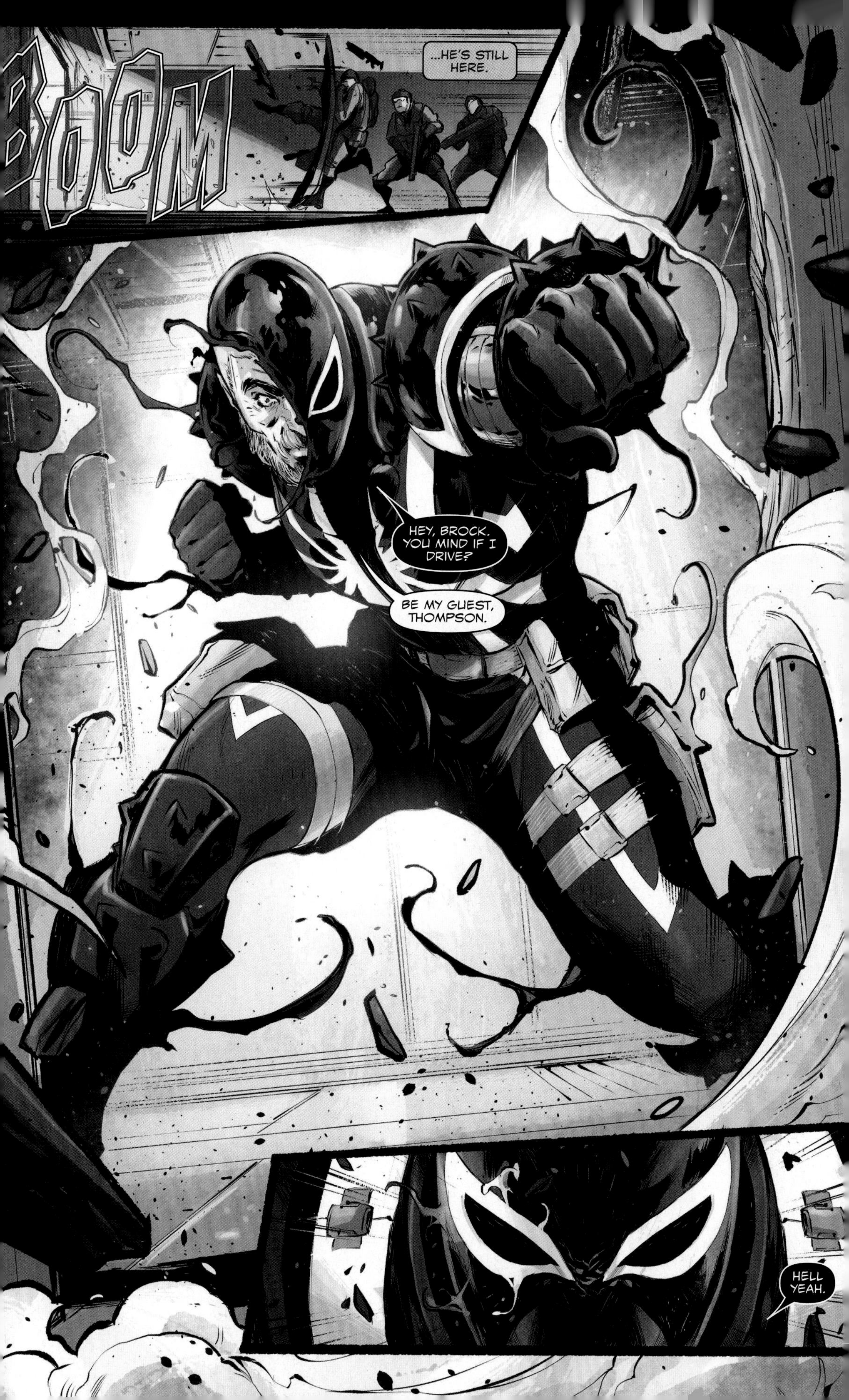
BOOM
...HE'S STILL HERE.
HEY, BROCK. YOU MIND IF I DRIVE?
BE MY GUEST, THOMPSON.
HELL YEAH.

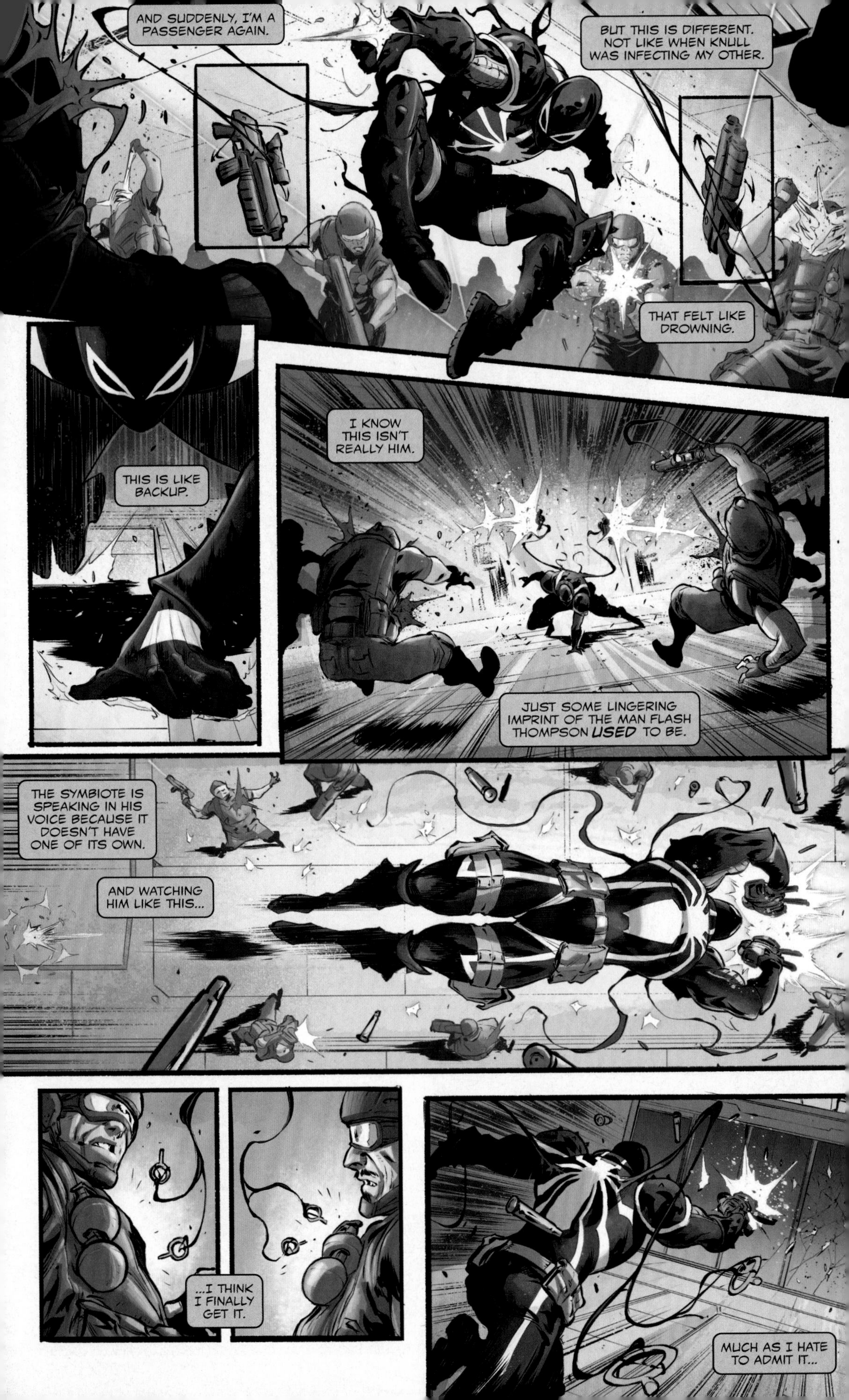
AND SUDDENLY, I'M A PASSENGER AGAIN.
BUT THIS IS DIFFERENT. NOT LIKE WHEN KNULL WAS INFECTING MY OTHER.
THAT FELT LIKE DROWNING.
THIS IS LIKE BACKUP.
I KNOW THIS ISN'T REALLY HIM.
JUST SOME LINGERING IMPRINT OF THE MAN FLASH THOMPSON USED TO BE.
THE SYMBIOTE IS SPEAKING IN HIS VOICE BECAUSE IT DOESN'T HAVE ONE OF ITS OWN.
AND WATCHING HIM LIKE THIS...
...I THINK I FINALLY GET IT.
MUCH AS I HATE TO ADMIT IT...

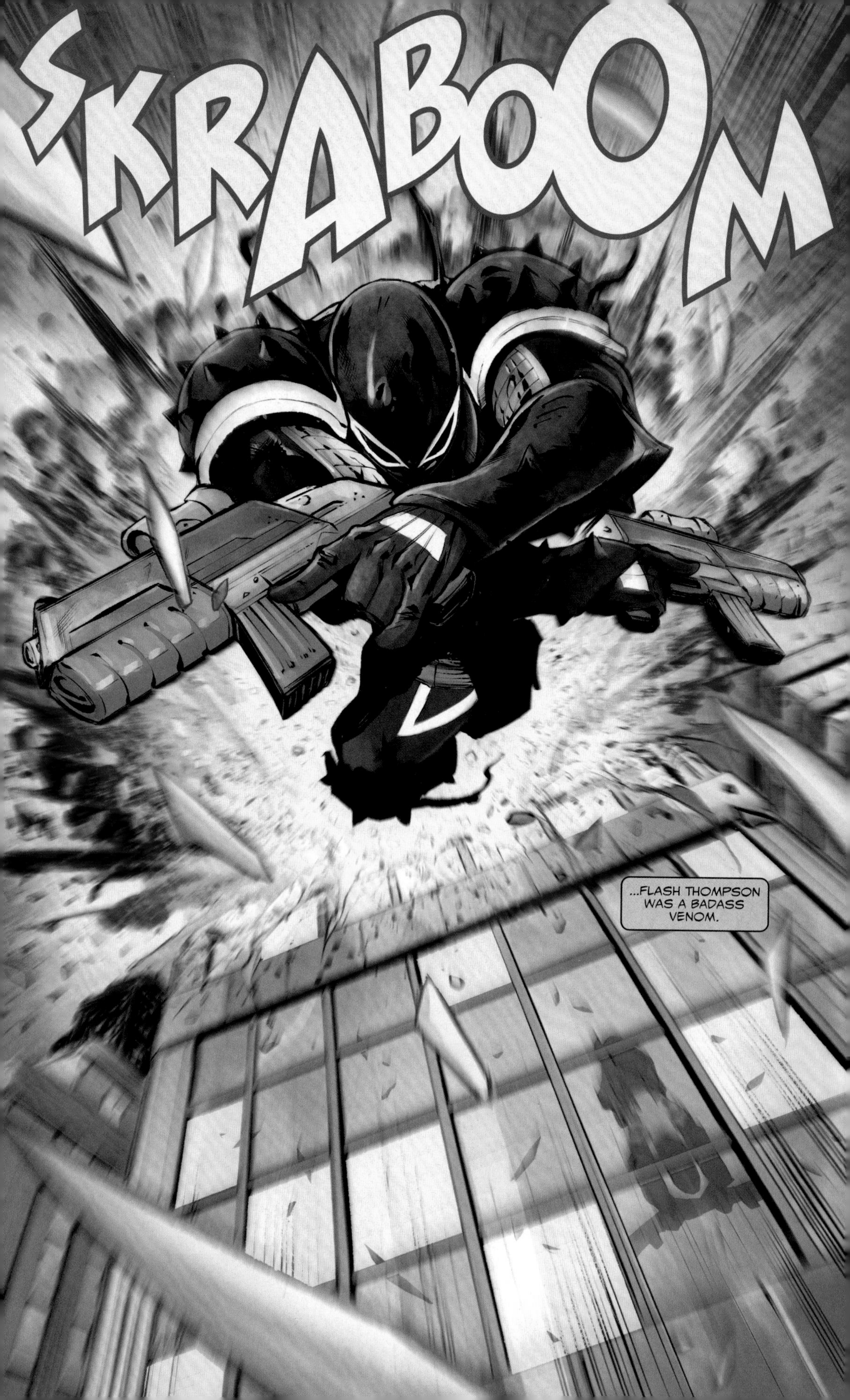
SKRABOOM
...FLASH THOMPSON WAS A BADASS VENOM.

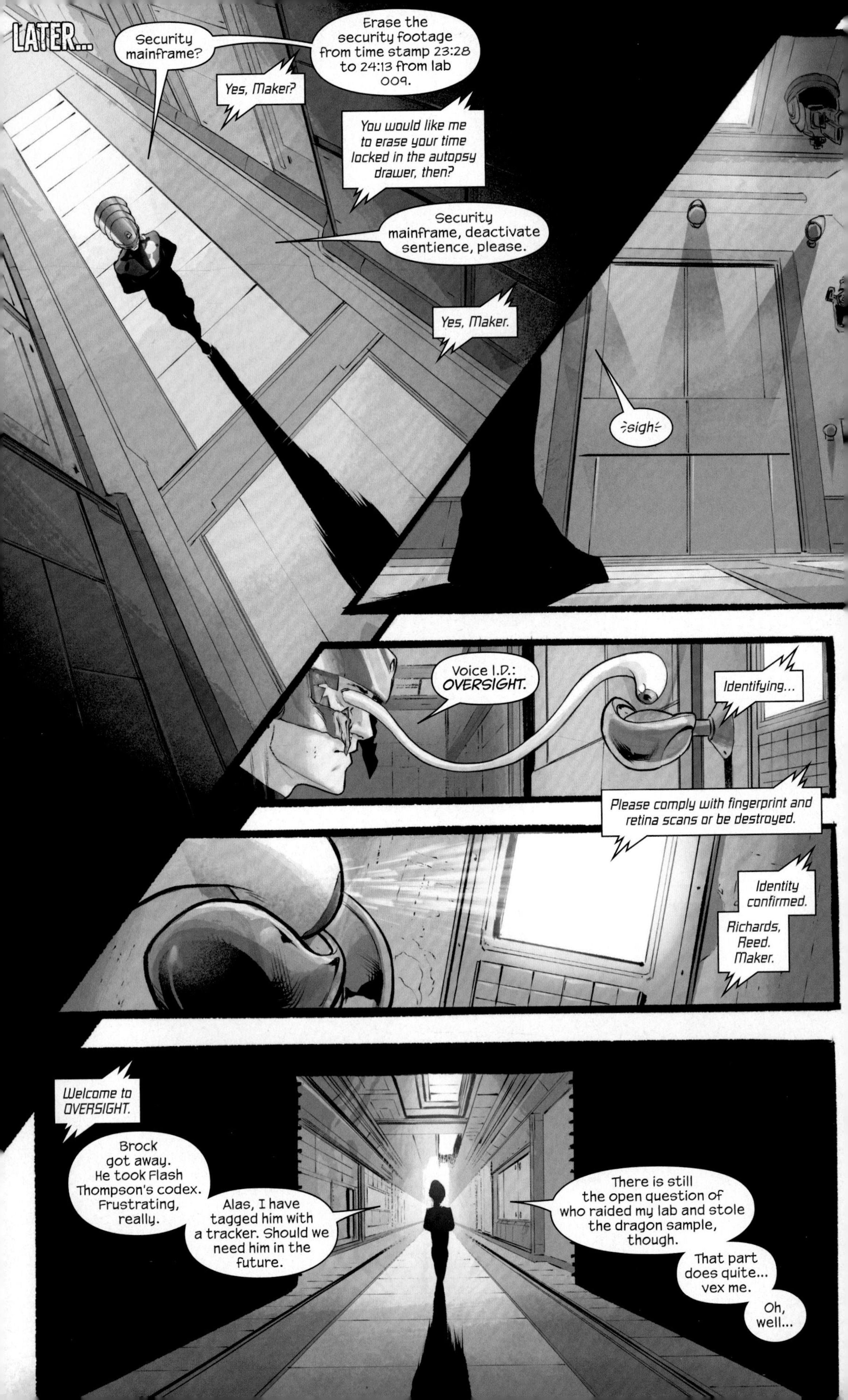
LATER...
Security mainframe?
Erase the security footage from time stamp 23:28 to 24:13 from lab 009.
Yes, Maker?
You would like me to erase your time locked in the autopsy drawer, then?
Security mainframe, deactivate sentience, please.
Yes, Maker.
sigh
Voice I.D.: OVERSIGHT.
Identifying...
Please comply with fingerprint and retina scans or be destroyed.
Identity confirmed.
Richards, Reed. Maker.
Welcome to OVERSIGHT.
Brock got away. He took Flash Thompson's codex. Frustrating, really.
Alas, I have tagged him with a tracker. Should we need him in the future.
There is still the open question of who raided my lab and stole the dragon sample, though.
That part does quite... vex me.
Oh, well...

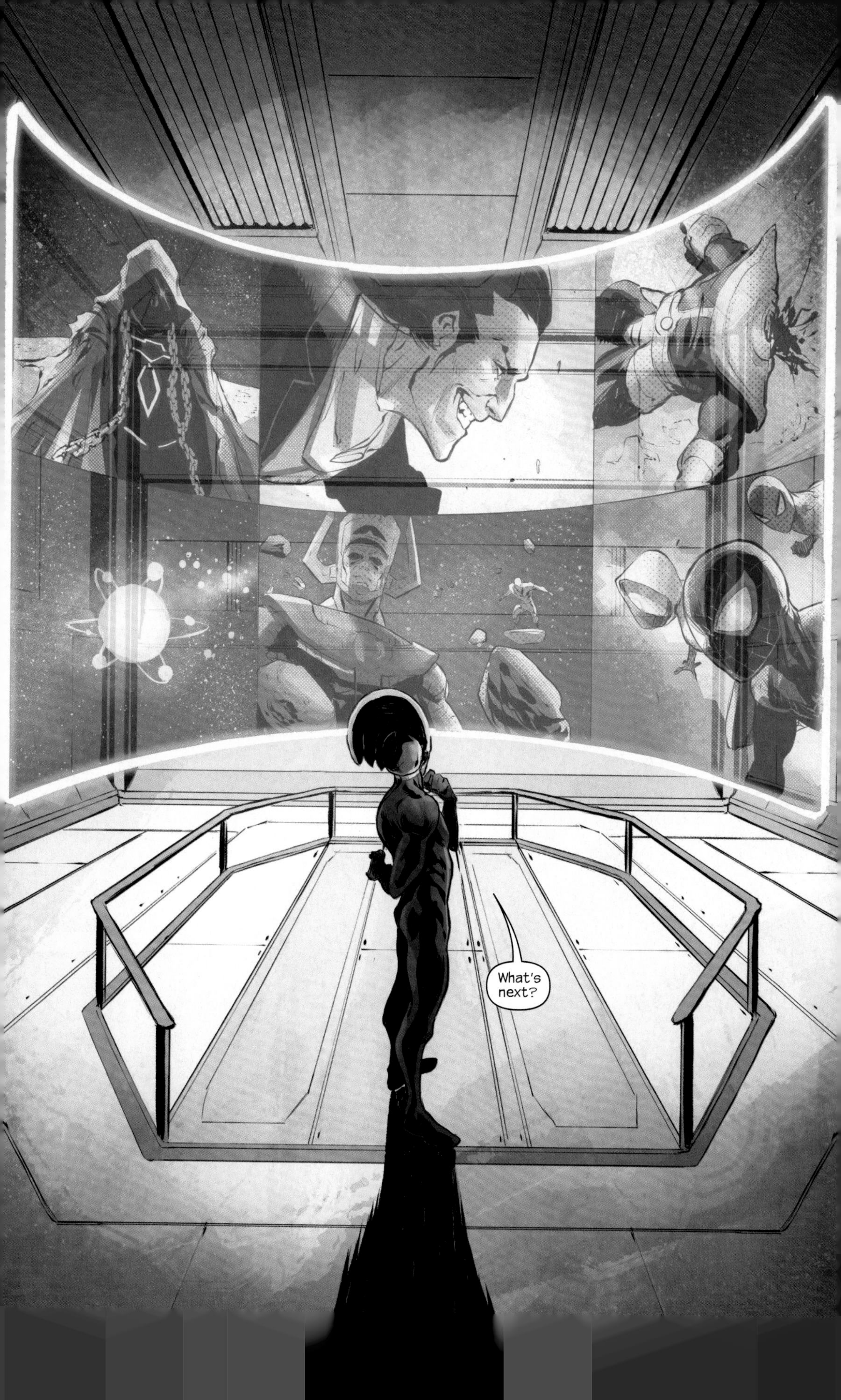
What's next?

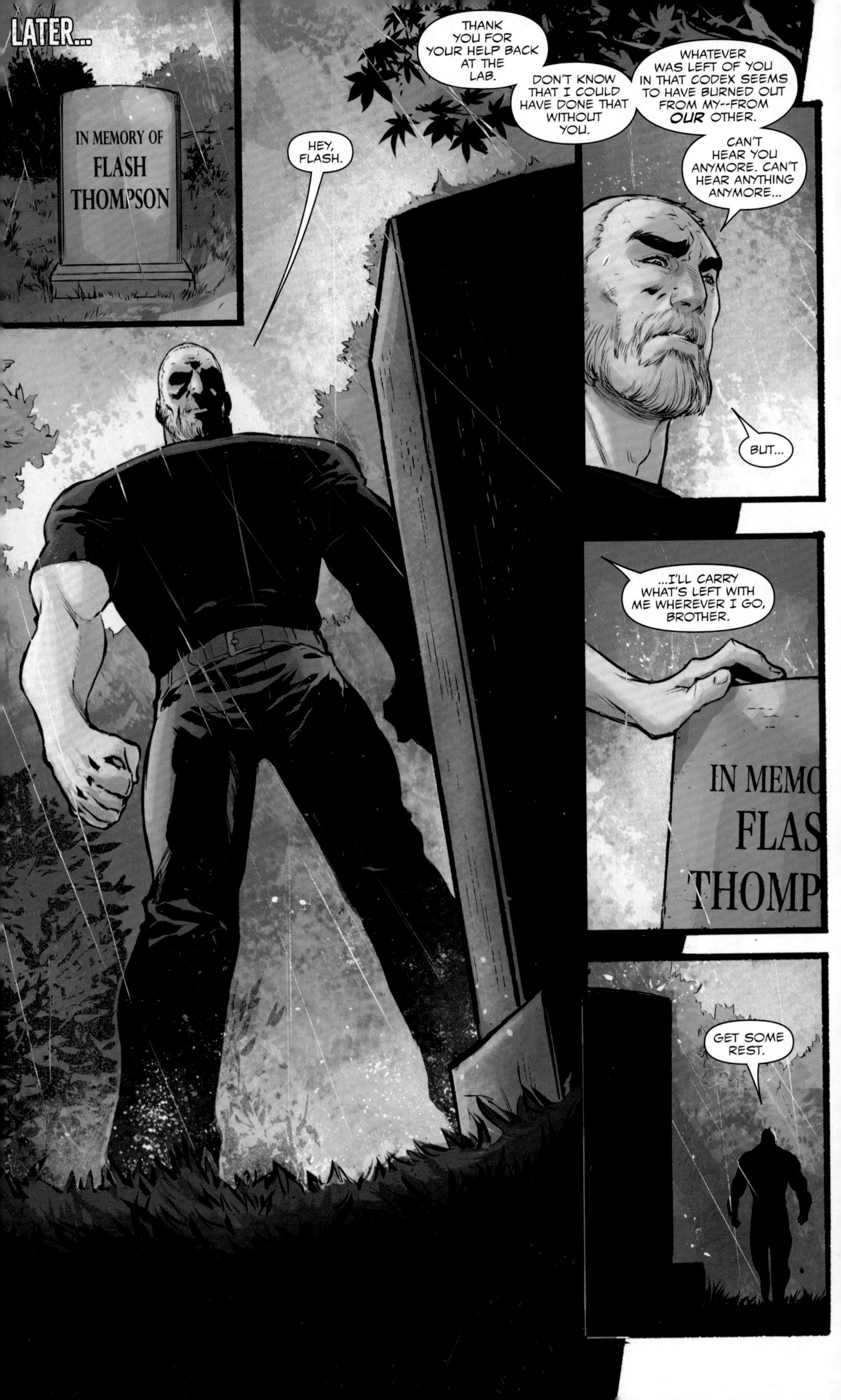
LATER...
IN MEMORY OF FLASH THOMPSON
HEY, FLASH.
THANK YOU FOR YOUR HELP BACK AT THE LAB.
DON'T KNOW THAT I COULD HAVE DONE THAT WITHOUT YOU.
WHATEVER WAS LEFT OF YOU IN THAT CODEX SEEMS TO HAVE BURNED OUT FROM MY--FROM OUR OTHER.
CAN'T HEAR YOU ANYMORE. CAN'T HEAR ANYTHING ANYMORE...
BUT...
...I'LL CARRY WHAT'S LEFT WITH ME WHEREVER I GO, BROTHER.
IN MEMO FLAS THOMP
GET SOME REST.

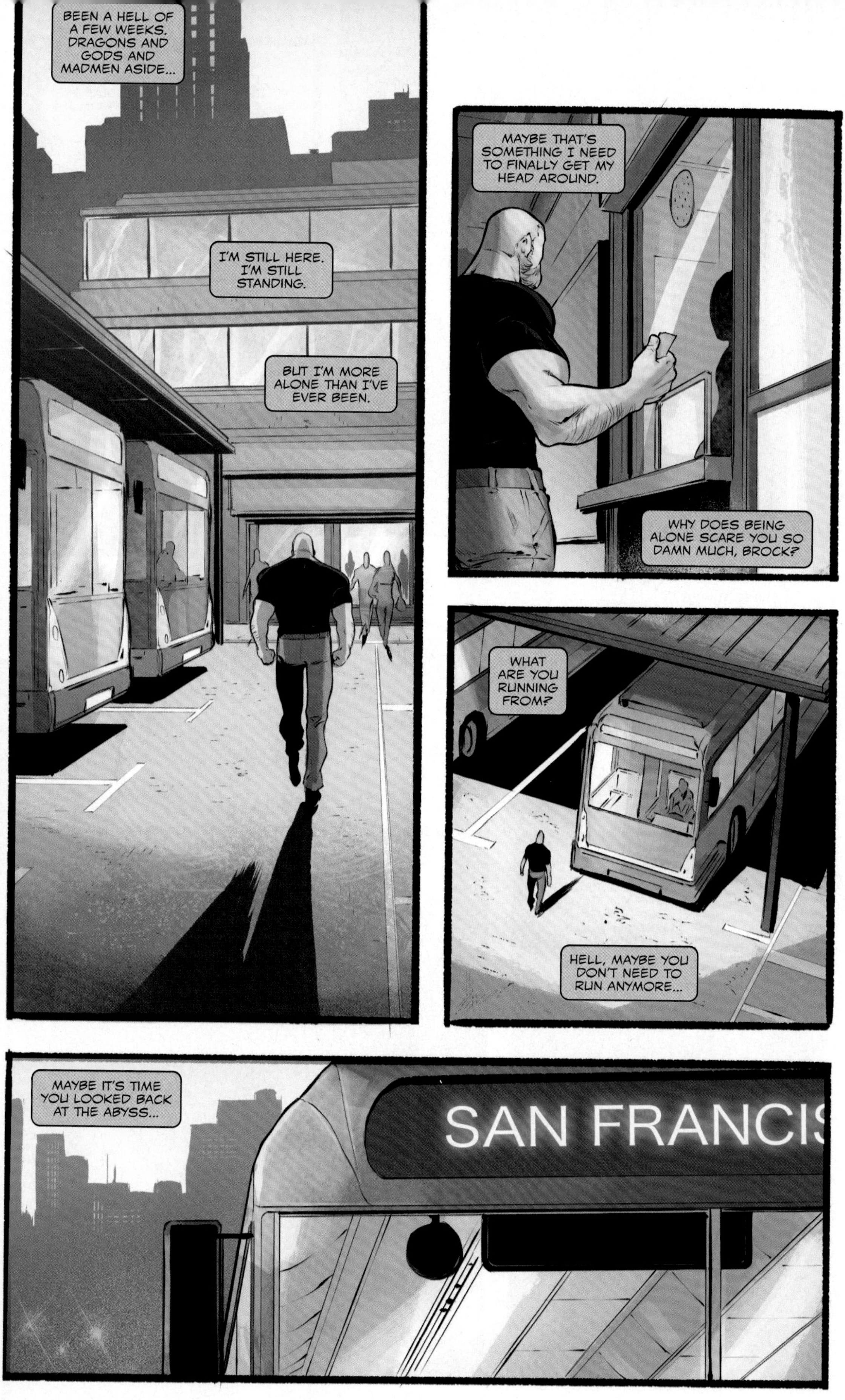
BEEN A HELL OF A FEW WEEKS. DRAGONS AND GODS AND MADMEN ASIDE...
I'M STILL HERE. I'M STILL STANDING.
BUT I'M MORE ALONE THAN I'VE EVER BEEN.
MAYBE THAT'S SOMETHING I NEED TO FINALLY GET MY HEAD AROUND.
WHY DOES BEING ALONE SCARE YOU SO DAMN MUCH, BROCK?
WHAT ARE YOU RUNNING FROM?
HELL, MAYBE YOU DON'T NEED TO RUN ANYMORE...
MAYBE IT'S TIME YOU LOOKED BACK AT THE ABYSS...
SAN FRANCIS

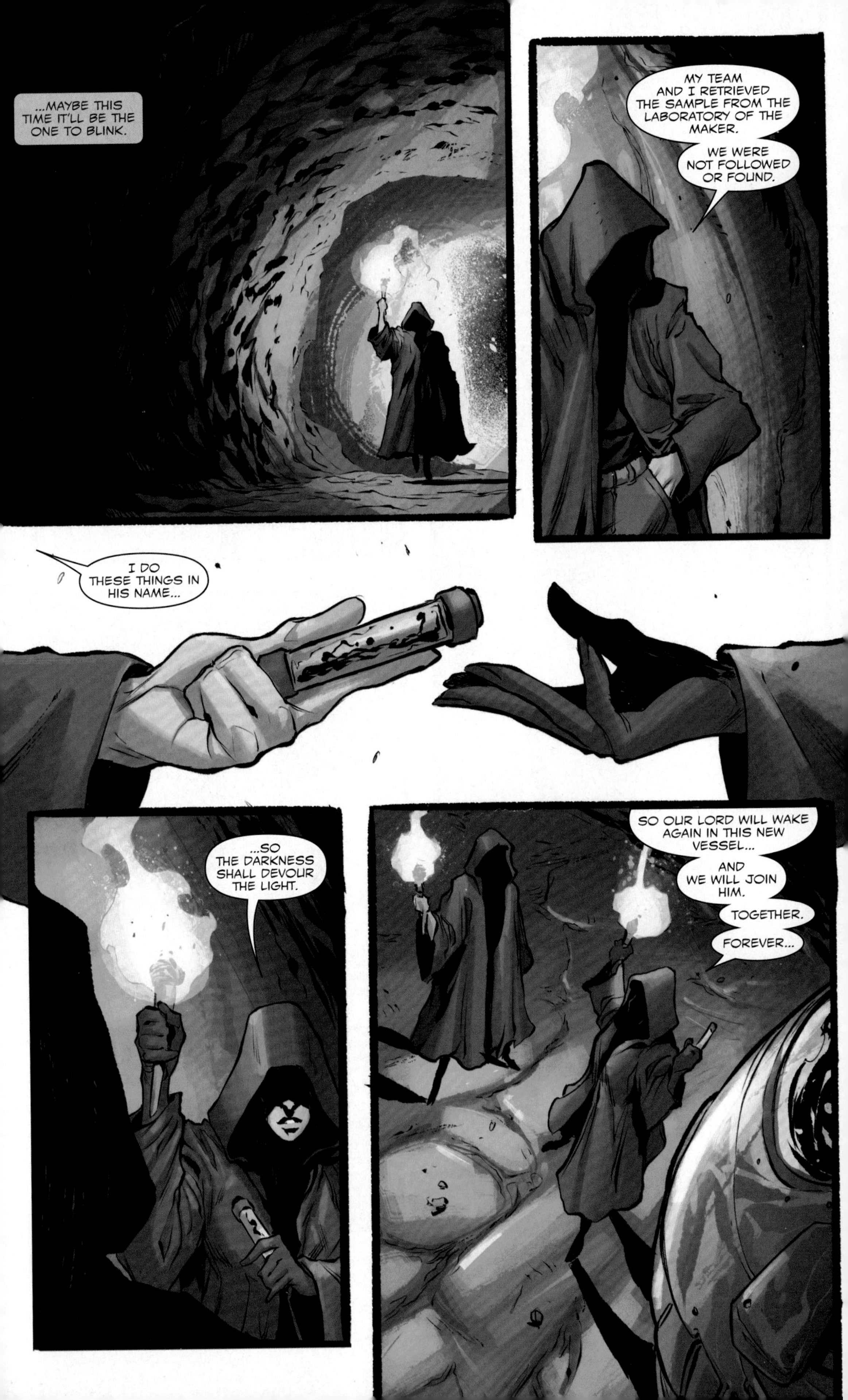
...MAYBE THIS TIME IT'LL BE THE ONE TO BLINK.
MY TEAM AND I RETRIEVED THE SAMPLE FROM THE LABORATORY OF THE MAKER.
WE WERE NOT FOLLOWED OR FOUND.
I DO THESE THINGS IN HIS NAME...
...SO THE DARKNESS SHALL DEVOUR THE LIGHT.
SO OUR LORD WILL WAKE AGAIN IN THIS NEW VESSEL...
AND WE WILL JOIN HIM.
TOGETHER.
FOREVER...

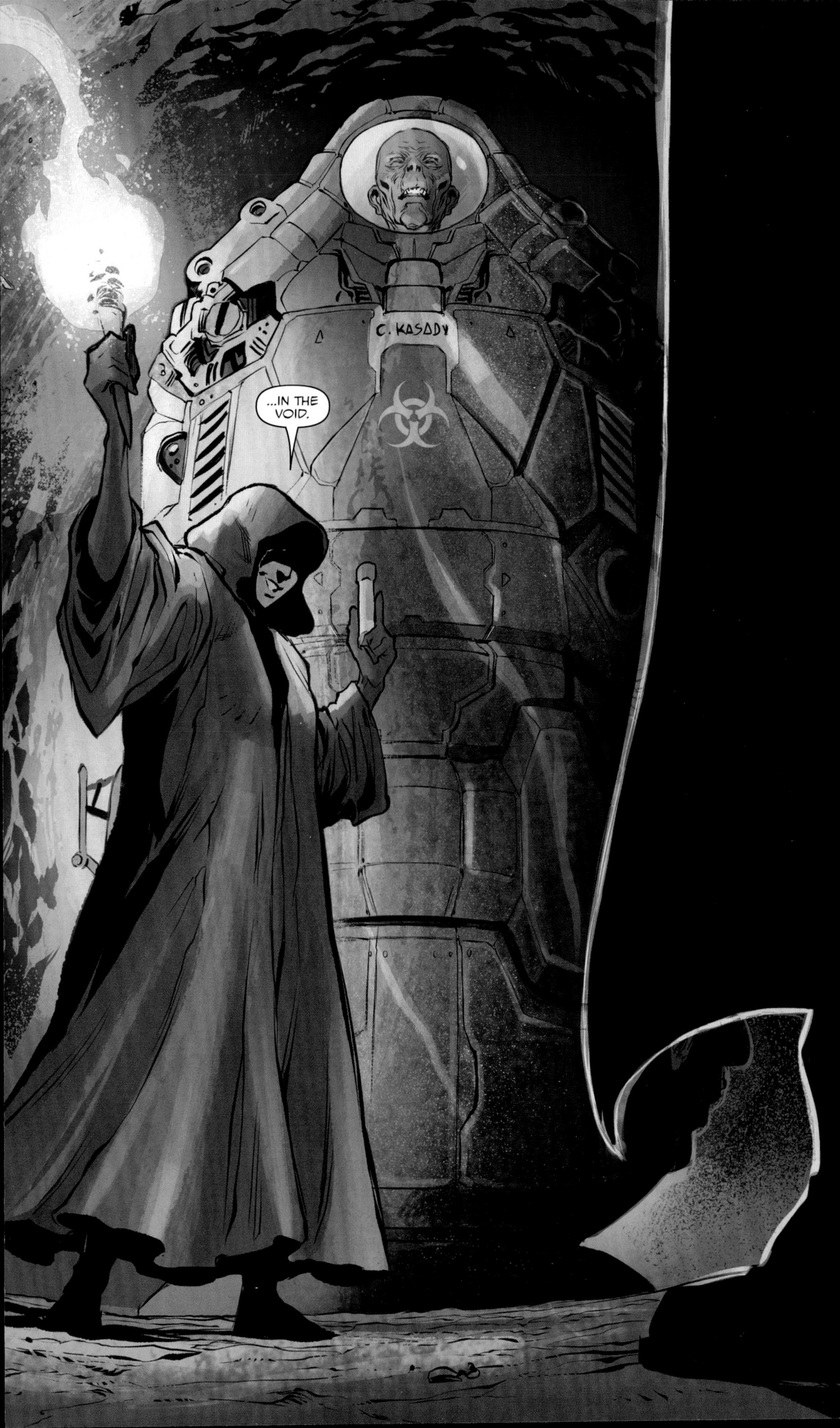
C. KASADY
...IN THE VOID.

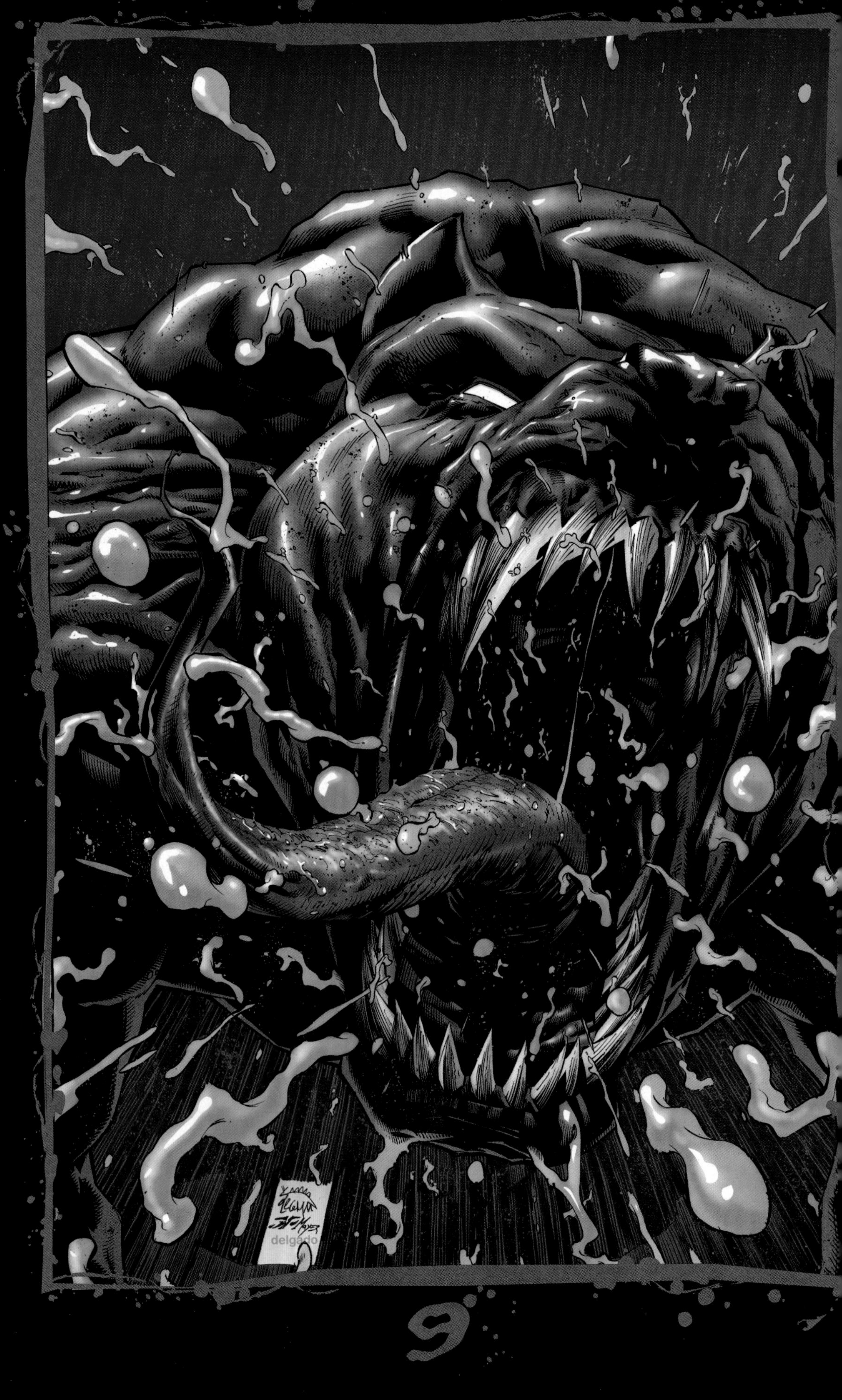
9

WHEN YOU LOVE SOMEONE, WHEN YOUR LIVES ARE TIED TOGETHER, YOUR BODIES SHARE THE HAPPINESS YOU CREATE.

THE BOTH OF YOU BECOME A HIVE MIND OF THE JOY AND THE LAUGHTER, THE BIG THINGS AND THE SMALL.

EVERYTHING THE TWO OF YOU DO GOES INTO THAT SAME, SHARED PLACE.

AND WHEN YOUR OTHER HALF DIES...

...THE HIVE MIND OF YOUR LIFE TOGETHER... BECOMES YOURS TO CARRY AND KEEP, ALONE.

THAT FEELING. THE MASSIVE, UNMANAGEABLE WEIGHT...

...THE SUDDEN, SOLE RESPONSIBILITY OF KEEPING THE MEMORIES OF THE LIFE YOU SHARED ALIVE...

...THAT'S WHAT GRIEF IS. THAT'S DESPAIR.

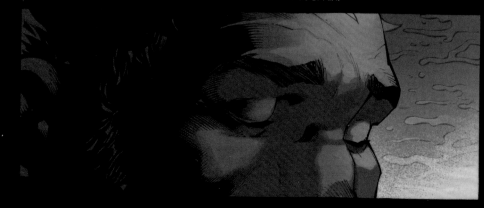

THAT'S LIFE FOR THOSE LEFT BEHIND.

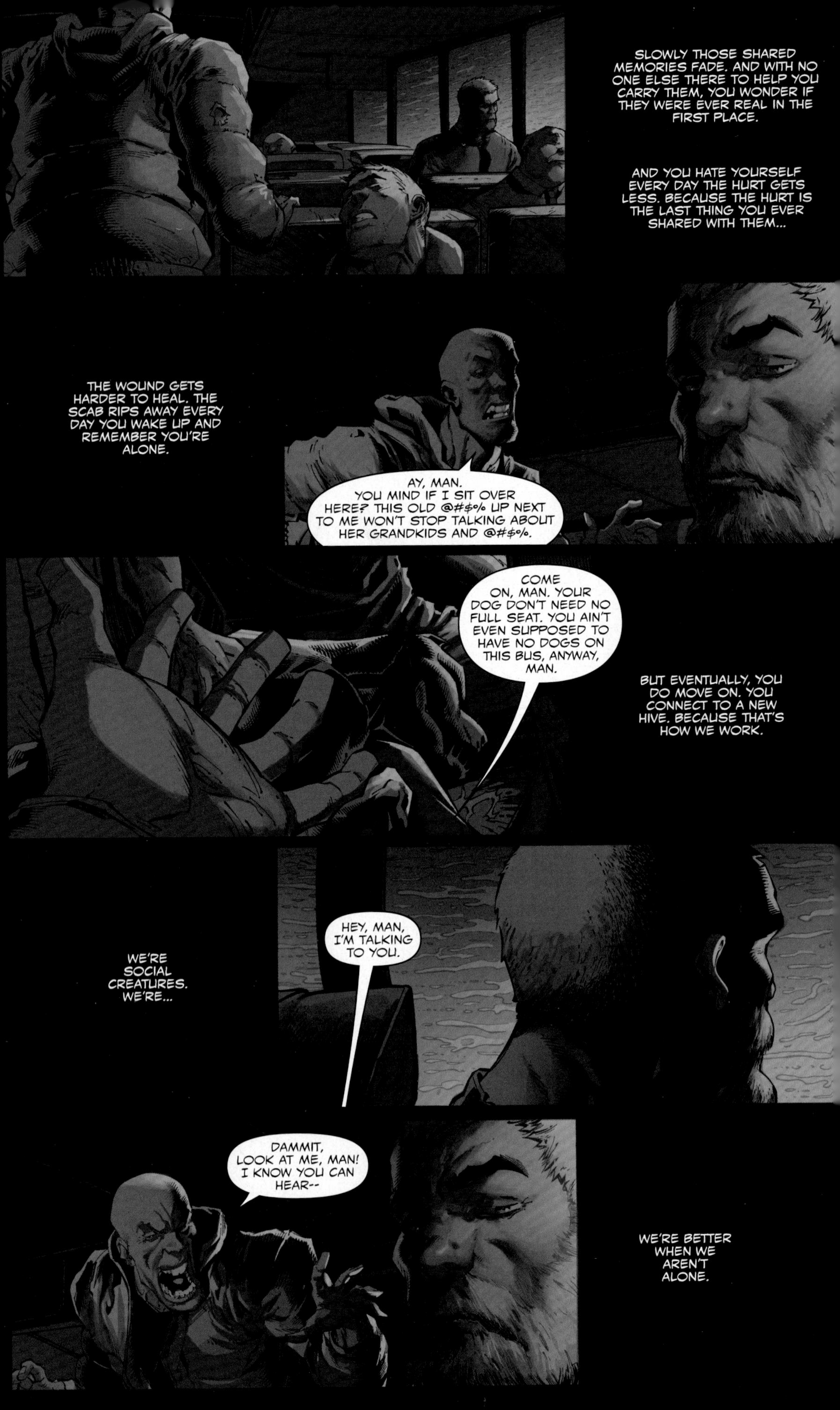
SLOWLY THOSE SHARED MEMORIES FADE. AND WITH NO ONE ELSE THERE TO HELP YOU CARRY THEM, YOU WONDER IF THEY WERE EVER REAL IN THE FIRST PLACE.
AND YOU HATE YOURSELF EVERY DAY THE HURT GETS LESS. BECAUSE THE HURT IS THE LAST THING YOU EVER SHARED WITH THEM...
THE WOUND GETS HARDER TO HEAL. THE SCAB RIPS AWAY EVERY DAY YOU WAKE UP AND REMEMBER YOU'RE ALONE.
AY, MAN. YOU MIND IF I SIT OVER HERE? THIS OLD @#$%% UP NEXT TO ME WON'T STOP TALKING ABOUT HER GRANDKIDS AND @#$%%.
COME ON, MAN. YOUR DOG DON'T NEED NO FULL SEAT. YOU AIN'T EVEN SUPPOSED TO HAVE NO DOGS ON THIS BUS, ANYWAY, MAN.
BUT EVENTUALLY, YOU DO MOVE ON. YOU CONNECT TO A NEW HIVE. BECAUSE THAT'S HOW WE WORK.
WE'RE SOCIAL CREATURES. WE'RE...
HEY, MAN, I'M TALKING TO YOU.
DAMMIT, LOOK AT ME, MAN! I KNOW YOU CAN HEAR--
WE'RE BETTER WHEN WE AREN'T ALONE.

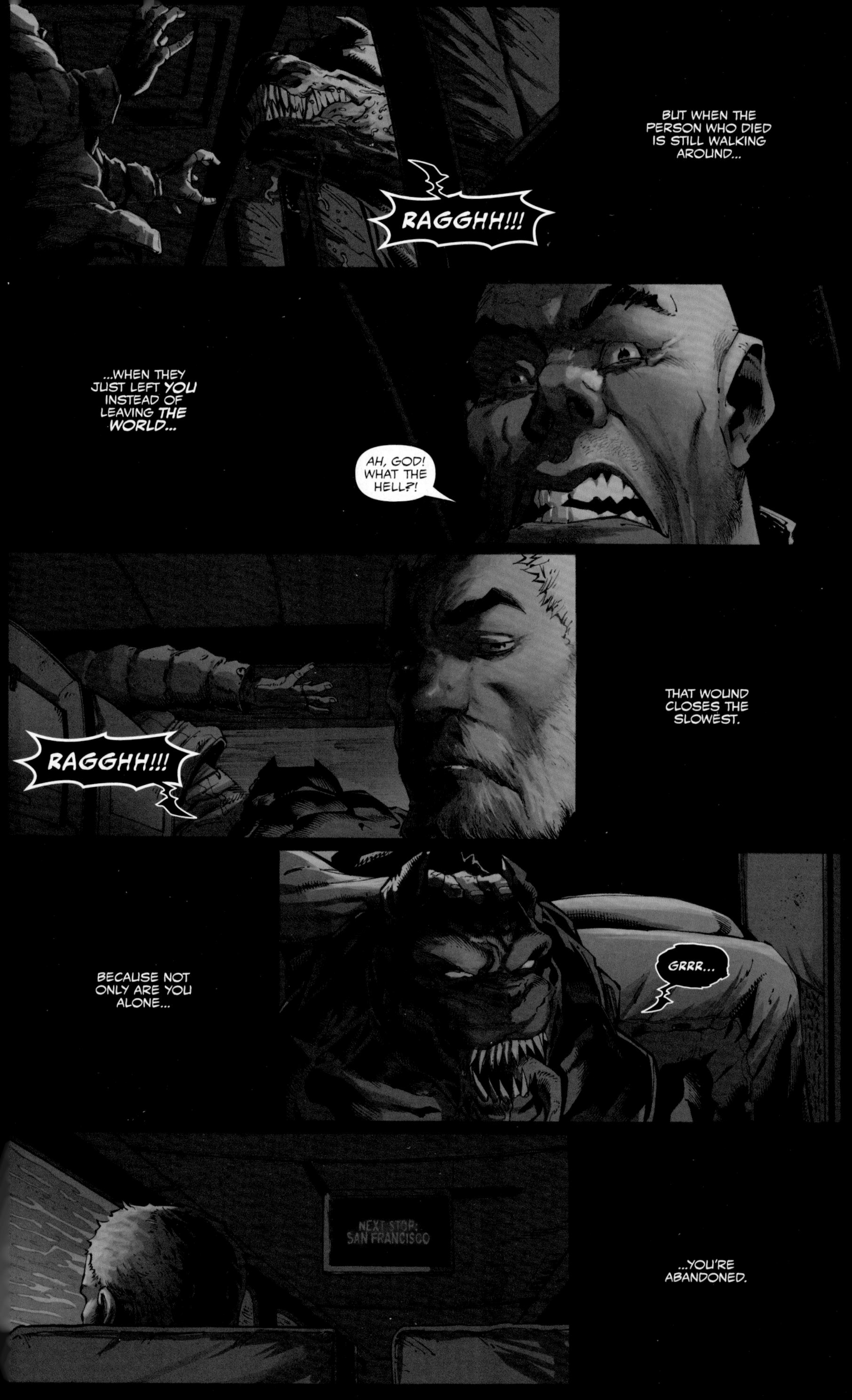
BUT WHEN THE PERSON WHO DIED IS STILL WALKING AROUND...
RAGGHH!!!
...WHEN THEY JUST LEFT YOU INSTEAD OF LEAVING THE WORLD...
AH, GOD! WHAT THE HELL?!
RAGGHH!!!
THAT WOUND CLOSES THE SLOWEST.
BECAUSE NOT ONLY ARE YOU ALONE...
GRRR...
NEXT STOP: SAN FRANCISCO
...YOU'RE ABANDONED.

THE
ABYSS

CHAPTER ONE.

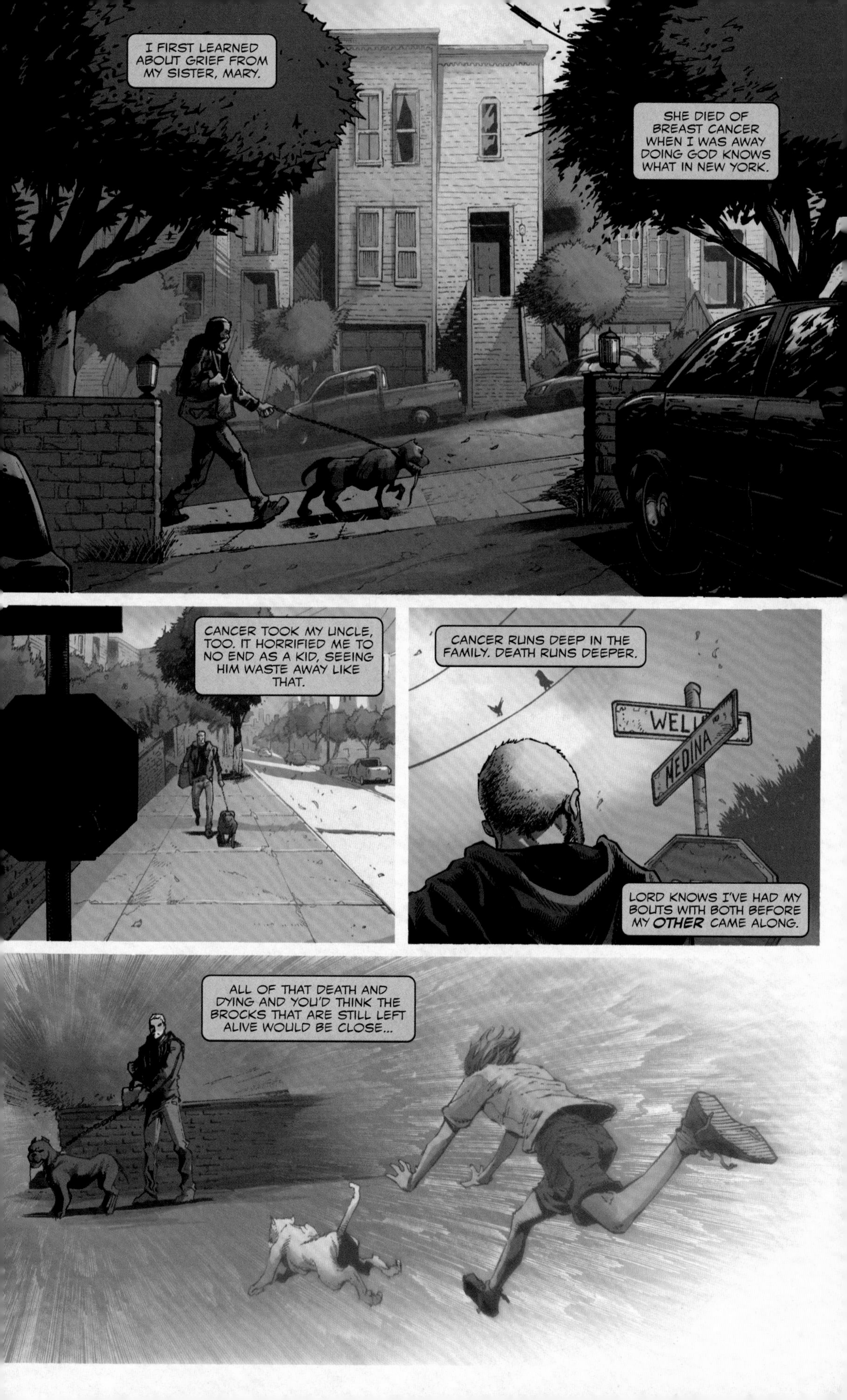
I FIRST LEARNED ABOUT GRIEF FROM MY SISTER, MARY.
SHE DIED OF BREAST CANCER WHEN I WAS AWAY DOING GOD KNOWS WHAT IN NEW YORK.
CANCER TOOK MY UNCLE, TOO. IT HORRIFIED ME TO NO END AS A KID, SEEING HIM WASTE AWAY LIKE THAT.
CANCER RUNS DEEP IN THE FAMILY. DEATH RUNS DEEPER.
WELL
MEDINA
LORD KNOWS I'VE HAD MY BOUTS WITH BOTH BEFORE MY *OTHER* CAME ALONG.
ALL OF THAT DEATH AND DYING AND YOU'D THINK THE BROCKS THAT ARE STILL LEFT ALIVE WOULD BE CLOSE...

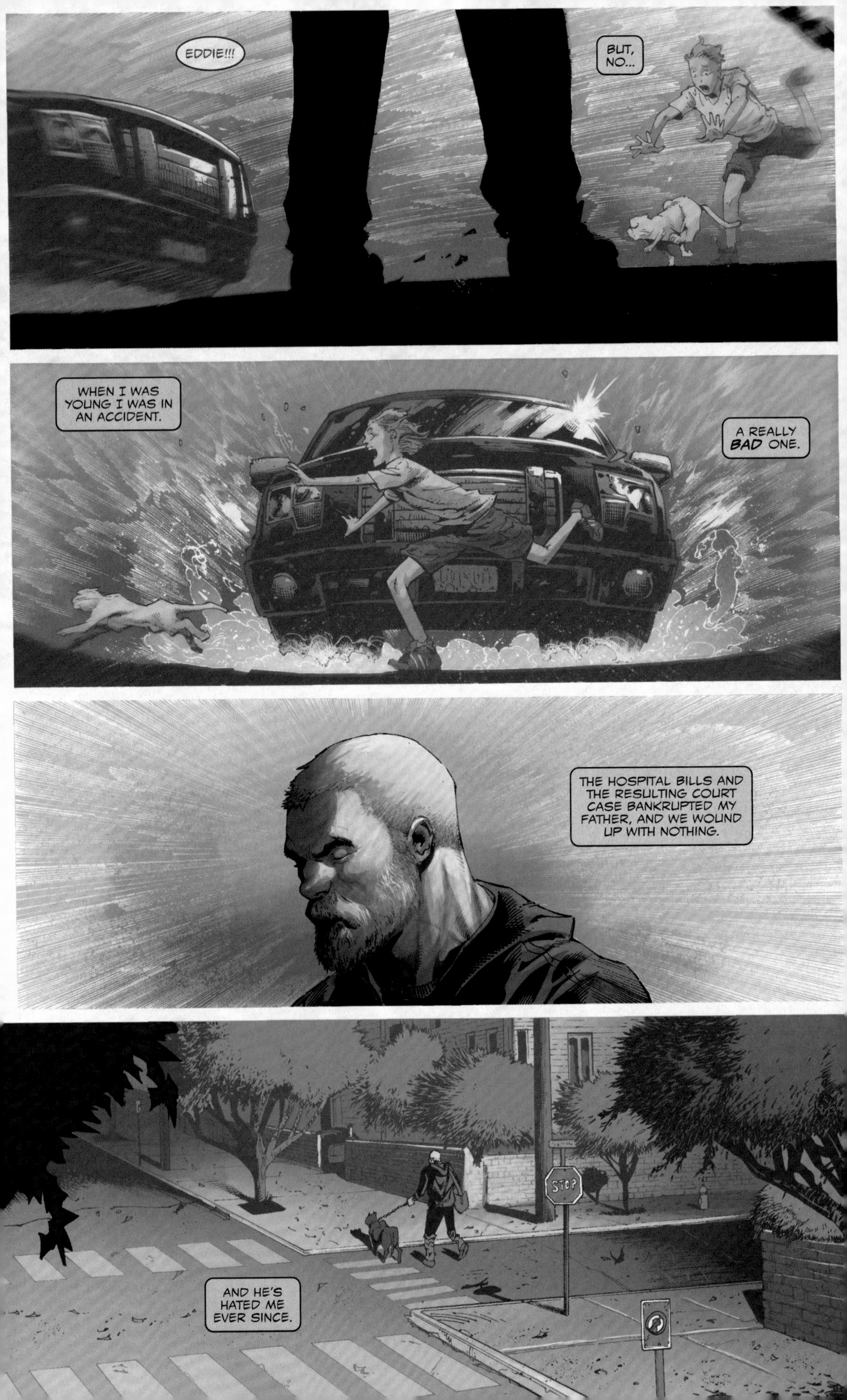

EDDIE!!!
BUT, NO...
WHEN I WAS YOUNG I WAS IN AN ACCIDENT.
A REALLY BAD ONE.
THE HOSPITAL BILLS AND THE RESULTING COURT CASE BANKRUPTED MY FATHER, AND WE WOUND UP WITH NOTHING.
AND HE'S HATED ME EVER SINCE.
STOP

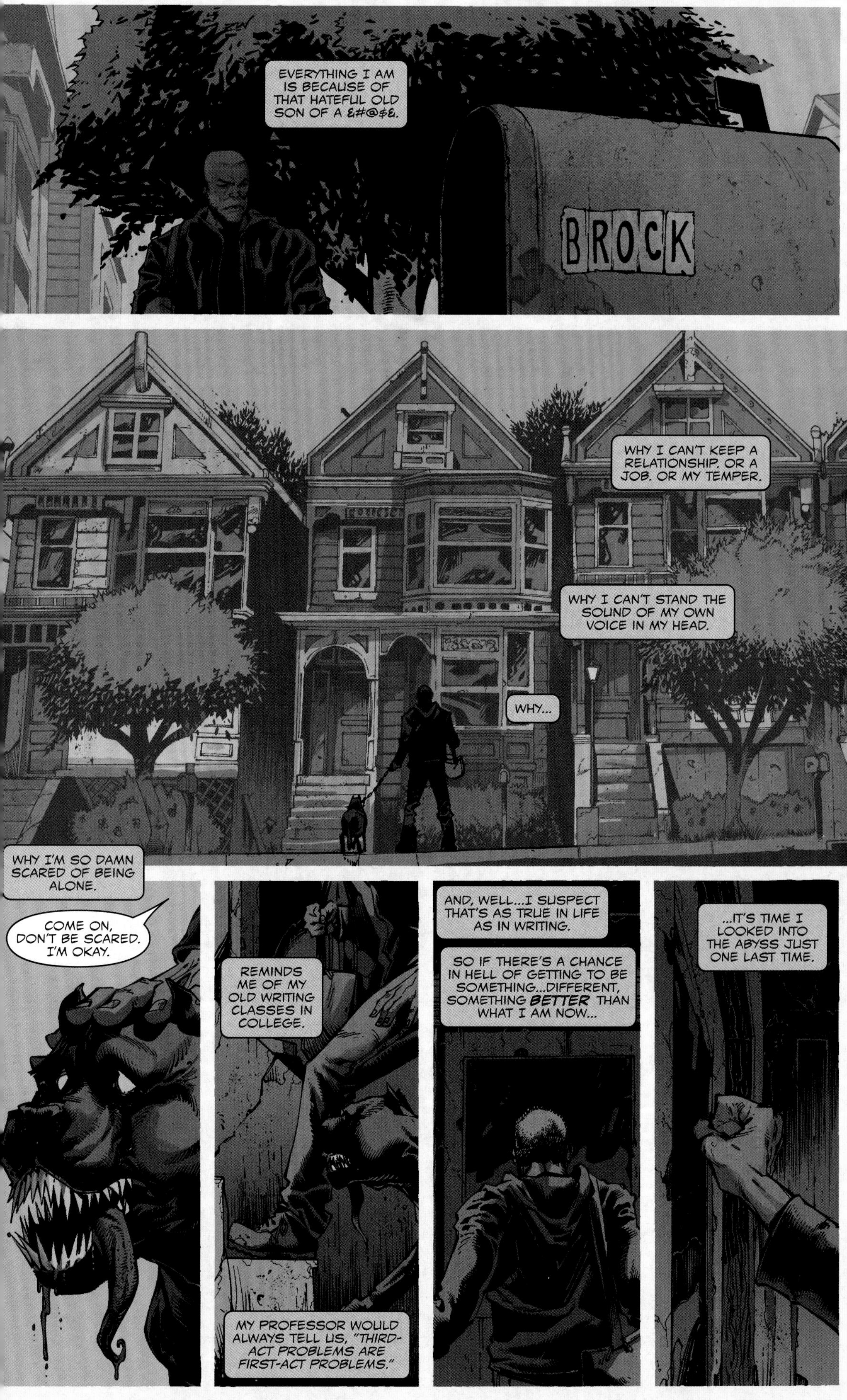
EVERYTHING I AM IS BECAUSE OF THAT HATEFUL OLD SON OF A &#@$&.
BROCK
WHY I CAN'T KEEP A RELATIONSHIP. OR A JOB. OR MY TEMPER.
WHY I CAN'T STAND THE SOUND OF MY OWN VOICE IN MY HEAD.
WHY...
WHY I'M SO DAMN SCARED OF BEING ALONE.
COME ON, DON'T BE SCARED. I'M OKAY.
REMINDS ME OF MY OLD WRITING CLASSES IN COLLEGE.
MY PROFESSOR WOULD ALWAYS TELL US, "THIRD-ACT PROBLEMS ARE FIRST-ACT PROBLEMS."
AND, WELL...I SUSPECT THAT'S AS TRUE IN LIFE AS IN WRITING.
SO IF THERE'S A CHANCE IN HELL OF GETTING TO BE SOMETHING...DIFFERENT, SOMETHING BETTER THAN WHAT I AM NOW...
...IT'S TIME I LOOKED INTO THE ABYSS JUST ONE LAST TIME.

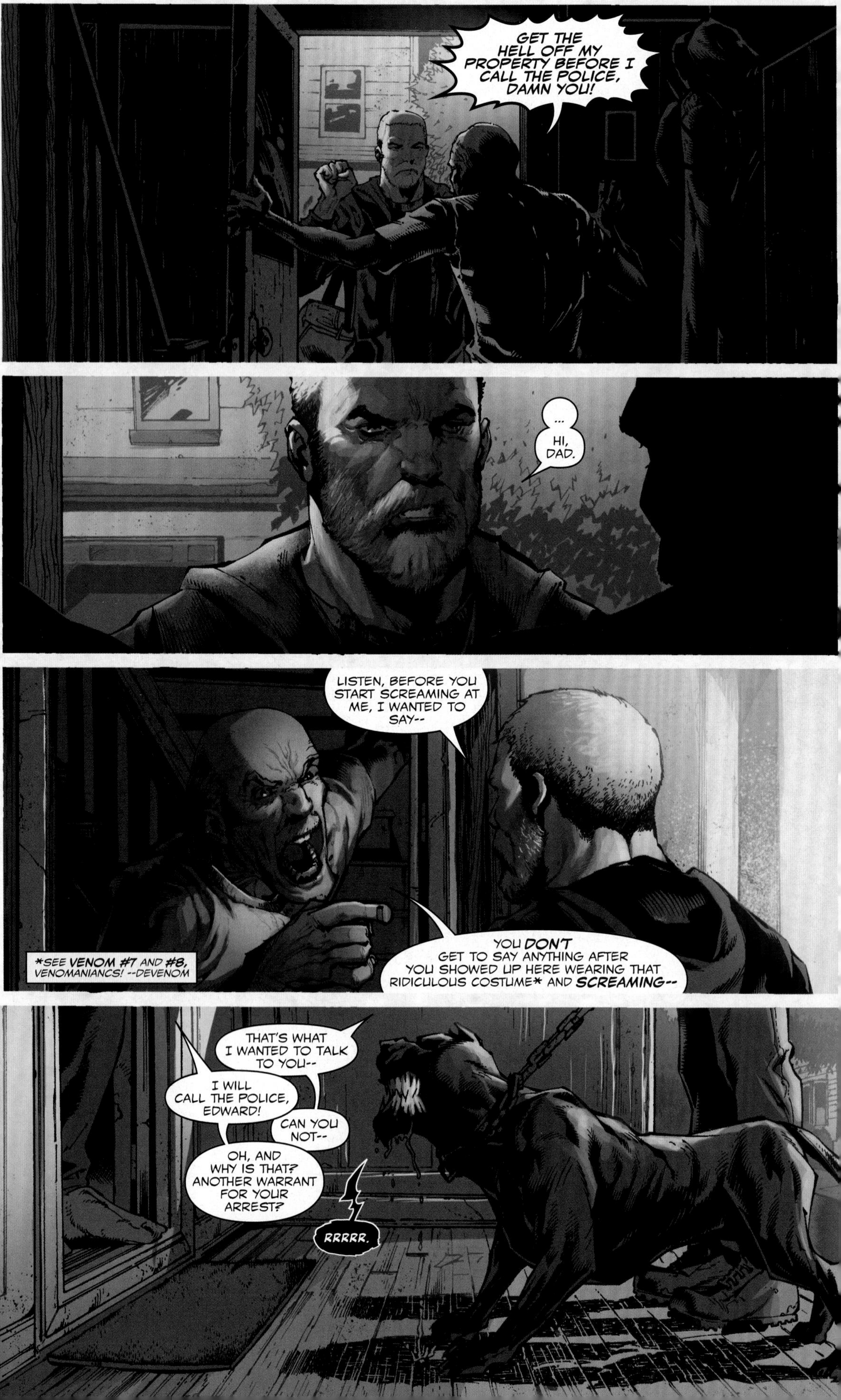
GET THE HELL OFF MY PROPERTY BEFORE I CALL THE POLICE, DAMN YOU!
... HI, DAD.
LISTEN, BEFORE YOU START SCREAMING AT ME, I WANTED TO SAY--
YOU DON'T GET TO SAY ANYTHING AFTER YOU SHOWED UP HERE WEARING THAT RIDICULOUS COSTUME* AND SCREAMING--
*SEE VENOM #7 AND #8, VENOMANIANCS! --DEVENOM
THAT'S WHAT I WANTED TO TALK TO YOU--
I WILL CALL THE POLICE, EDWARD!
CAN YOU NOT--
OH, AND WHY IS THAT? ANOTHER WARRANT FOR YOUR ARREST?
RRRRR.

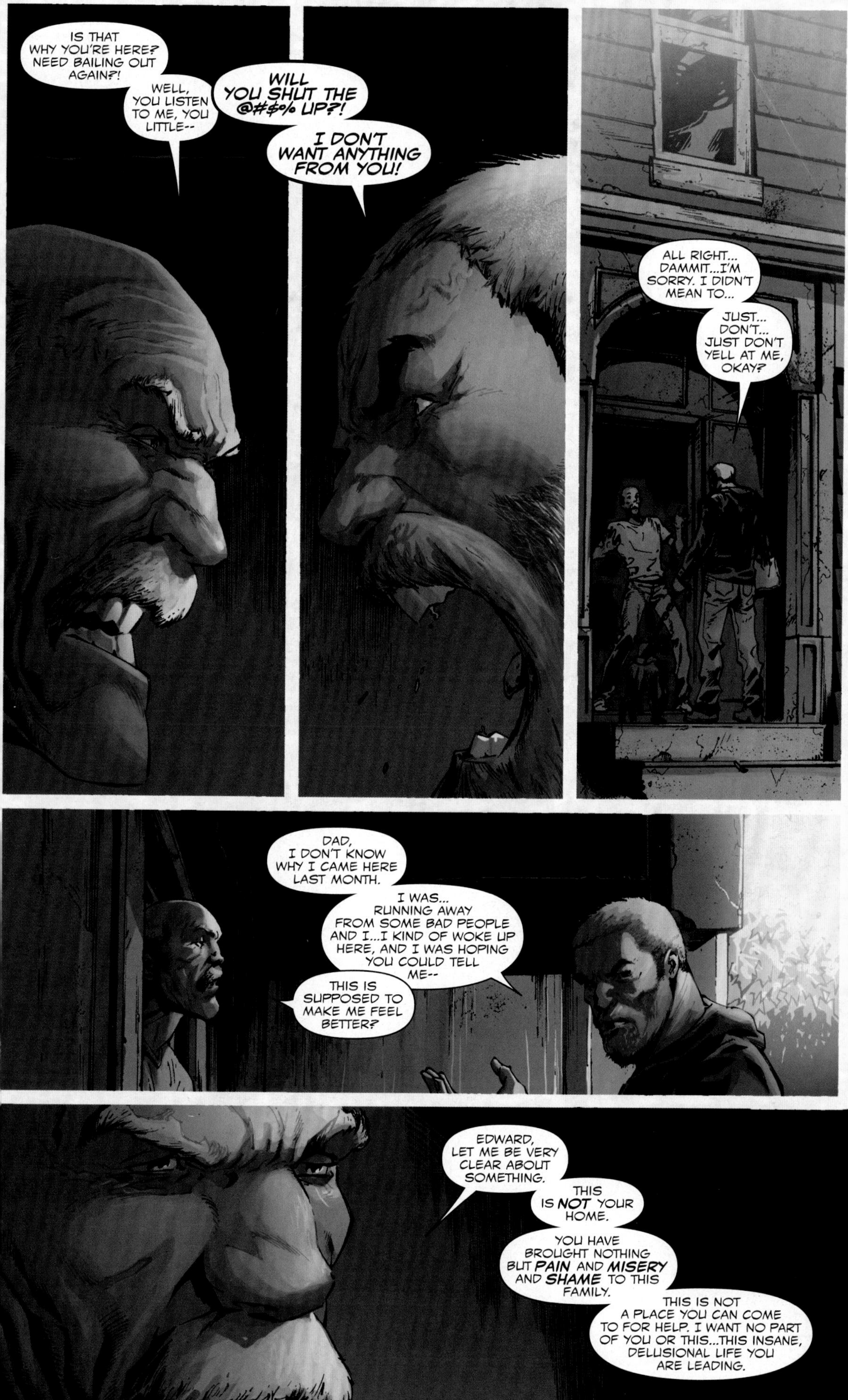
IS THAT WHY YOU'RE HERE? NEED BAILING OUT AGAIN?!
WELL, YOU LISTEN TO ME, YOU LITTLE--
WILL YOU SHUT THE @#$%/o UP?!
I DON'T WANT ANYTHING FROM YOU!
ALL RIGHT... DAMMIT...I'M SORRY. I DIDN'T MEAN TO...
JUST... DON'T... JUST DON'T YELL AT ME, OKAY?
DAD, I DON'T KNOW WHY I CAME HERE LAST MONTH.
I WAS... RUNNING AWAY FROM SOME BAD PEOPLE AND I...I KIND OF WOKE UP HERE, AND I WAS HOPING YOU COULD TELL ME--
THIS IS SUPPOSED TO MAKE ME FEEL BETTER?
EDWARD, LET ME BE VERY CLEAR ABOUT SOMETHING.
THIS IS NOT YOUR HOME.
YOU HAVE BROUGHT NOTHING BUT PAIN AND MISERY AND SHAME TO THIS FAMILY.
THIS IS NOT A PLACE YOU CAN COME TO FOR HELP. I WANT NO PART OF YOU OR THIS...THIS INSANE, DELUSIONAL LIFE YOU ARE LEADING.

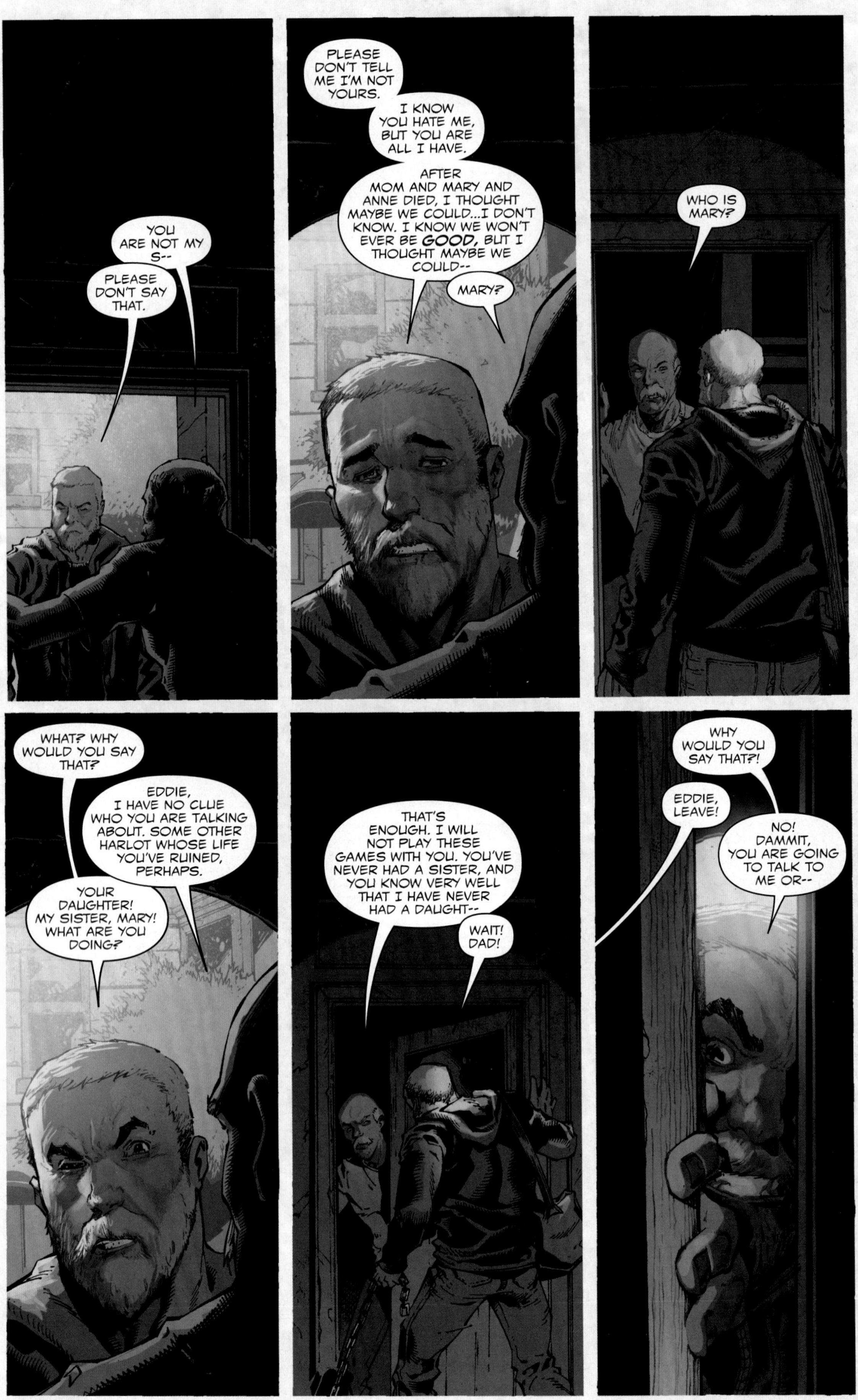
YOU ARE NOT MY S--
PLEASE DON'T SAY THAT.
PLEASE DON'T TELL ME I'M NOT YOURS.
I KNOW YOU HATE ME, BUT YOU ARE ALL I HAVE.
AFTER MOM AND MARY AND ANNE DIED, I THOUGHT MAYBE WE COULD...I DON'T KNOW. I KNOW WE WON'T EVER BE GOOD, BUT I THOUGHT MAYBE WE COULD--
MARY?
WHO IS MARY?
WHAT? WHY WOULD YOU SAY THAT?
EDDIE, I HAVE NO CLUE WHO YOU ARE TALKING ABOUT. SOME OTHER HARLOT WHOSE LIFE YOU'VE RUINED, PERHAPS.
YOUR DAUGHTER! MY SISTER, MARY! WHAT ARE YOU DOING?
THAT'S ENOUGH. I WILL NOT PLAY THESE GAMES WITH YOU. YOU'VE NEVER HAD A SISTER, AND YOU KNOW VERY WELL THAT I HAVE NEVER HAD A DAUGHT--
WAIT! DAD!
WHY WOULD YOU SAY THAT?!
EDDIE, LEAVE!
NO! DAMMIT, YOU ARE GOING TO TALK TO ME OR--

DAD?!

NOW THAT IS IT!

YOU GET THE HELL OUT OF HERE THIS INSTANT OR I SWEAR TO GOD, EDDIE, I WILL MAKE SURE YOU ARE PUT AWAY FOR--

NO!!!

OH...OH GOD...

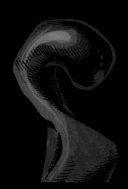

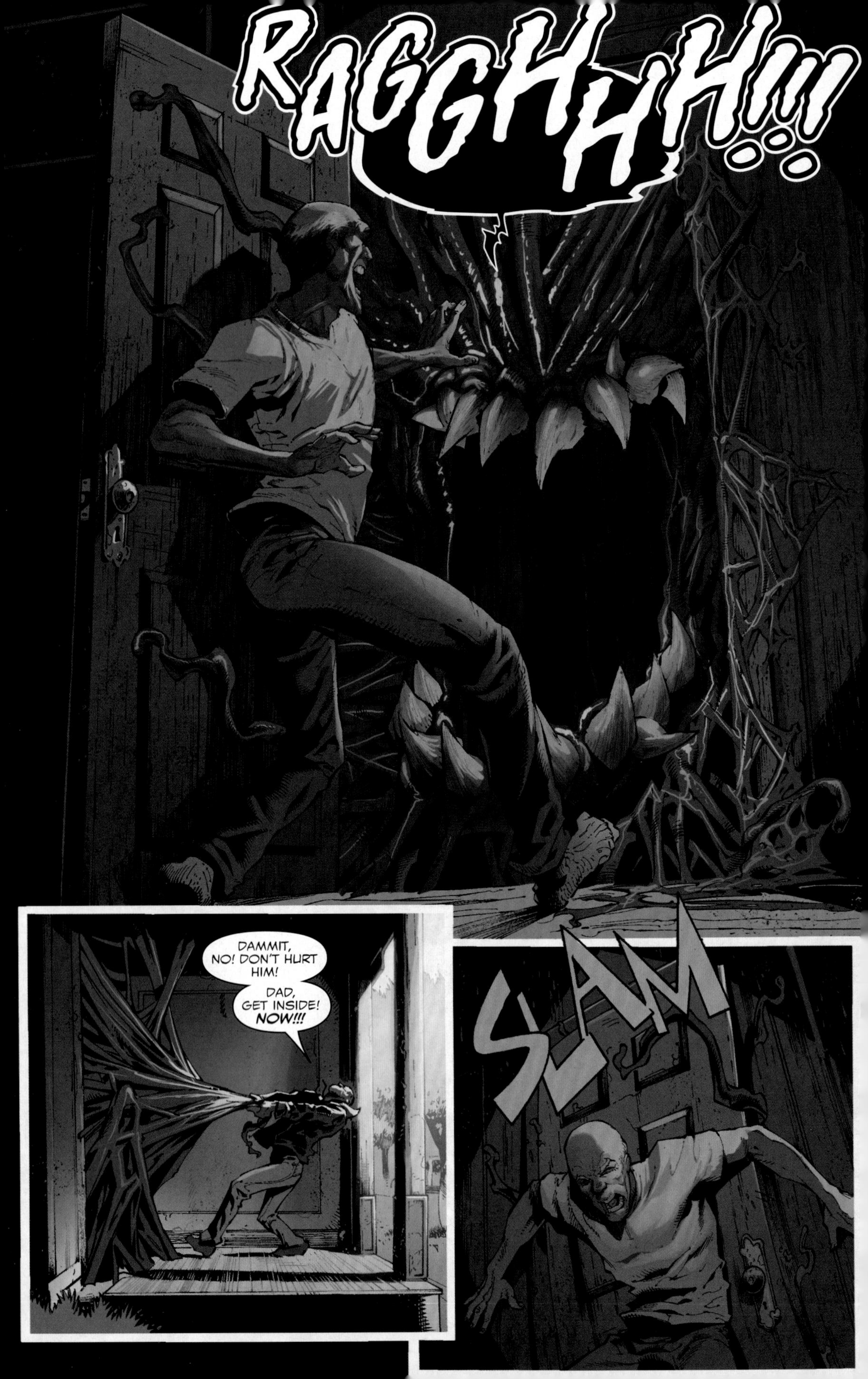
RAGGHHH!!!
DAMMIT, NO! DON'T HURT HIM!
DAD, GET INSIDE! NOW!!!
SLAM

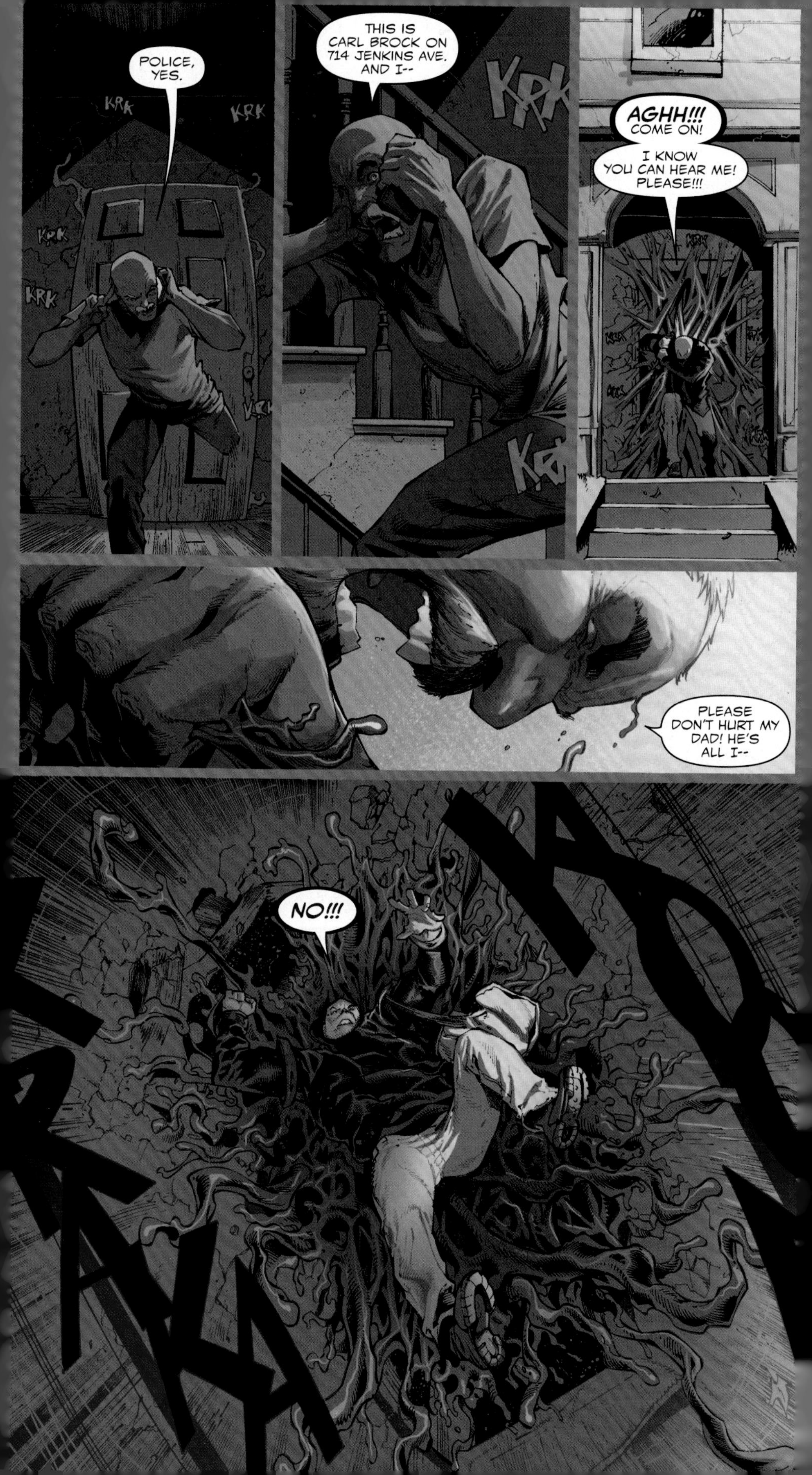
KRK
KRK
KRK
KRK
POLICE, YES.
KRK
THIS IS CARL BROCK ON 714 JENKINS AVE. AND I--
KRK
KRK
AGHH!!! COME ON!
I KNOW YOU CAN HEAR ME! PLEASE!!!
PLEASE DON'T HURT MY DAD! HE'S ALL I--
NO!!!

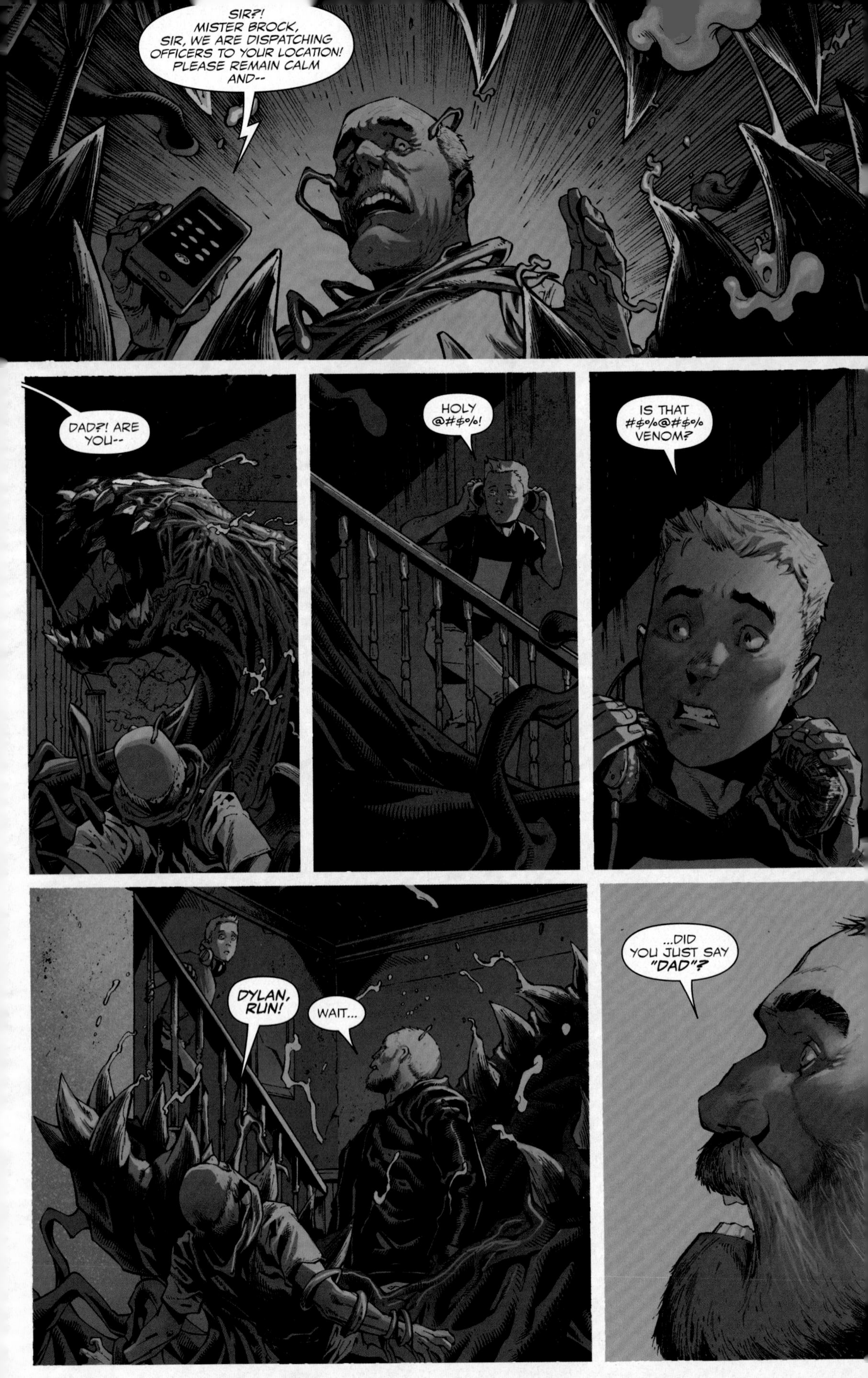
SIR?! MISTER BROCK, SIR, WE ARE DISPATCHING OFFICERS TO YOUR LOCATION! PLEASE REMAIN CALM AND--
DAD?! ARE YOU--
HOLY @#$%!
IS THAT #$%@#$% VENOM?
DYLAN, RUN!
WAIT...
...DID YOU JUST SAY "DAD"?

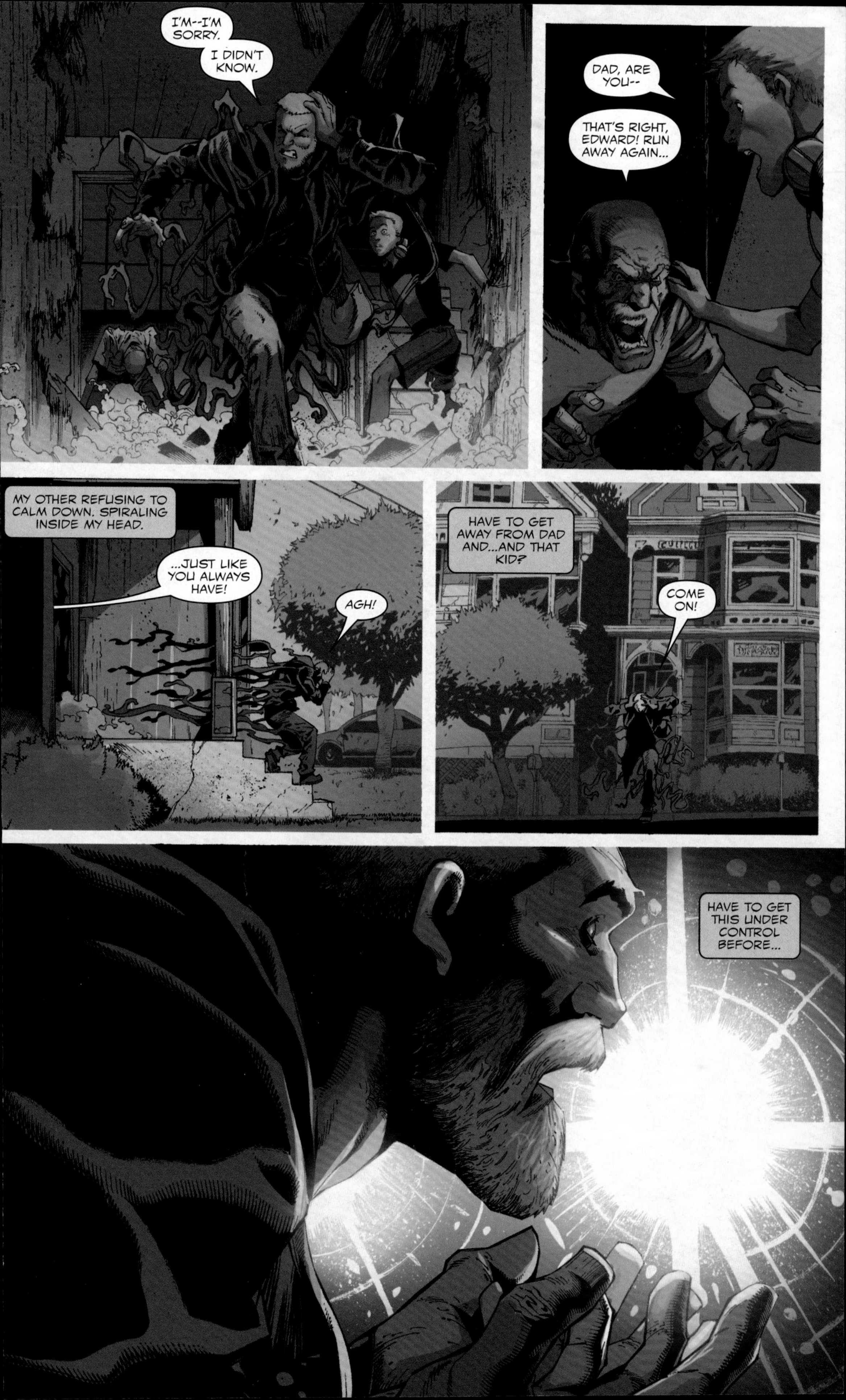
I'M--I'M SORRY.
I DIDN'T KNOW.
DAD, ARE YOU--
THAT'S RIGHT, EDWARD! RUN AWAY AGAIN...
MY OTHER REFUSING TO CALM DOWN. SPIRALING INSIDE MY HEAD.
...JUST LIKE YOU ALWAYS HAVE!
AGH!
HAVE TO GET AWAY FROM DAD AND...AND THAT KID?
COME ON!
HAVE TO GET THIS UNDER CONTROL BEFORE...

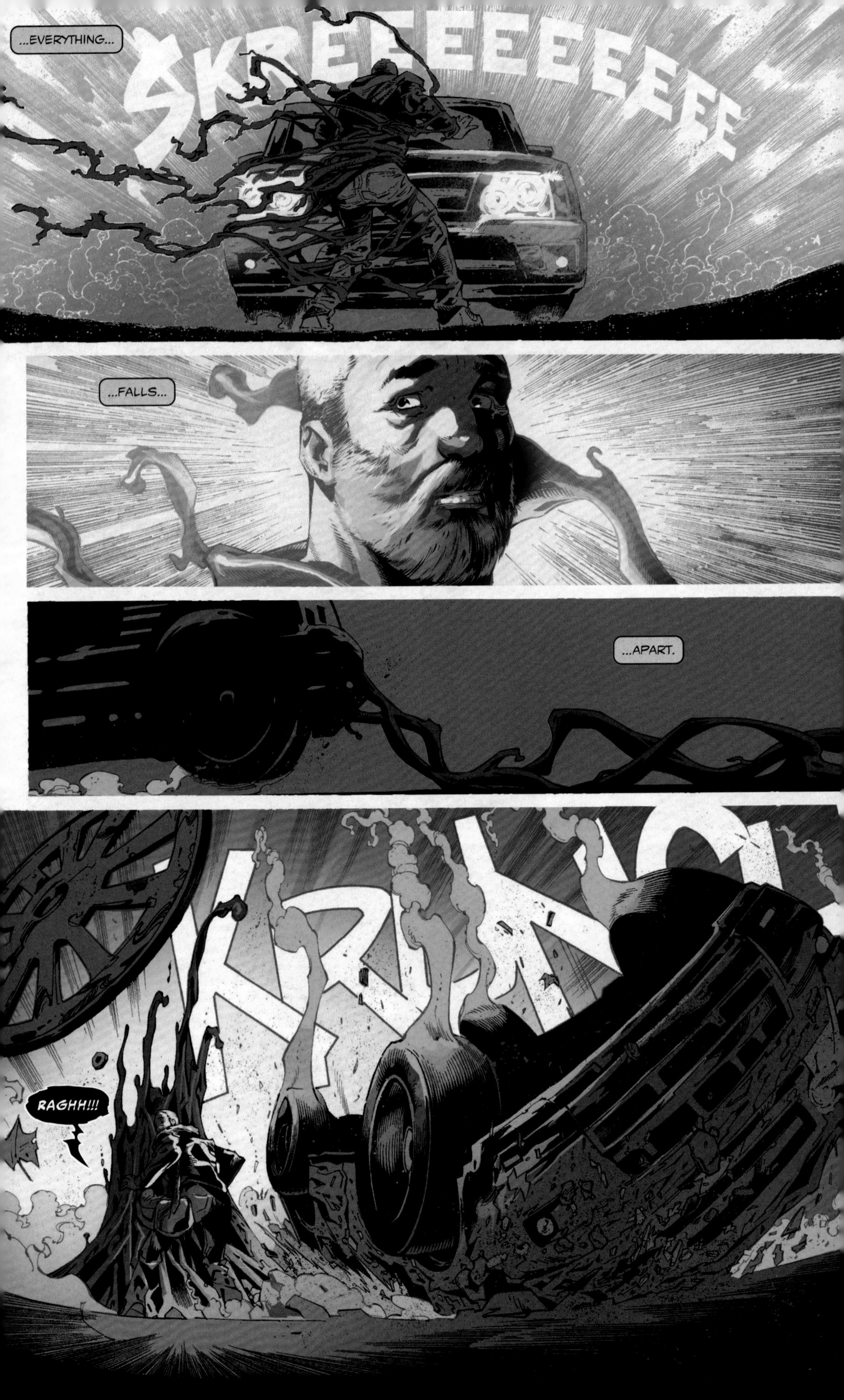
...EVERYTHING...
SKREEEEEEEEEE
...FALLS...
...APART.
RAGHH!!!

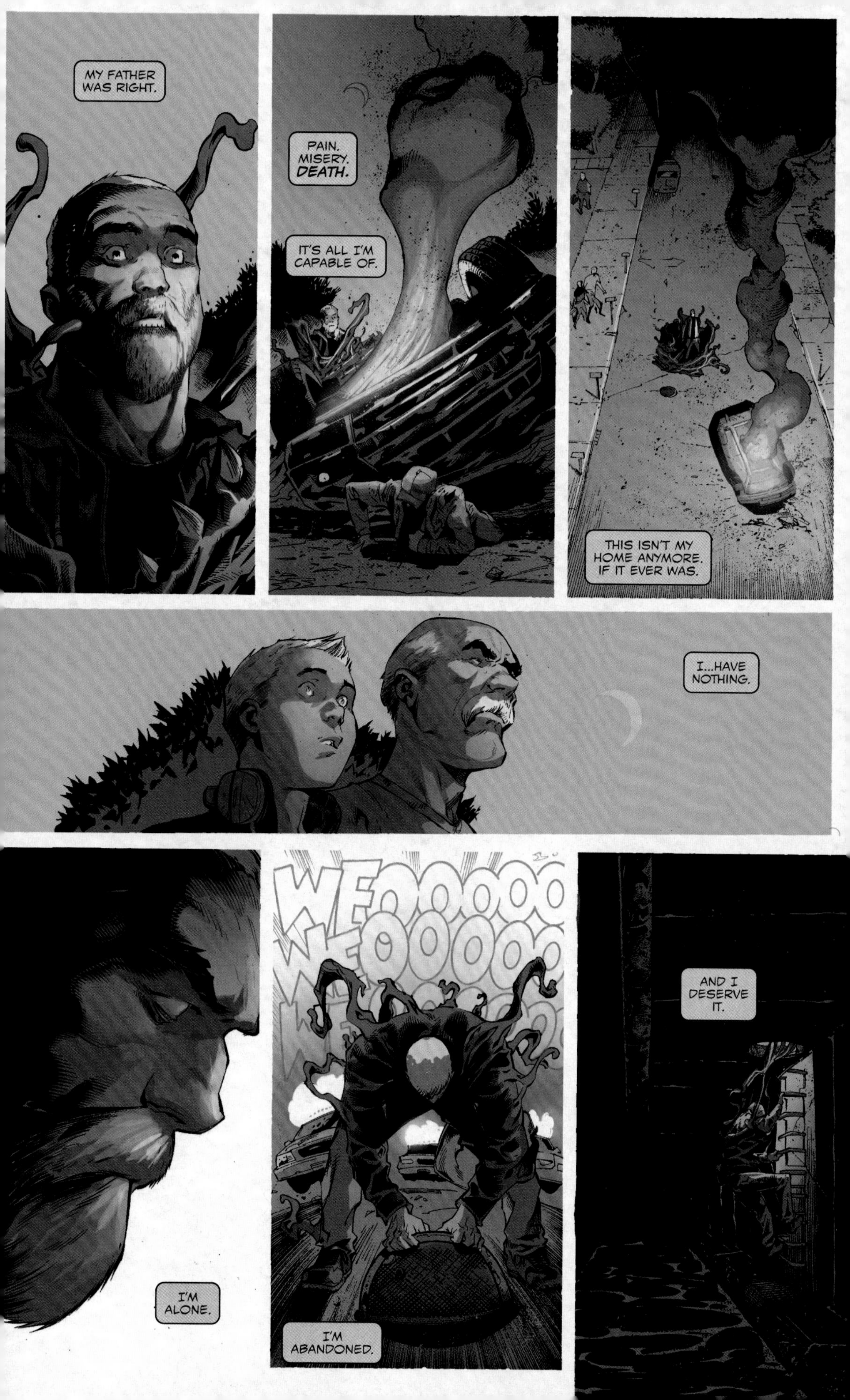
MY FATHER WAS RIGHT.
PAIN. MISERY. DEATH.
IT'S ALL I'M CAPABLE OF.
THIS ISN'T MY HOME ANYMORE. IF IT EVER WAS.
I...HAVE NOTHING.
I'M ALONE.
WEOOOOO
WEOOOOO
I'M ABANDONED.
AND I DESERVE IT.

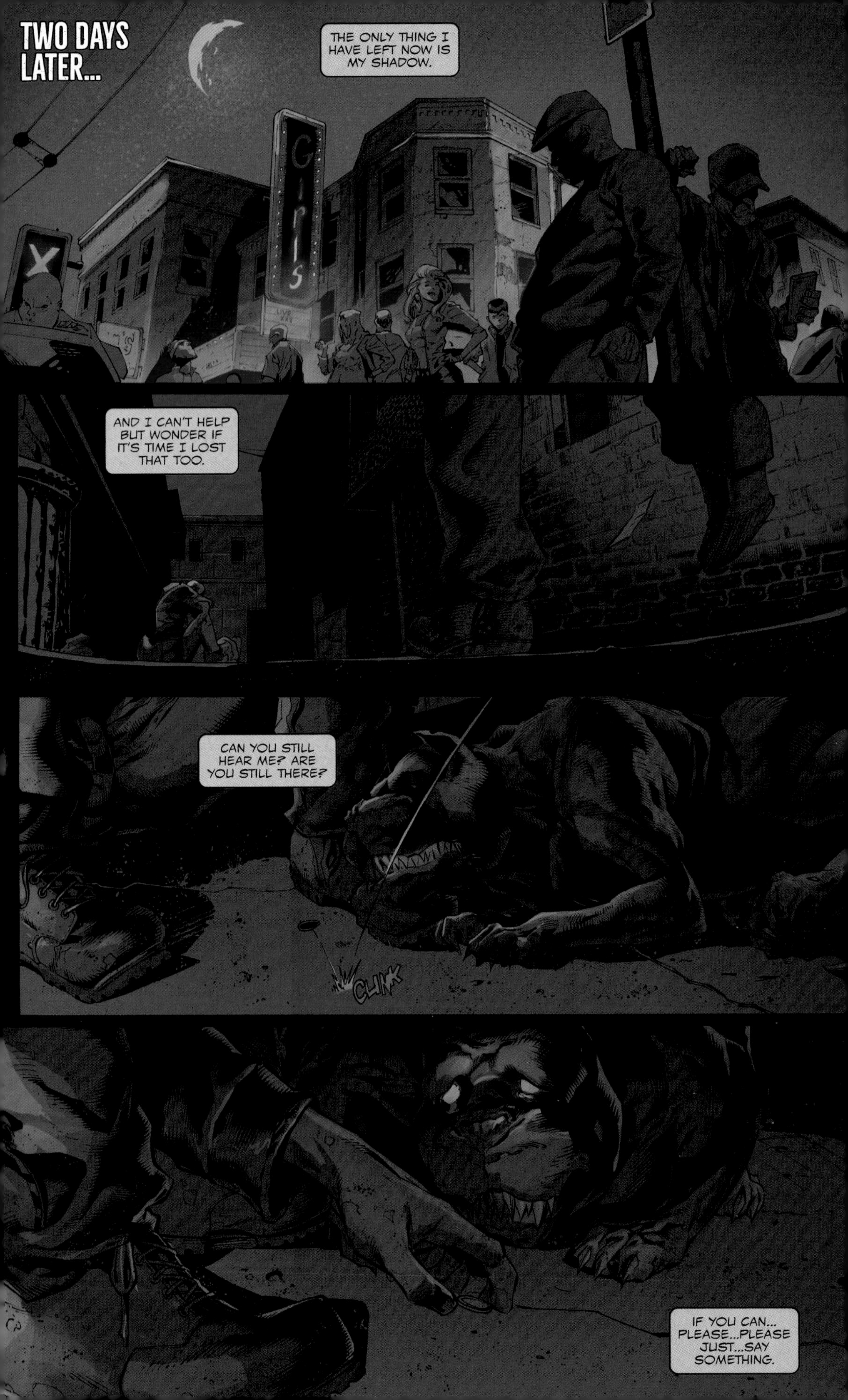
TWO DAYS LATER...
THE ONLY THING I HAVE LEFT NOW IS MY SHADOW.
AND I CAN'T HELP BUT WONDER IF IT'S TIME I LOST THAT TOO.
CAN YOU STILL HEAR ME? ARE YOU STILL THERE?
CLINK
IF YOU CAN... PLEASE...PLEASE JUST...SAY SOMETHING.

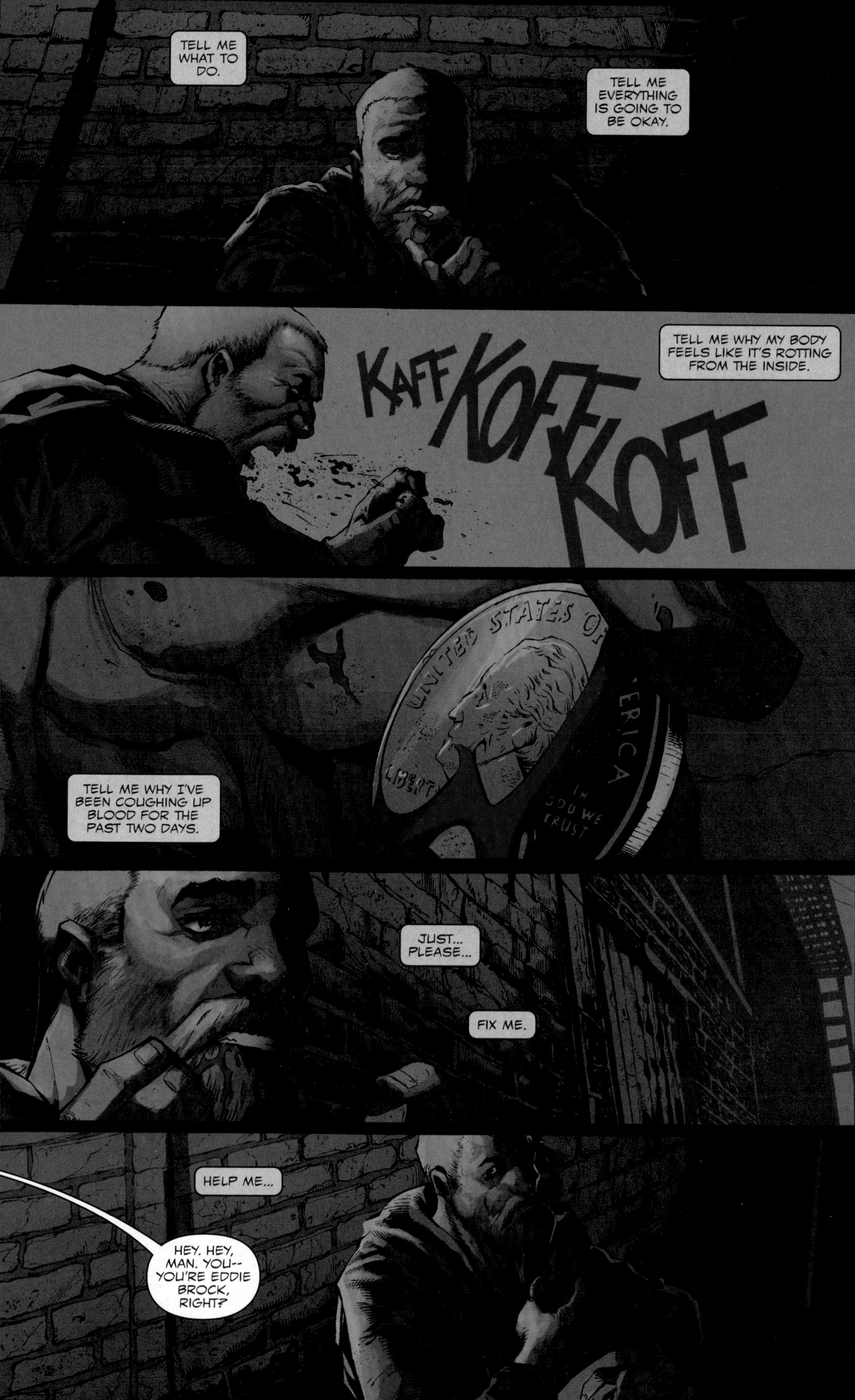
TELL ME WHAT TO DO.
TELL ME EVERYTHING IS GOING TO BE OKAY.
TELL ME WHY MY BODY FEELS LIKE IT'S ROTTING FROM THE INSIDE.
KAFF KOFF KOFF
UNITED STATES OF AMERICA
LIBERTY
IN GOD WE TRUST
TELL ME WHY I'VE BEEN COUGHING UP BLOOD FOR THE PAST TWO DAYS.
JUST... PLEASE...
FIX ME.
HELP ME...
HEY. HEY, MAN. YOU-- YOU'RE EDDIE BROCK, RIGHT?

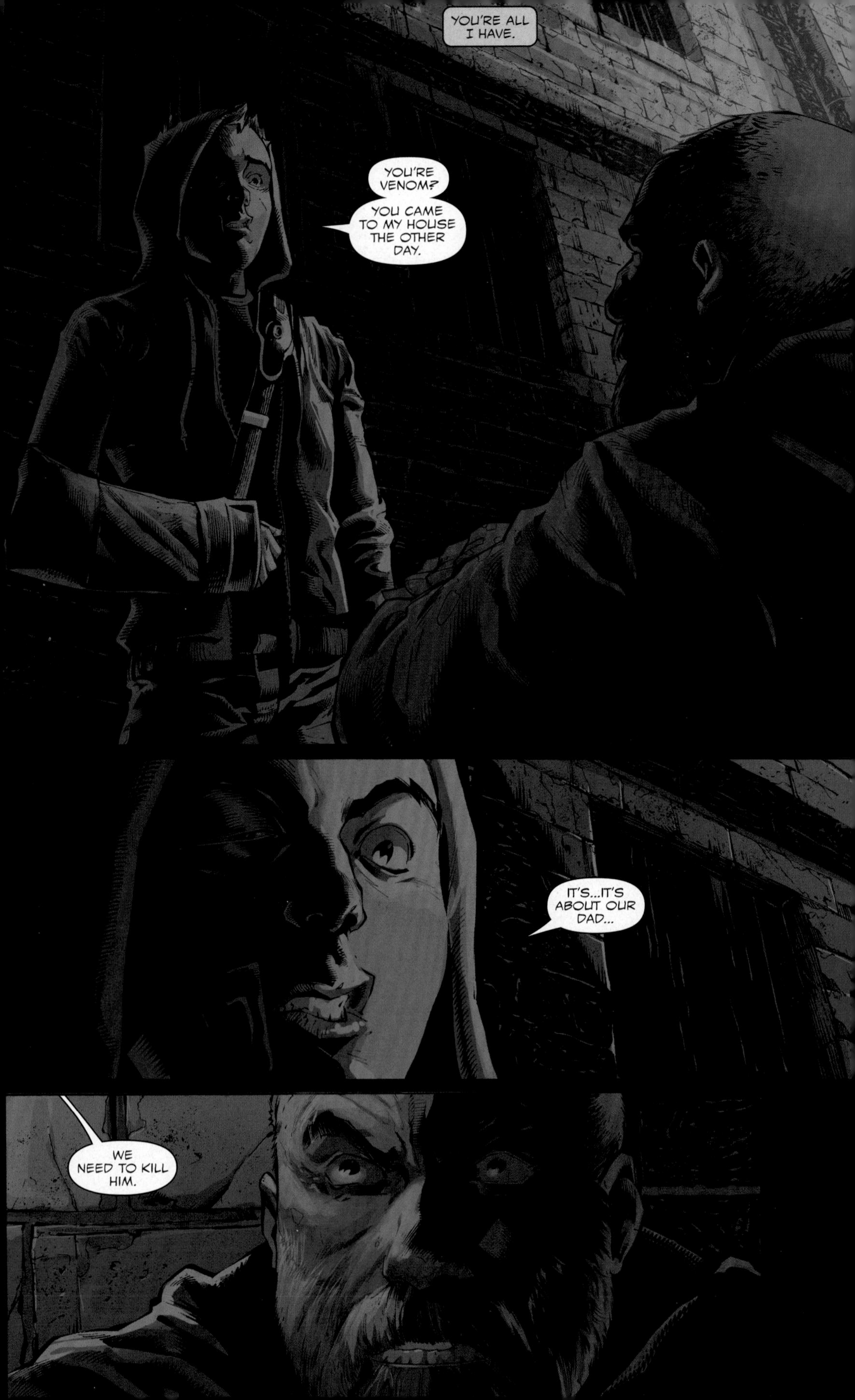
YOU'RE ALL I HAVE.
YOU'RE VENOM?
YOU CAME TO MY HOUSE THE OTHER DAY.
IT'S...IT'S ABOUT OUR DAD...
WE NEED TO KILL HIM.

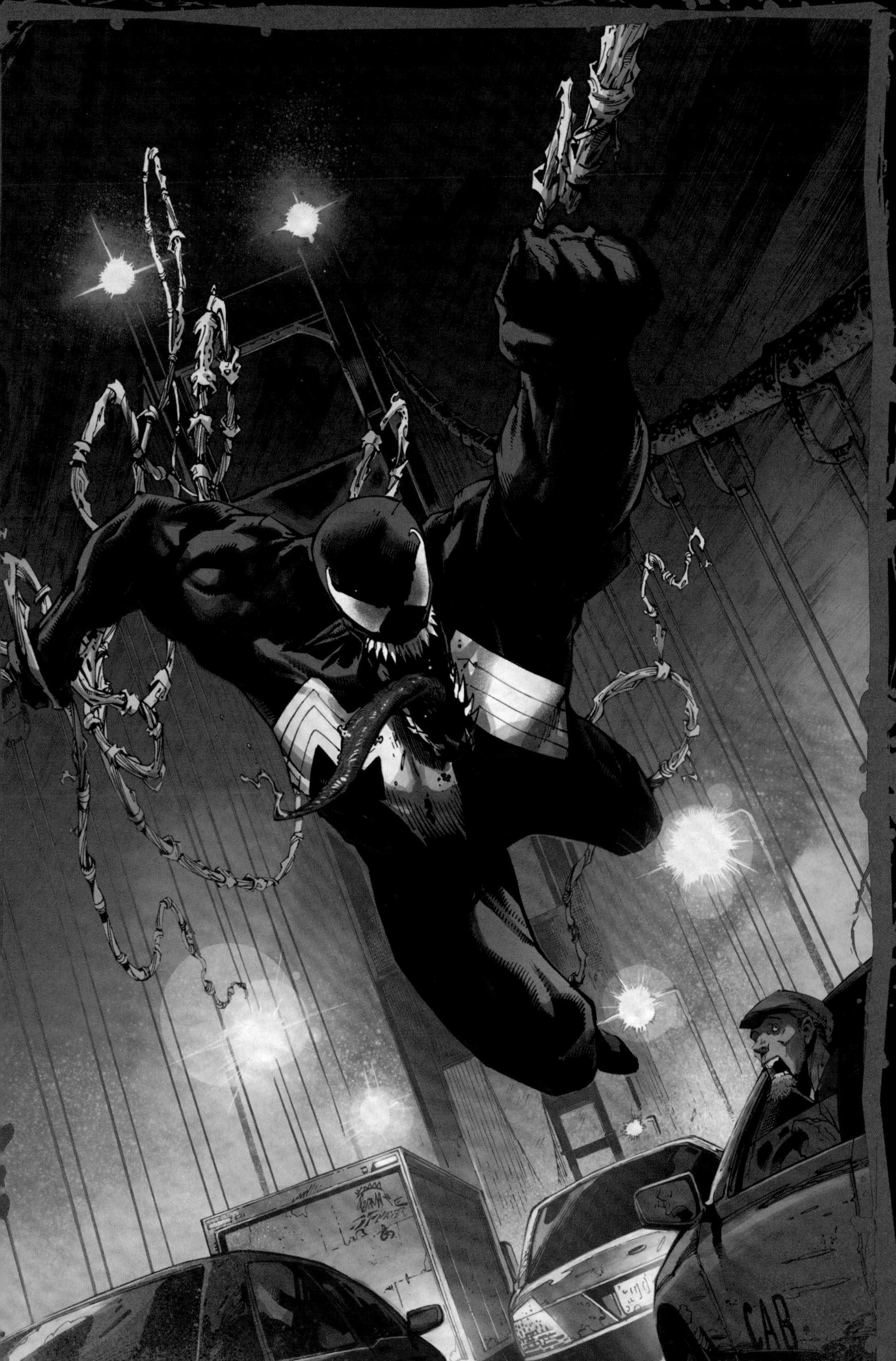
CAB

I FOUGHT A GOD WEARING A DAMN DRAGON AS A SUIT OF ARMOR NOT A MONTH AGO.

TRUE STORY.

SINCE THEN, I'VE BEEN BURNED ALIVE, HUNTED ACROSS THE COUNTRY AND EXPERIMENTED ON BY A SADISTIC, ALTERNATE-UNIVERSE REED RICHARDS...

ALL TO FIND OUT THAT MY SYMBIOTE IS BRAIN-DEAD AND NO LONGER CAPABLE OF SPEECH OR FEELINGS.

OH, AND MY DAD PUNCHED ME TOO.

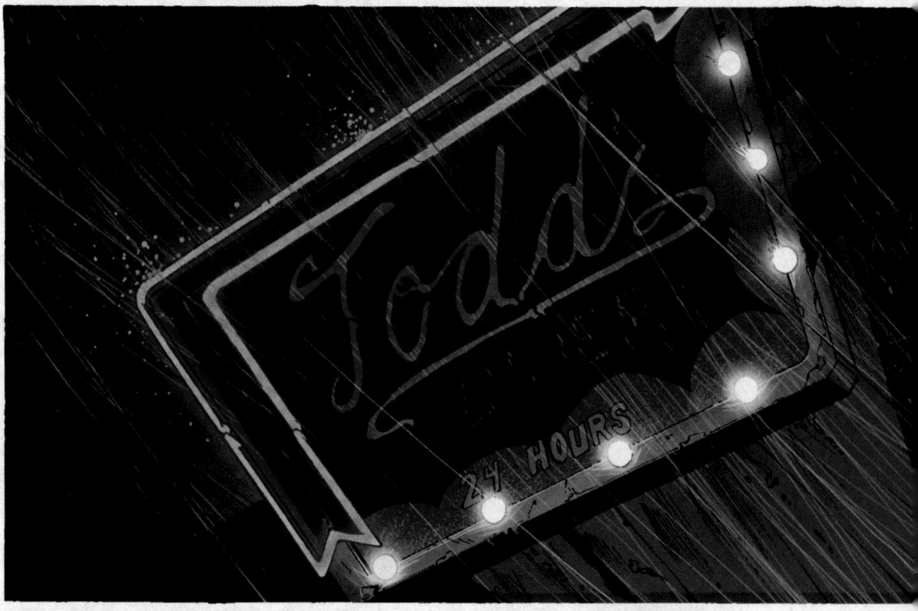

Todd's
24 HOURS

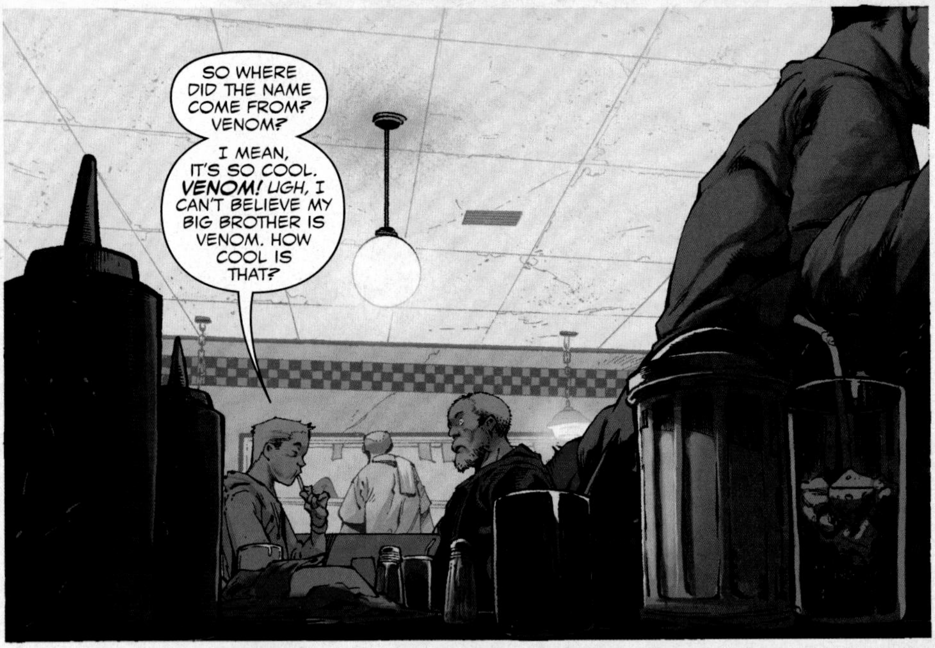

SO WHERE DID THE NAME COME FROM? VENOM?
I MEAN, IT'S SO COOL. *VENOM!* UGH, I CAN'T BELIEVE MY BIG BROTHER IS VENOM. HOW COOL IS THAT?

I THINK ABOUT ALL OF THAT. ABOUT ALL OF THAT PAIN AND MISERY AND HORROR...

...AND THEN I LOOK INTO THIS KID'S EYES.

DYLAN BROCK. MY NEW LITTLE HALF BROTHER...

AND ALL I CAN THINK...

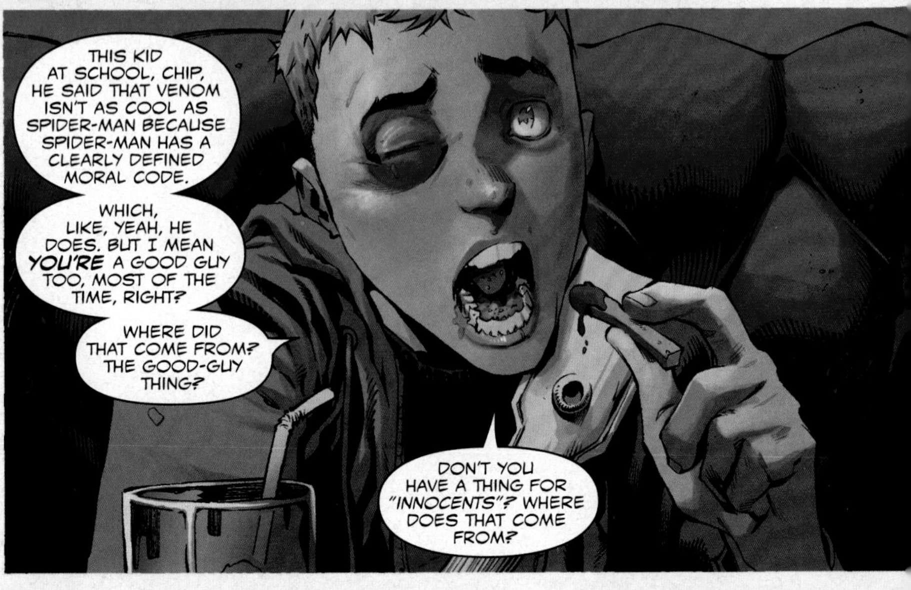

THIS KID AT SCHOOL, CHIP, HE SAID THAT VENOM ISN'T AS COOL AS SPIDER-MAN BECAUSE SPIDER-MAN HAS A CLEARLY DEFINED MORAL CODE.
WHICH, LIKE, YEAH, HE DOES. BUT I MEAN ***YOU'RE*** A GOOD GUY TOO, MOST OF THE TIME, RIGHT?
WHERE DID THAT COME FROM? THE GOOD-GUY THING?
DON'T YOU HAVE A THING FOR "INNOCENTS"? WHERE DOES THAT COME FROM?

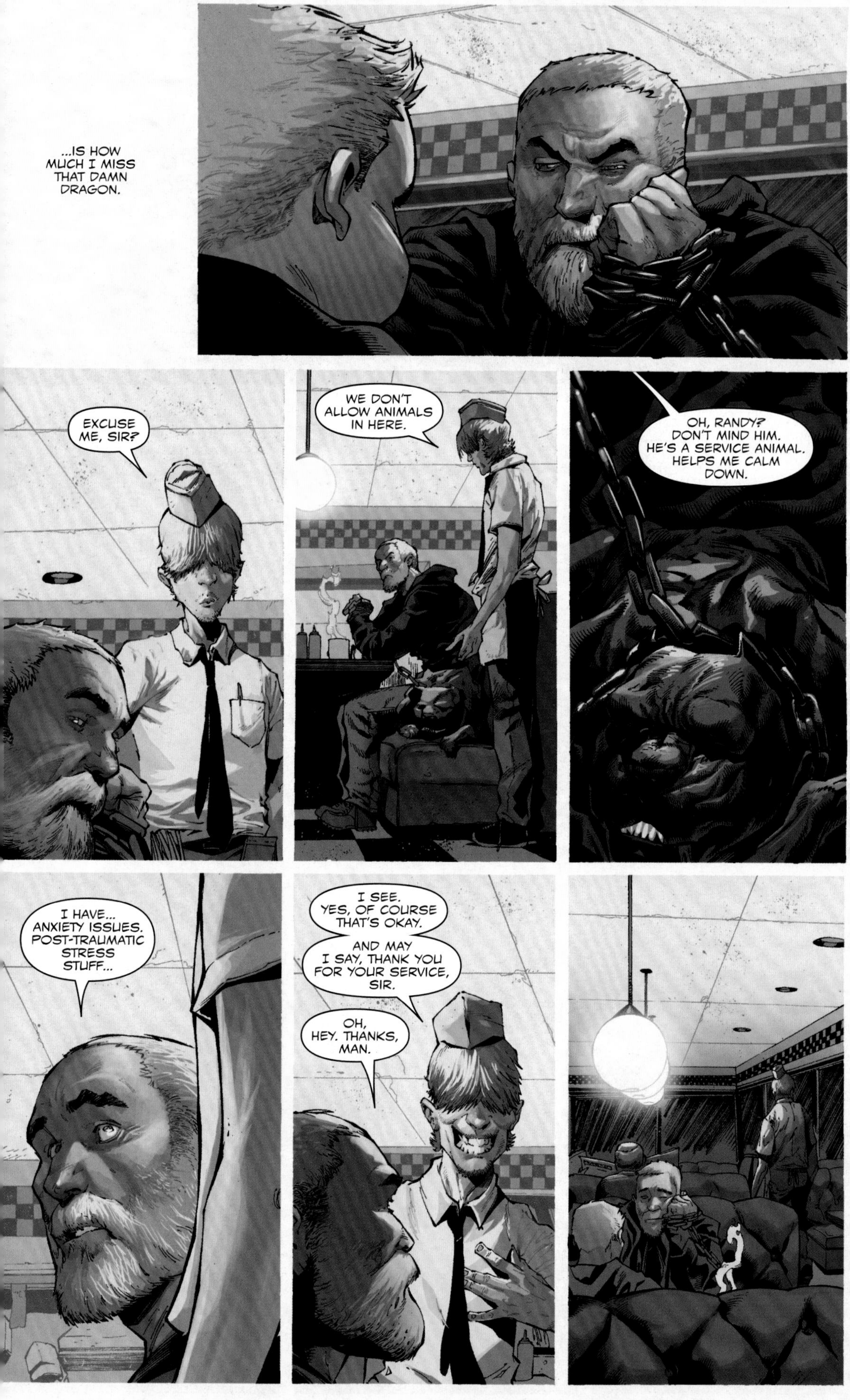
...IS HOW MUCH I MISS THAT DAMN DRAGON.
EXCUSE ME, SIR?
WE DON'T ALLOW ANIMALS IN HERE.
OH, RANDY? DON'T MIND HIM. HE'S A SERVICE ANIMAL. HELPS ME CALM DOWN.
I HAVE... ANXIETY ISSUES. POST-TRAUMATIC STRESS STUFF...
I SEE. YES, OF COURSE THAT'S OKAY.
AND MAY I SAY, THANK YOU FOR YOUR SERVICE, SIR.
OH, HEY. THANKS, MAN.

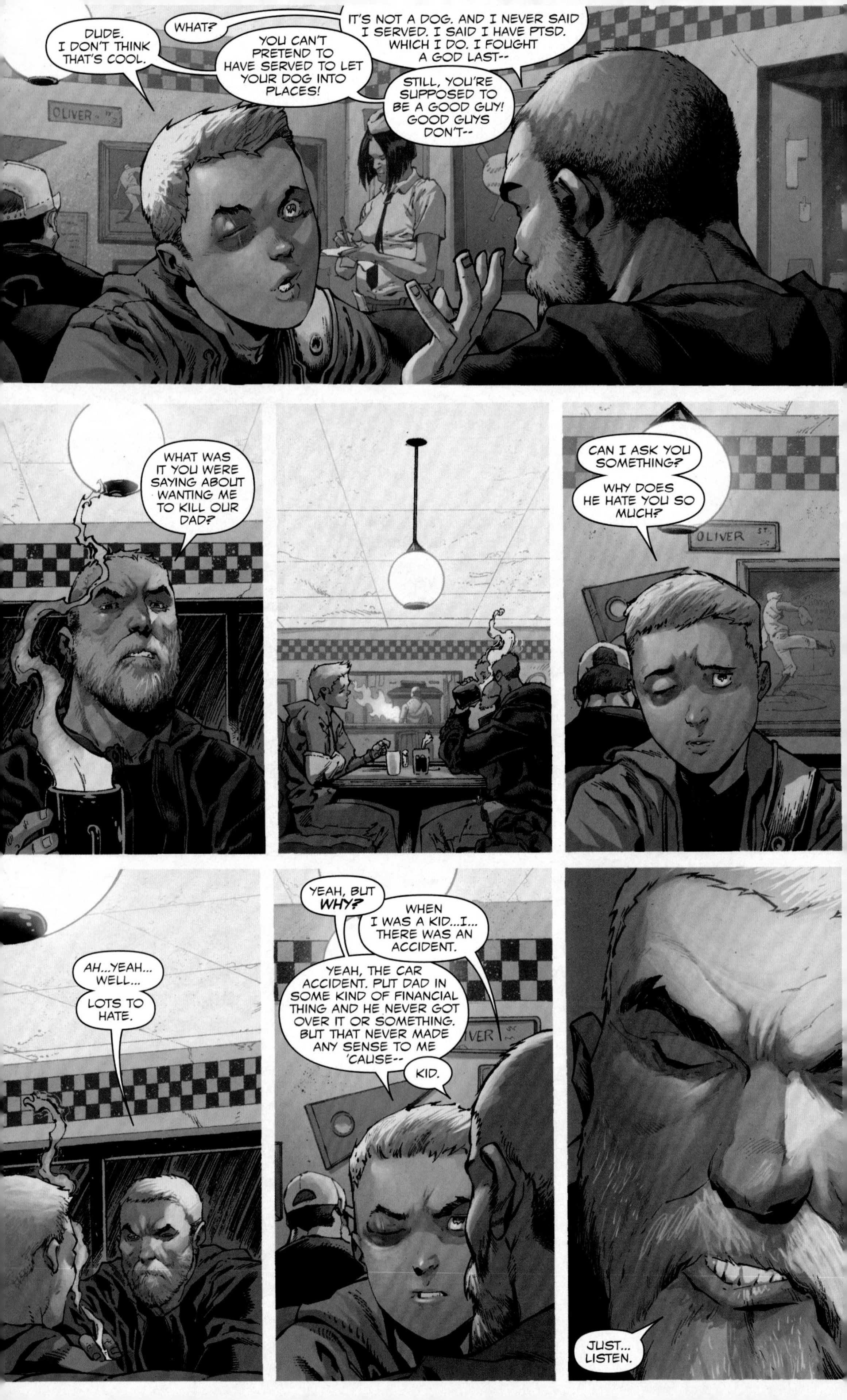
DUDE. I DON'T THINK THAT'S COOL.
WHAT?
YOU CAN'T PRETEND TO HAVE SERVED TO LET YOUR DOG INTO PLACES!
IT'S NOT A DOG. AND I NEVER SAID I SERVED. I SAID I HAVE PTSD. WHICH I DO. I FOUGHT A GOD LAST--
STILL, YOU'RE SUPPOSED TO BE A GOOD GUY! GOOD GUYS DON'T--
OLIVER
WHAT WAS IT YOU WERE SAYING ABOUT WANTING ME TO KILL OUR DAD?
CAN I ASK YOU SOMETHING?
WHY DOES HE HATE YOU SO MUCH?
OLIVER ST.
AH...YEAH... WELL...
LOTS TO HATE.
YEAH, BUT *WHY?*
WHEN I WAS A KID...I... THERE WAS AN ACCIDENT.
YEAH, THE CAR ACCIDENT. PUT DAD IN SOME KIND OF FINANCIAL THING AND HE NEVER GOT OVER IT OR SOMETHING. BUT THAT NEVER MADE ANY SENSE TO ME 'CAUSE--
KID.
JUST... LISTEN.

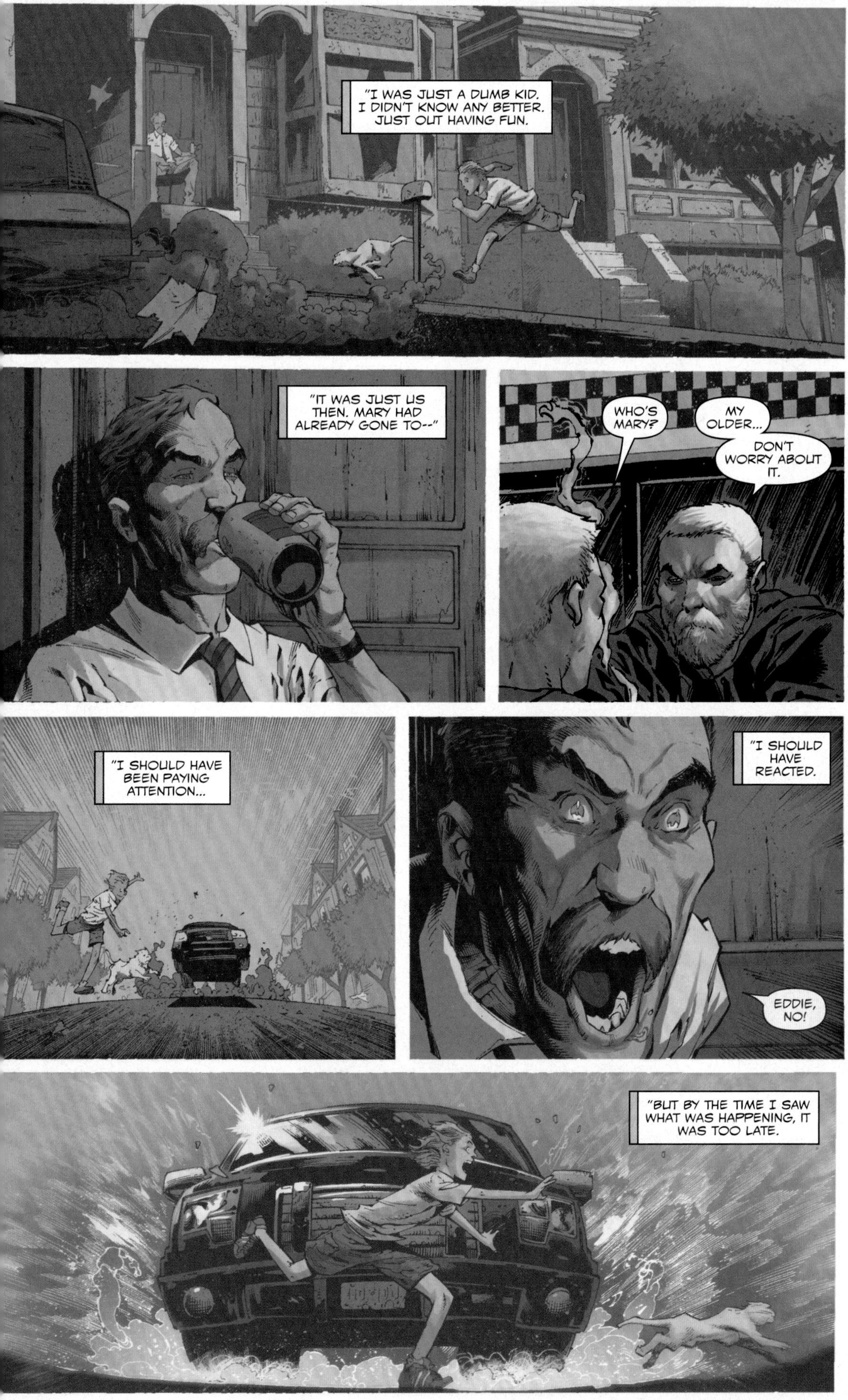
"I WAS JUST A DUMB KID. I DIDN'T KNOW ANY BETTER. JUST OUT HAVING FUN.
"IT WAS JUST US THEN. MARY HAD ALREADY GONE TO--"
WHO'S MARY?
MY OLDER...
DON'T WORRY ABOUT IT.
"I SHOULD HAVE BEEN PAYING ATTENTION...
"I SHOULD HAVE REACTED.
EDDIE, NO!
"BUT BY THE TIME I SAW WHAT WAS HAPPENING, IT WAS TOO LATE.

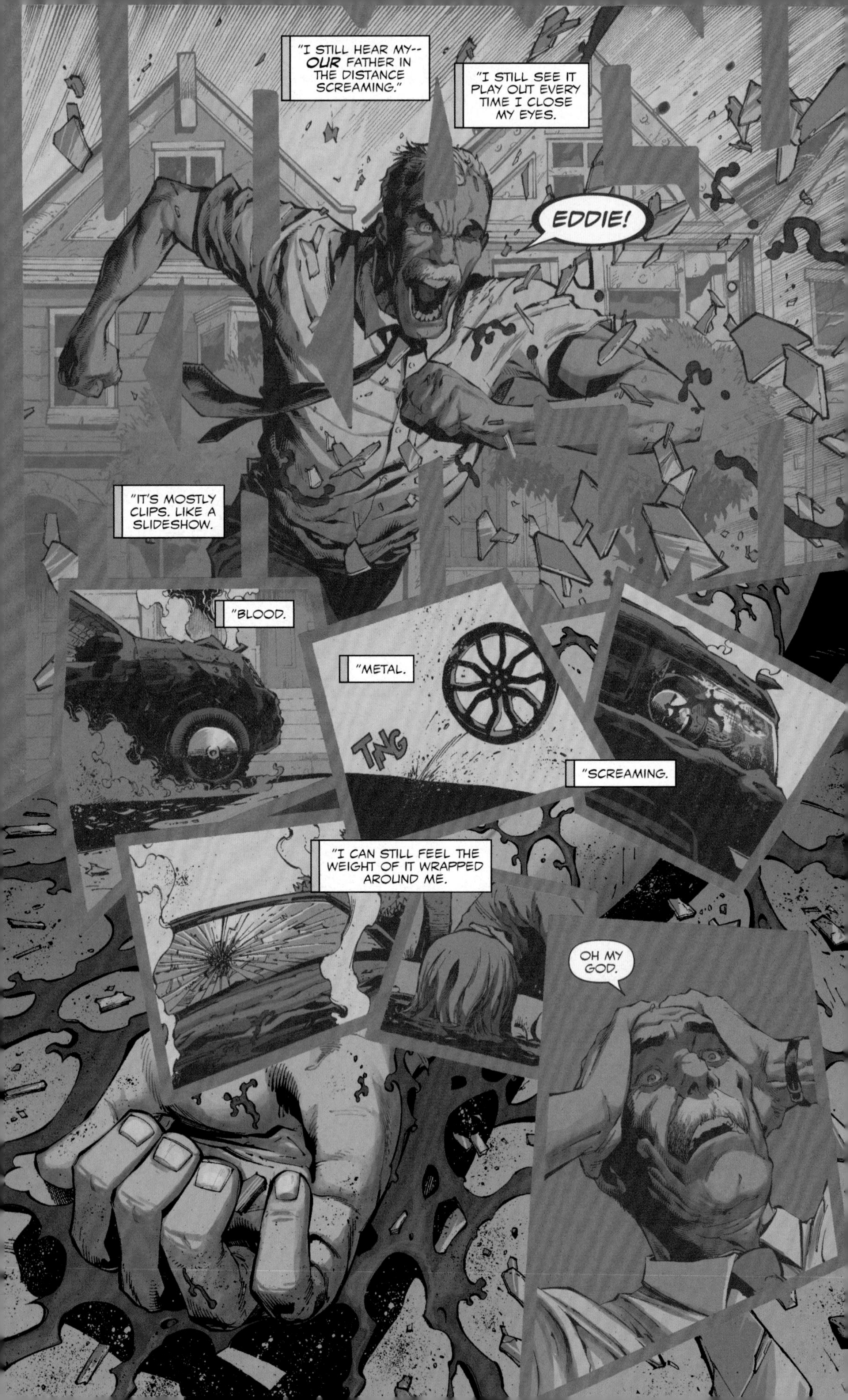
"I STILL HEAR MY-- OUR FATHER IN THE DISTANCE SCREAMING."
"I STILL SEE IT PLAY OUT EVERY TIME I CLOSE MY EYES.
EDDIE!
"IT'S MOSTLY CLIPS. LIKE A SLIDESHOW.
"BLOOD.
"METAL.
TNG
"SCREAMING.
"I CAN STILL FEEL THE WEIGHT OF IT WRAPPED AROUND ME.
OH MY GOD.

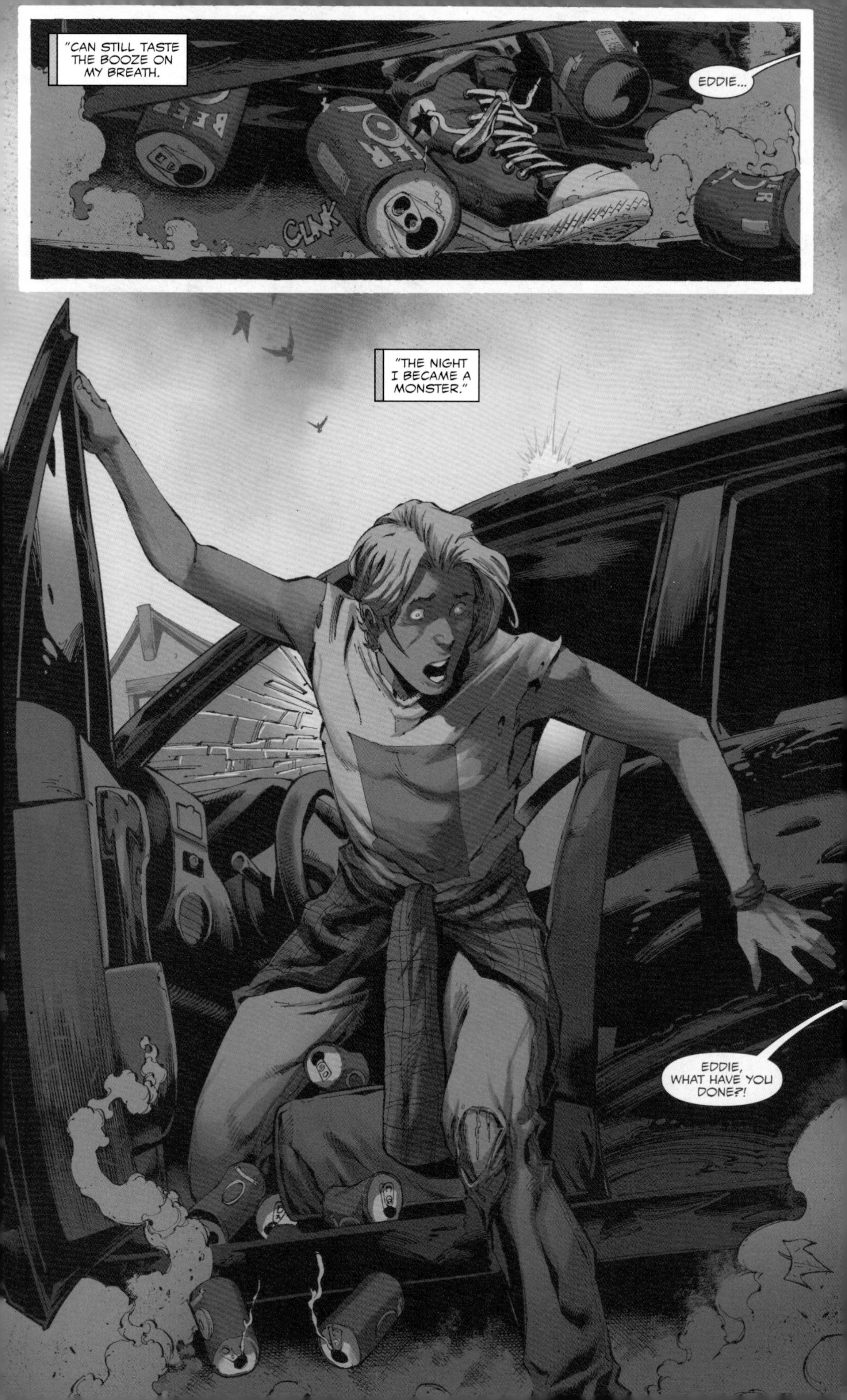
"CAN STILL TASTE THE BOOZE ON MY BREATH.
EDDIE...
CLNK
"THE NIGHT I BECAME A MONSTER."
EDDIE, WHAT HAVE YOU DONE?!

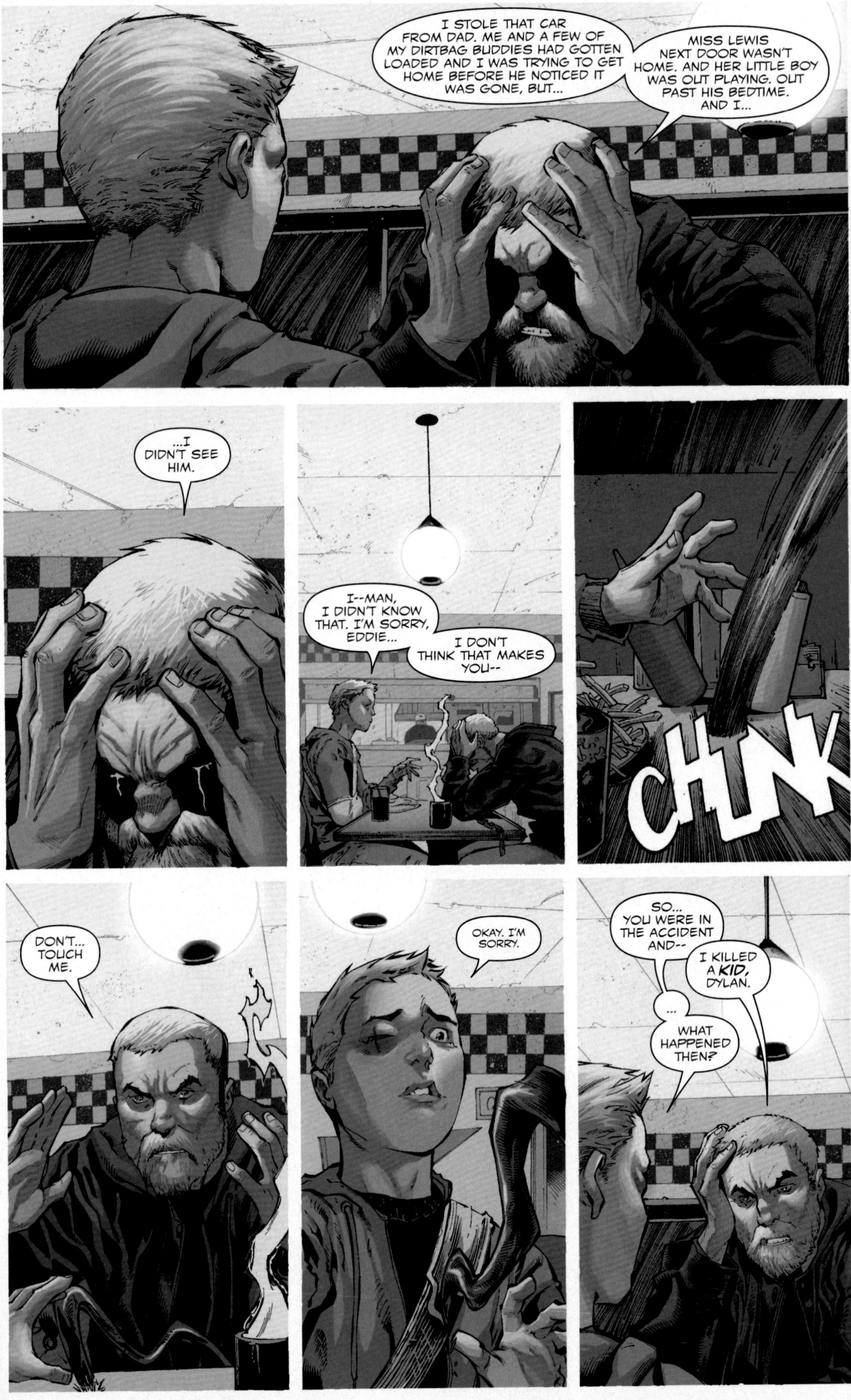
I STOLE THAT CAR FROM DAD. ME AND A FEW OF MY DIRTBAG BUDDIES HAD GOTTEN LOADED AND I WAS TRYING TO GET HOME BEFORE HE NOTICED IT WAS GONE, BUT...
MISS LEWIS NEXT DOOR WASN'T HOME. AND HER LITTLE BOY WAS OUT PLAYING. OUT PAST HIS BEDTIME. AND I...
...I DIDN'T SEE HIM.
I--MAN, I DIDN'T KNOW THAT. I'M SORRY, EDDIE...
I DON'T THINK THAT MAKES YOU--
CHUNK
DON'T... TOUCH ME.
OKAY. I'M SORRY.
SO... YOU WERE IN THE ACCIDENT AND--
I KILLED A KID, DYLAN.
...
WHAT HAPPENED THEN?

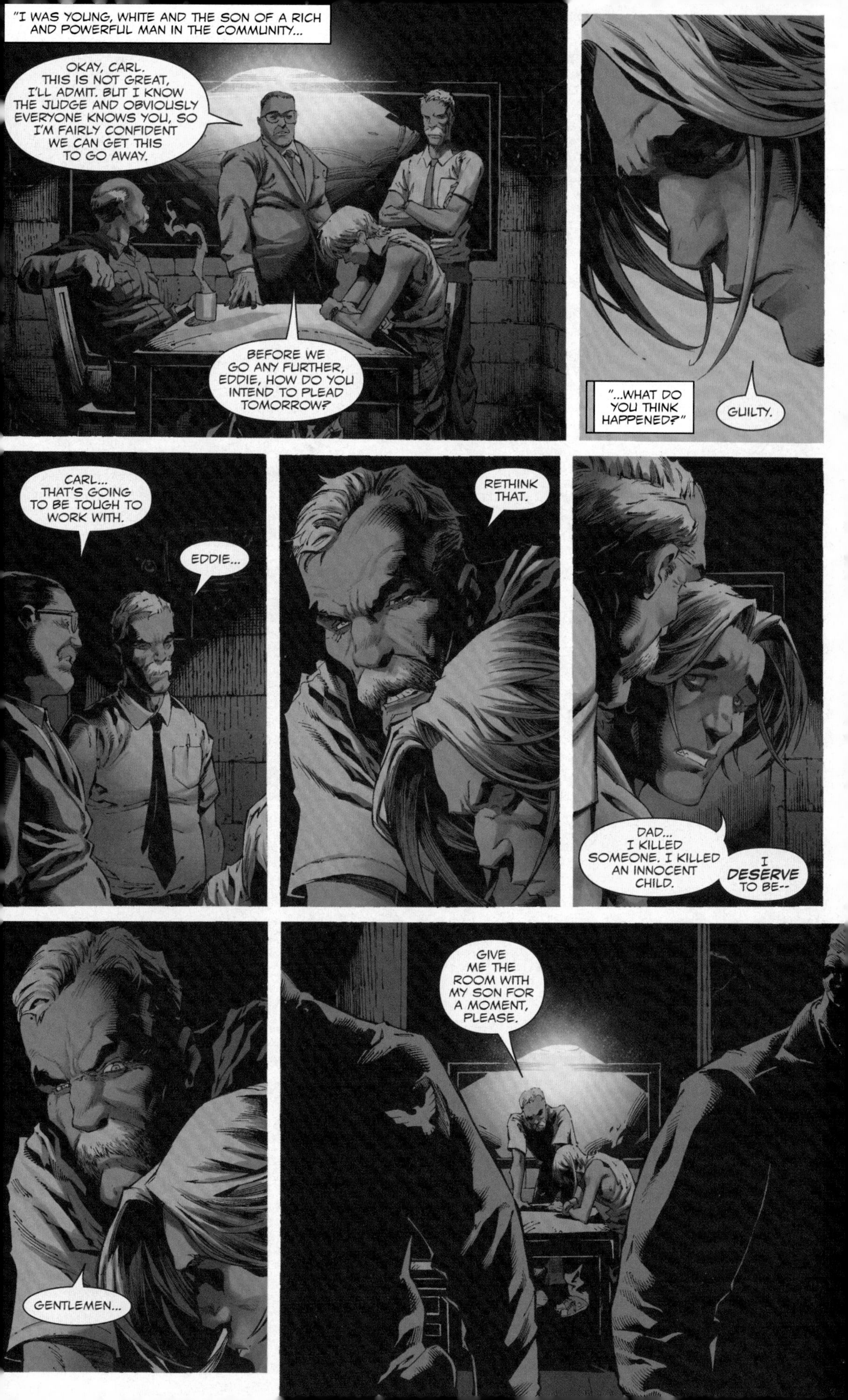
"I WAS YOUNG, WHITE AND THE SON OF A RICH AND POWERFUL MAN IN THE COMMUNITY...
OKAY, CARL. THIS IS NOT GREAT, I'LL ADMIT. BUT I KNOW THE JUDGE AND OBVIOUSLY EVERYONE KNOWS YOU, SO I'M FAIRLY CONFIDENT WE CAN GET THIS TO GO AWAY.
BEFORE WE GO ANY FURTHER, EDDIE, HOW DO YOU INTEND TO PLEAD TOMORROW?
"...WHAT DO YOU THINK HAPPENED?"
GUILTY.
CARL... THAT'S GOING TO BE TOUGH TO WORK WITH.
EDDIE...
RETHINK THAT.
DAD... I KILLED SOMEONE. I KILLED AN INNOCENT CHILD.
I DESERVE TO BE--
GENTLEMEN...
GIVE ME THE ROOM WITH MY SON FOR A MOMENT, PLEASE.

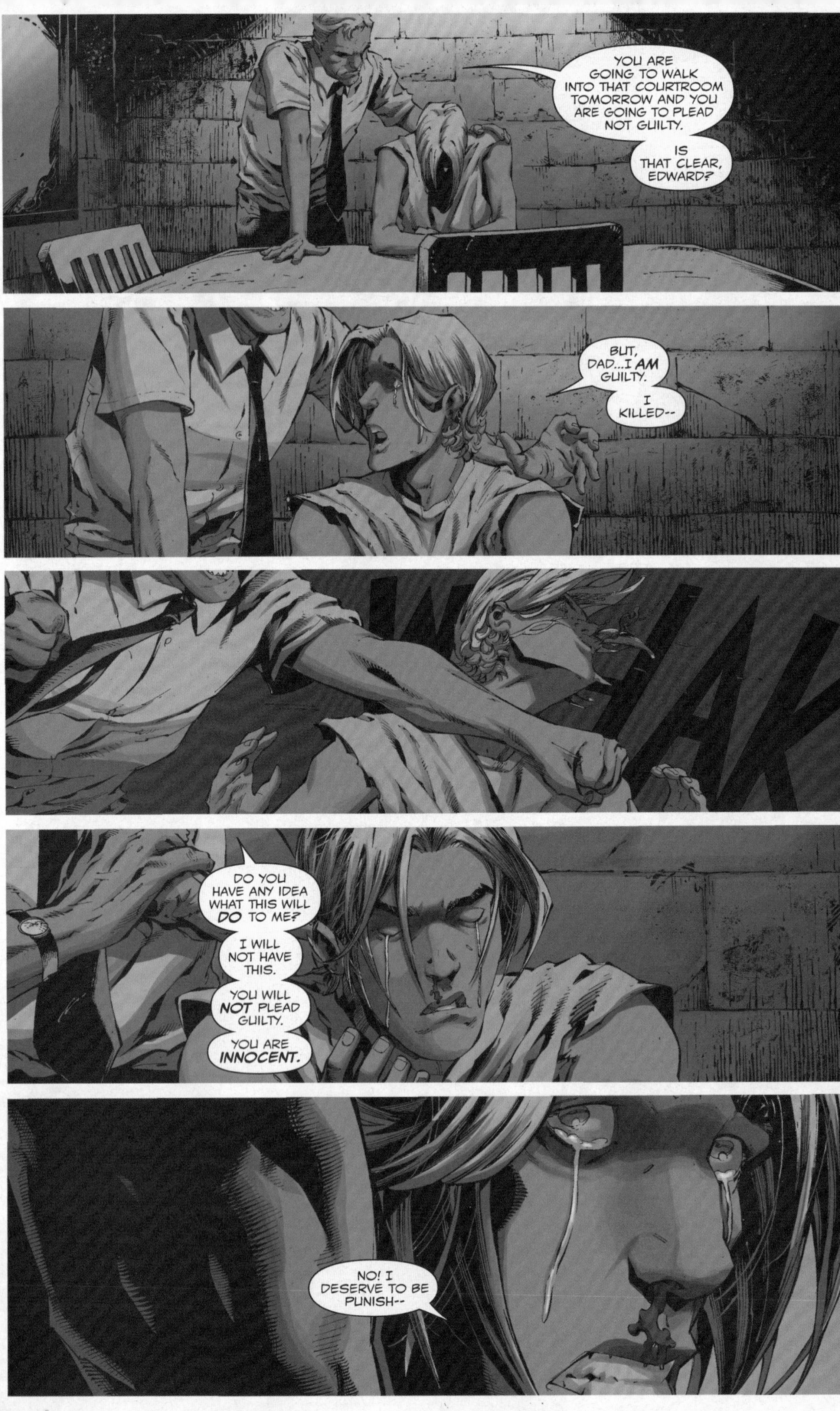
YOU ARE GOING TO WALK INTO THAT COURTROOM TOMORROW AND YOU ARE GOING TO PLEAD NOT GUILTY.
IS THAT CLEAR, EDWARD?
BUT, DAD...I **AM** GUILTY.
I KILLED--
DO YOU HAVE ANY IDEA WHAT THIS WILL **DO** TO ME?
I WILL NOT HAVE THIS.
YOU WILL **NOT** PLEAD GUILTY.
YOU ARE **INNOCENT.**
NO! I DESERVE TO BE PUNISH--

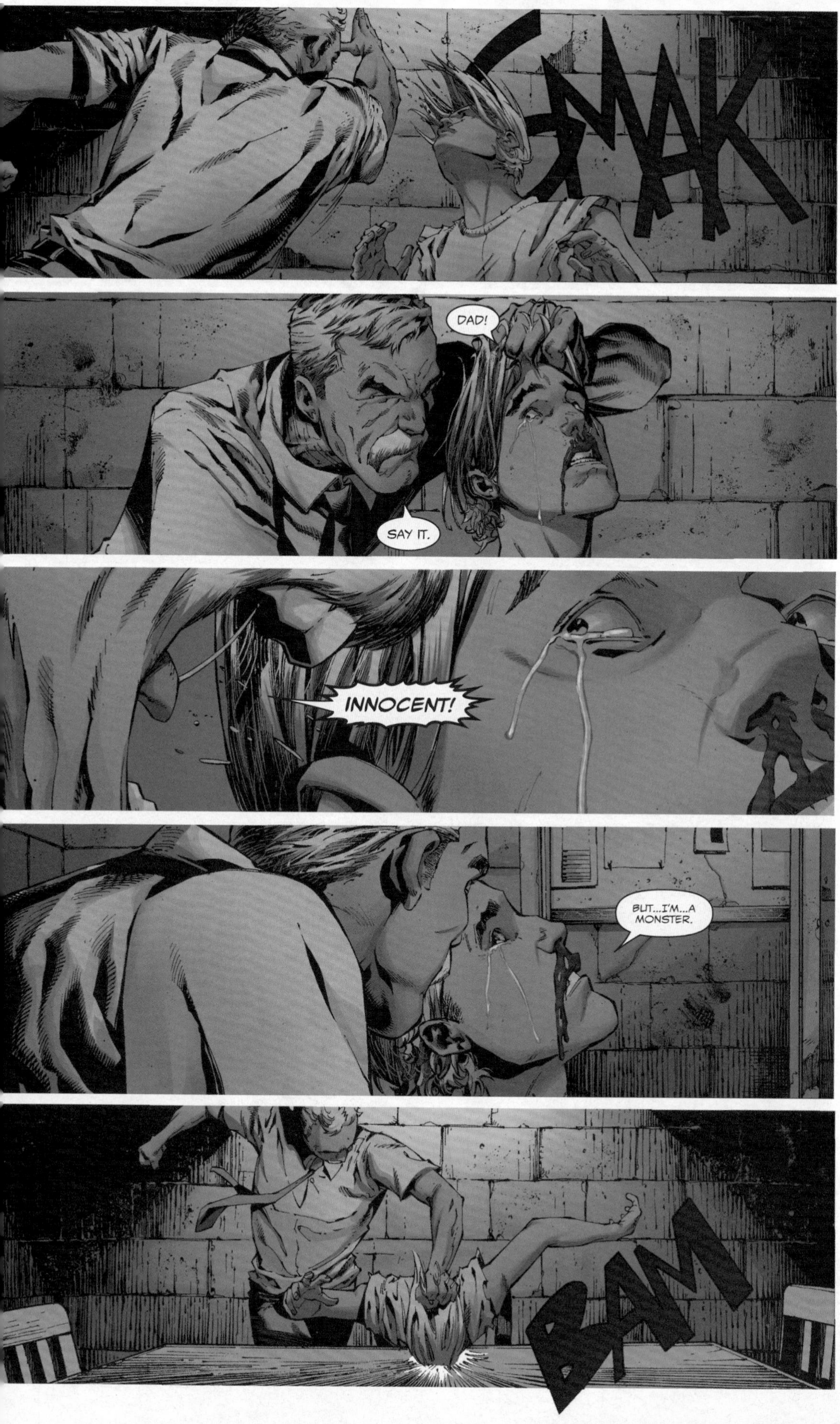
SMAK
DAD!
SAY IT.
INNOCENT!
BUT...I'M...A MONSTER.
BAM

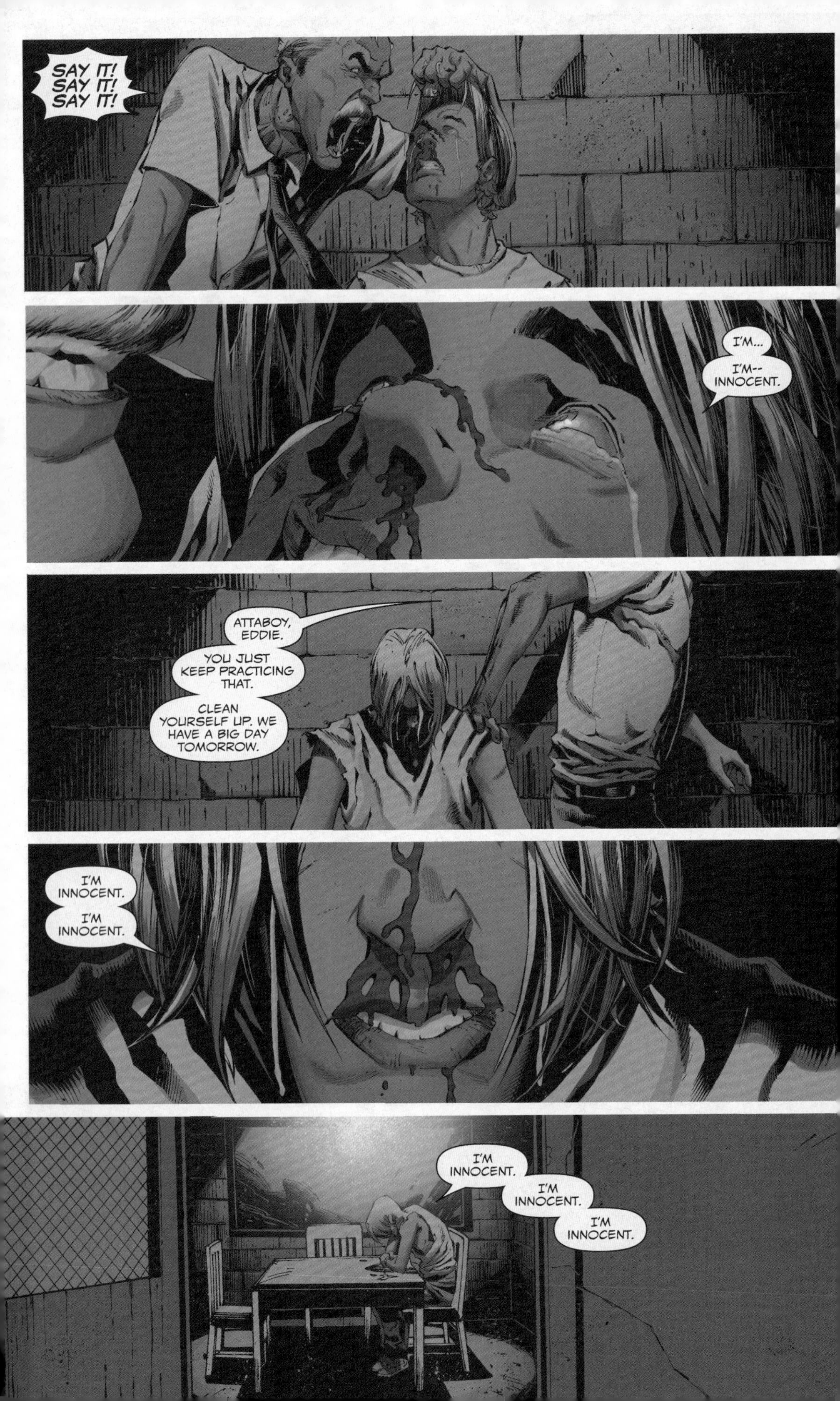
SAY IT! SAY IT! SAY IT!
I'M... I'M-- INNOCENT.
ATTABOY, EDDIE.
YOU JUST KEEP PRACTICING THAT.
CLEAN YOURSELF UP. WE HAVE A BIG DAY TOMORROW.
I'M INNOCENT.
I'M INNOCENT.
I'M INNOCENT.
I'M INNOCENT.
I'M INNOCENT.

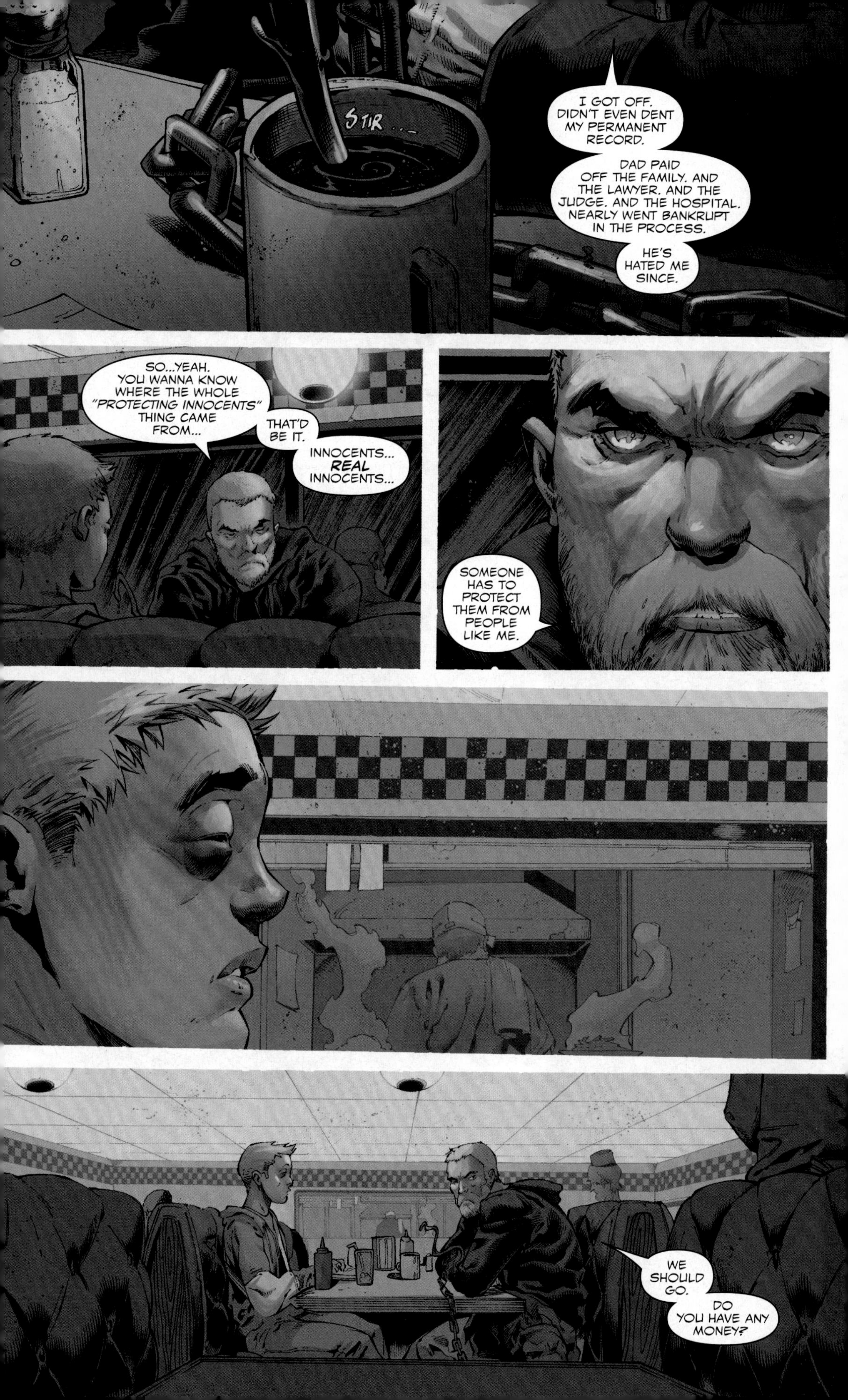
STIR...
I GOT OFF. DIDN'T EVEN DENT MY PERMANENT RECORD.
DAD PAID OFF THE FAMILY. AND THE LAWYER. AND THE JUDGE. AND THE HOSPITAL. NEARLY WENT BANKRUPT IN THE PROCESS.
HE'S HATED ME SINCE.
SO...YEAH. YOU WANNA KNOW WHERE THE WHOLE "PROTECTING INNOCENTS" THING CAME FROM...
THAT'D BE IT.
INNOCENTS... REAL INNOCENTS...
SOMEONE HAS TO PROTECT THEM FROM PEOPLE LIKE ME.
WE SHOULD GO.
DO YOU HAVE ANY MONEY?

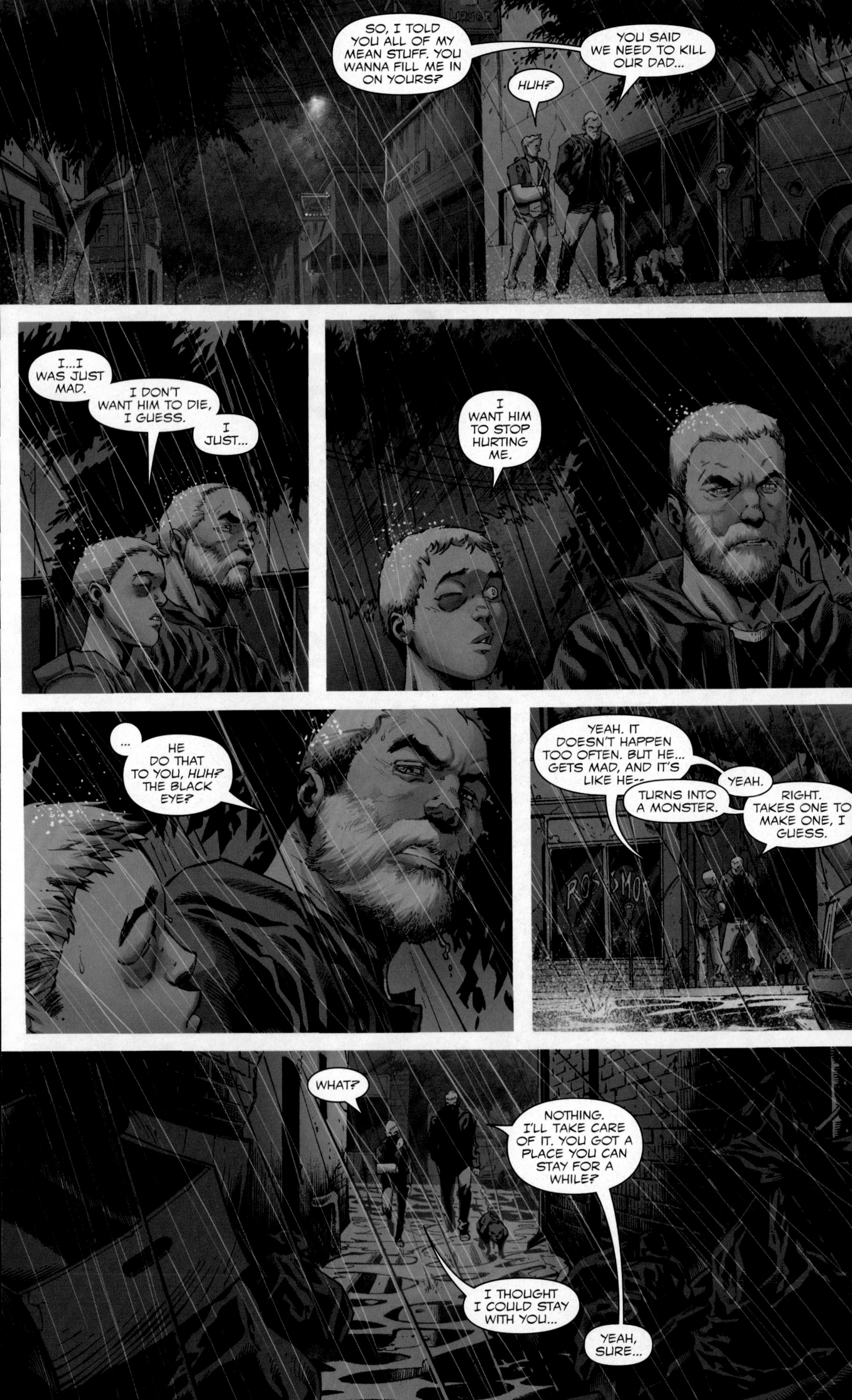
SO, I TOLD YOU ALL OF MY MEAN STUFF. YOU WANNA FILL ME IN ON YOURS?
HUH?
YOU SAID WE NEED TO KILL OUR DAD...
I...I WAS JUST MAD.
I DON'T WANT HIM TO DIE, I GUESS.
I JUST...
I WANT HIM TO STOP HURTING ME.
...
HE DO THAT TO YOU, HUH? THE BLACK EYE?
YEAH. IT DOESN'T HAPPEN TOO OFTEN. BUT HE... GETS MAD, AND IT'S LIKE HE--
TURNS INTO A MONSTER.
YEAH.
RIGHT. TAKES ONE TO MAKE ONE, I GUESS.
WHAT?
NOTHING. I'LL TAKE CARE OF IT. YOU GOT A PLACE YOU CAN STAY FOR A WHILE?
I THOUGHT I COULD STAY WITH YOU...
YEAH, SURE...

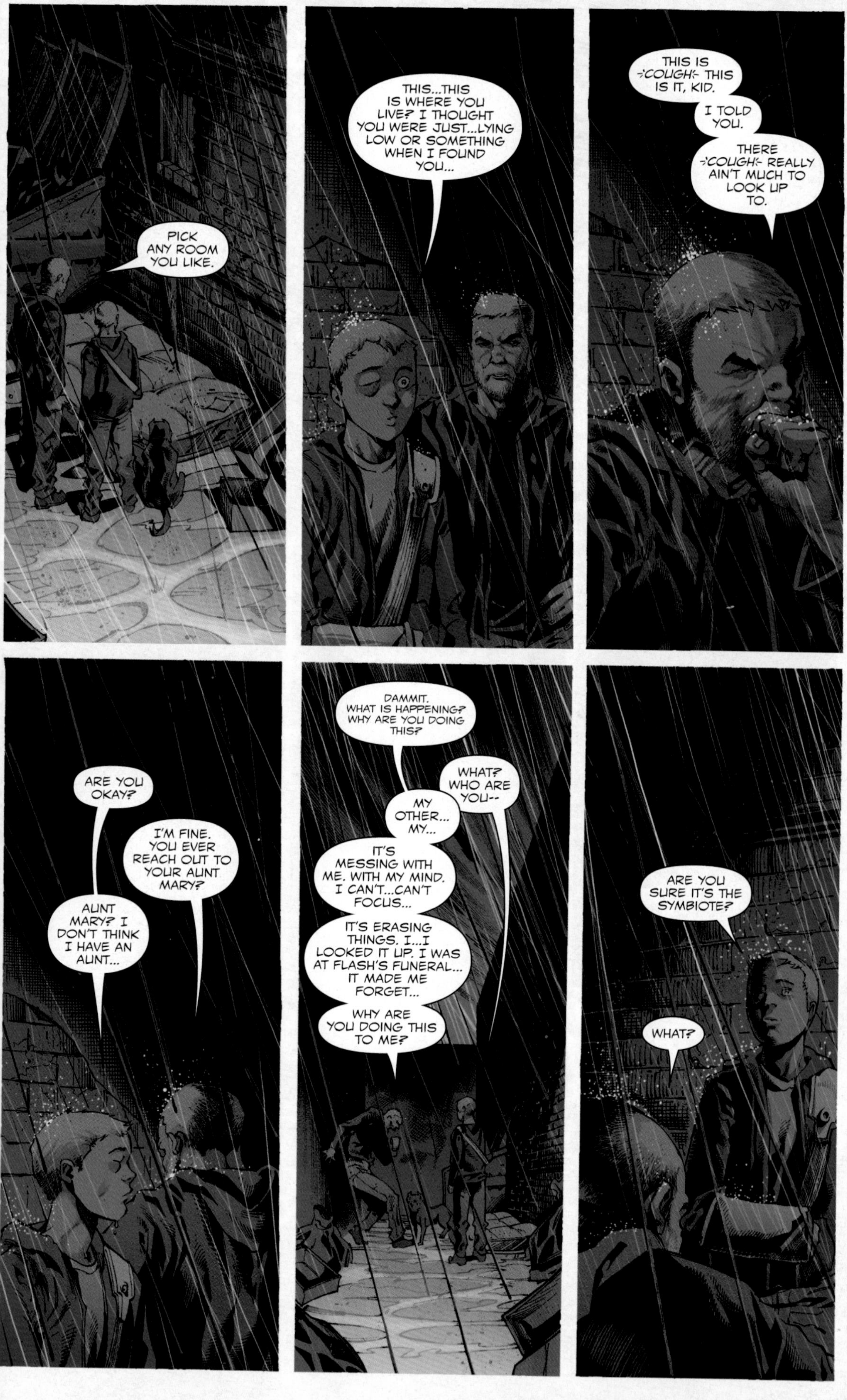
PICK ANY ROOM YOU LIKE.
THIS...THIS IS WHERE YOU LIVE? I THOUGHT YOU WERE JUST...LYING LOW OR SOMETHING WHEN I FOUND YOU...
THIS IS -COUGH- THIS IS IT, KID.
I TOLD YOU.
THERE -COUGH- REALLY AIN'T MUCH TO LOOK UP TO.
ARE YOU OKAY?
I'M FINE. YOU EVER REACH OUT TO YOUR AUNT MARY?
AUNT MARY? I DON'T THINK I HAVE AN AUNT...
DAMMIT. WHAT IS HAPPENING? WHY ARE YOU DOING THIS?
WHAT? WHO ARE YOU--
MY OTHER... MY...
IT'S MESSING WITH ME. WITH MY MIND. I CAN'T...CAN'T FOCUS...
IT'S ERASING THINGS. I...I LOOKED IT UP. I WAS AT FLASH'S FUNERAL... IT MADE ME FORGET...
WHY ARE YOU DOING THIS TO ME?
ARE YOU SURE IT'S THE SYMBIOTE?
WHAT?

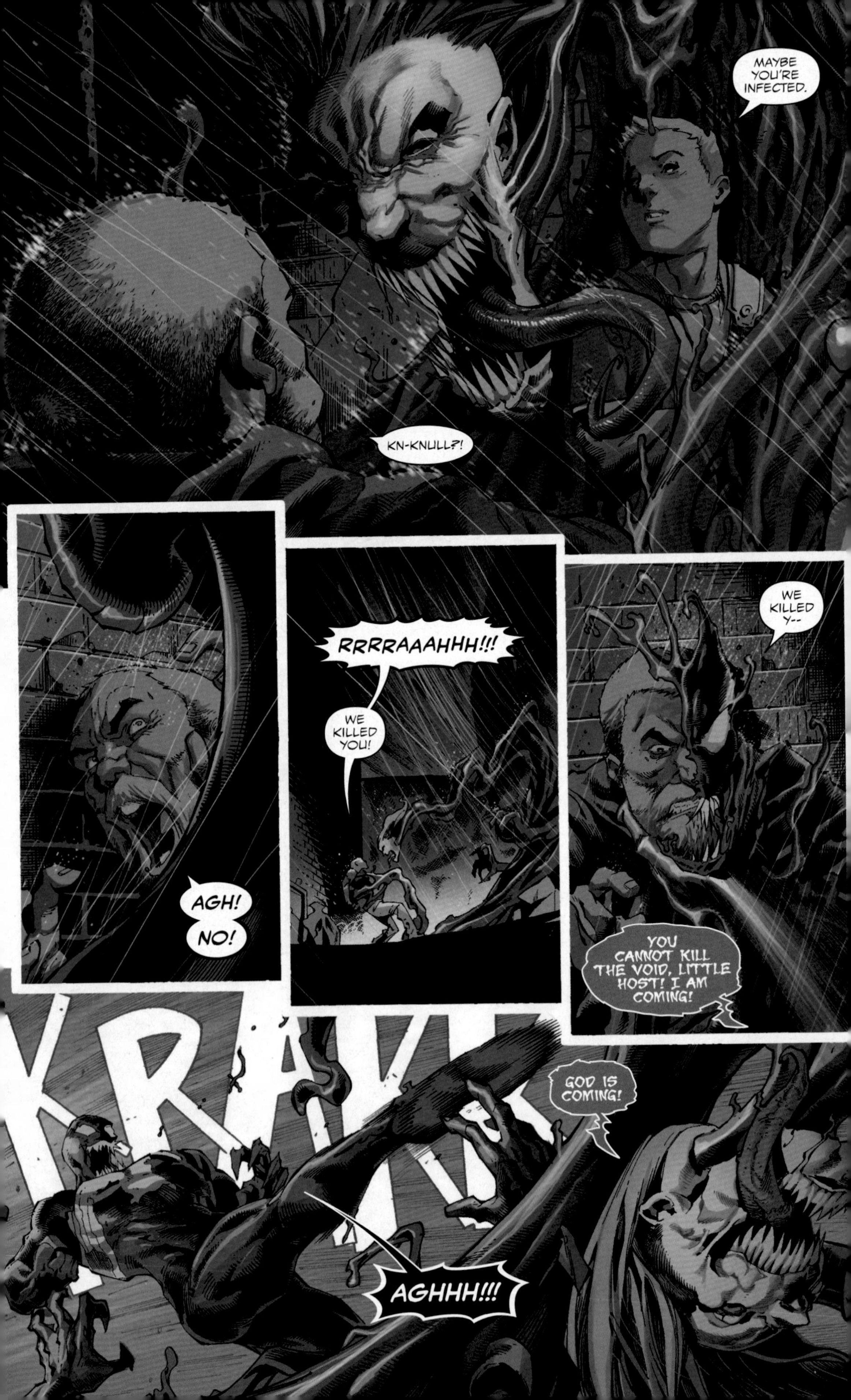
MAYBE YOU'RE INFECTED.
KN-KNULL?!
AGH! NO!
RRRRAAAHHH!!!
WE KILLED YOU!
WE KILLED Y--
YOU CANNOT KILL THE VOID, LITTLE HOST! I AM COMING!
GOD IS COMING!
AGHHH!!!

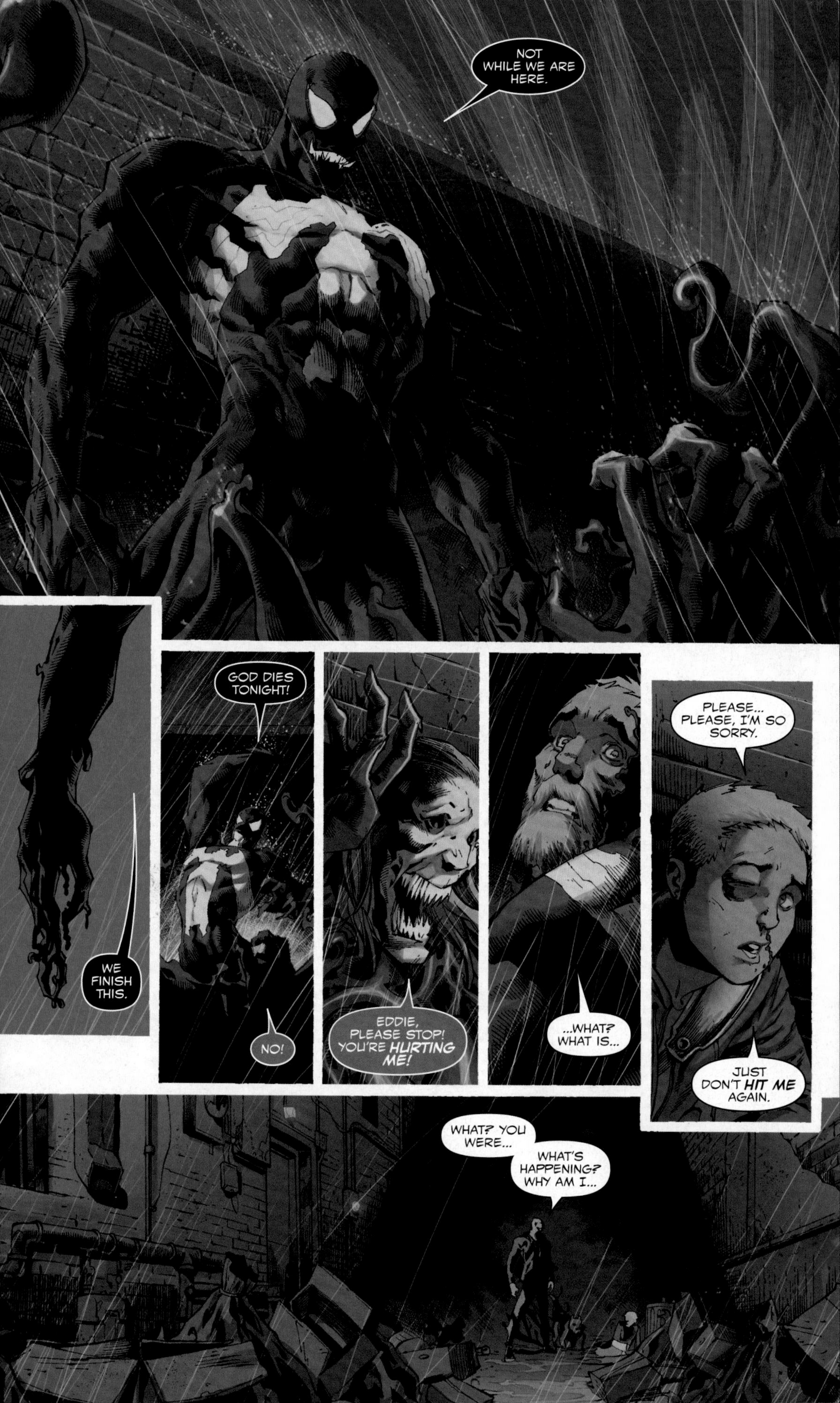
NOT WHILE WE ARE HERE.
WE FINISH THIS.
GOD DIES TONIGHT!
NO!
EDDIE, PLEASE STOP! YOU'RE HURTING ME!
...WHAT? WHAT IS...
PLEASE... PLEASE, I'M SO SORRY.
JUST DON'T HIT ME AGAIN.
WHAT? YOU WERE...
WHAT'S HAPPENING? WHY AM I...

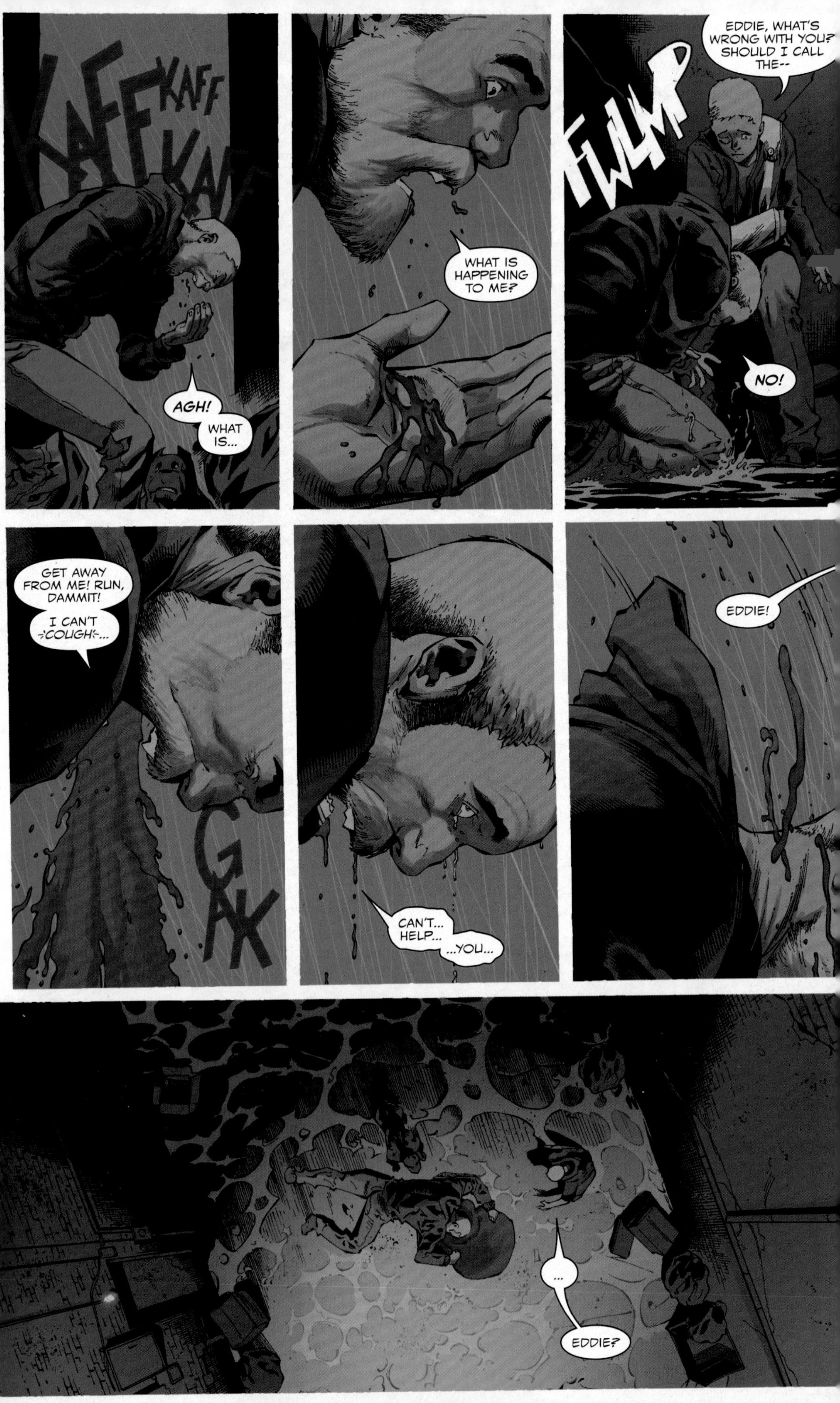
KAFF KAFF
KAFF KAFF
AGH!
WHAT IS...
WHAT IS HAPPENING TO ME?
FWUMP
EDDIE, WHAT'S WRONG WITH YOU? SHOULD I CALL THE--
NO!
GET AWAY FROM ME! RUN, DAMMIT!
I CAN'T -COUGH-...
GAK
CAN'T... HELP...
...YOU...
EDDIE!
...
EDDIE?

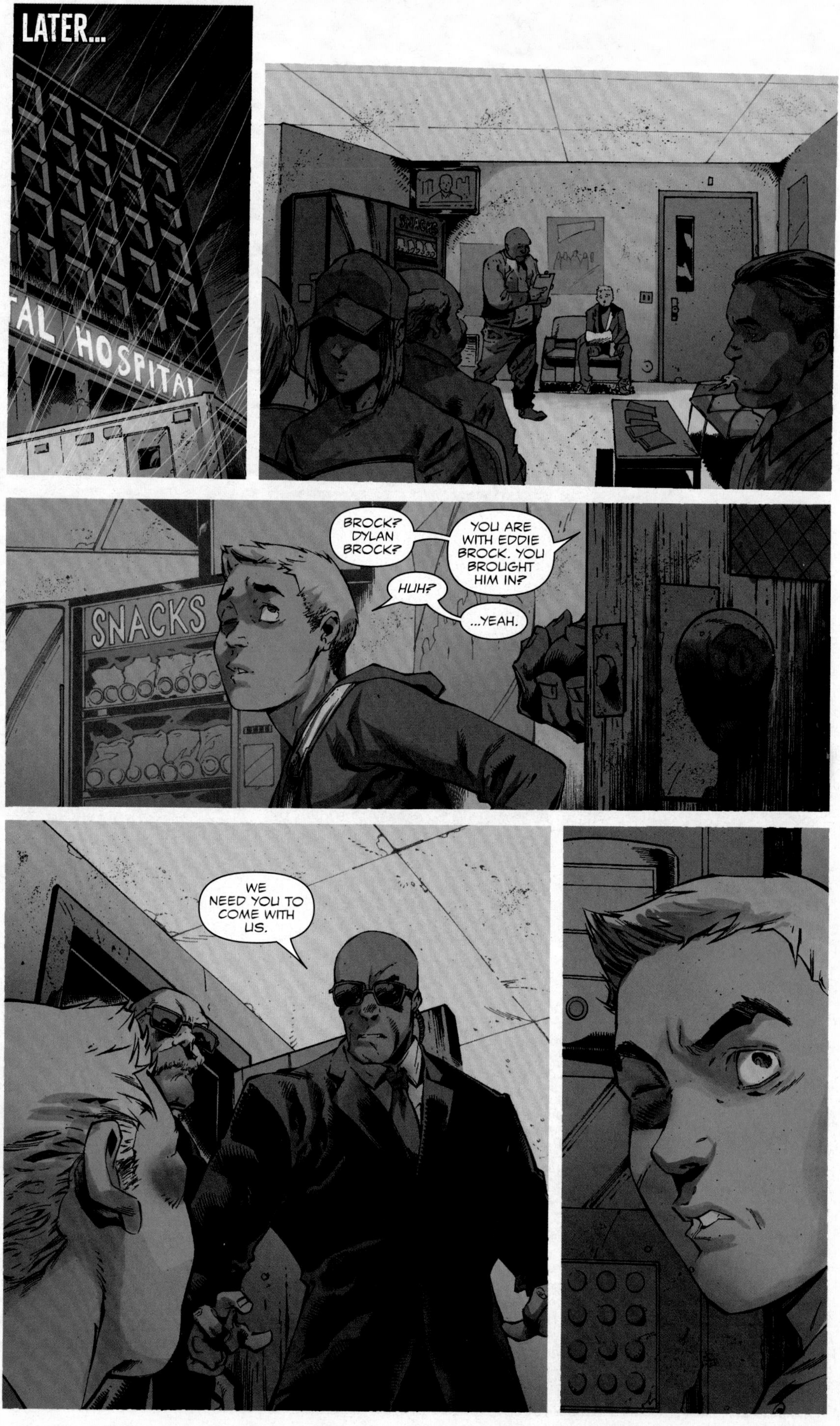
LATER...
HOSPITAL
SNACKS
BROCK? DYLAN BROCK?
YOU ARE WITH EDDIE BROCK. YOU BROUGHT HIM IN?
HUH?
...YEAH.
WE NEED YOU TO COME WITH US.

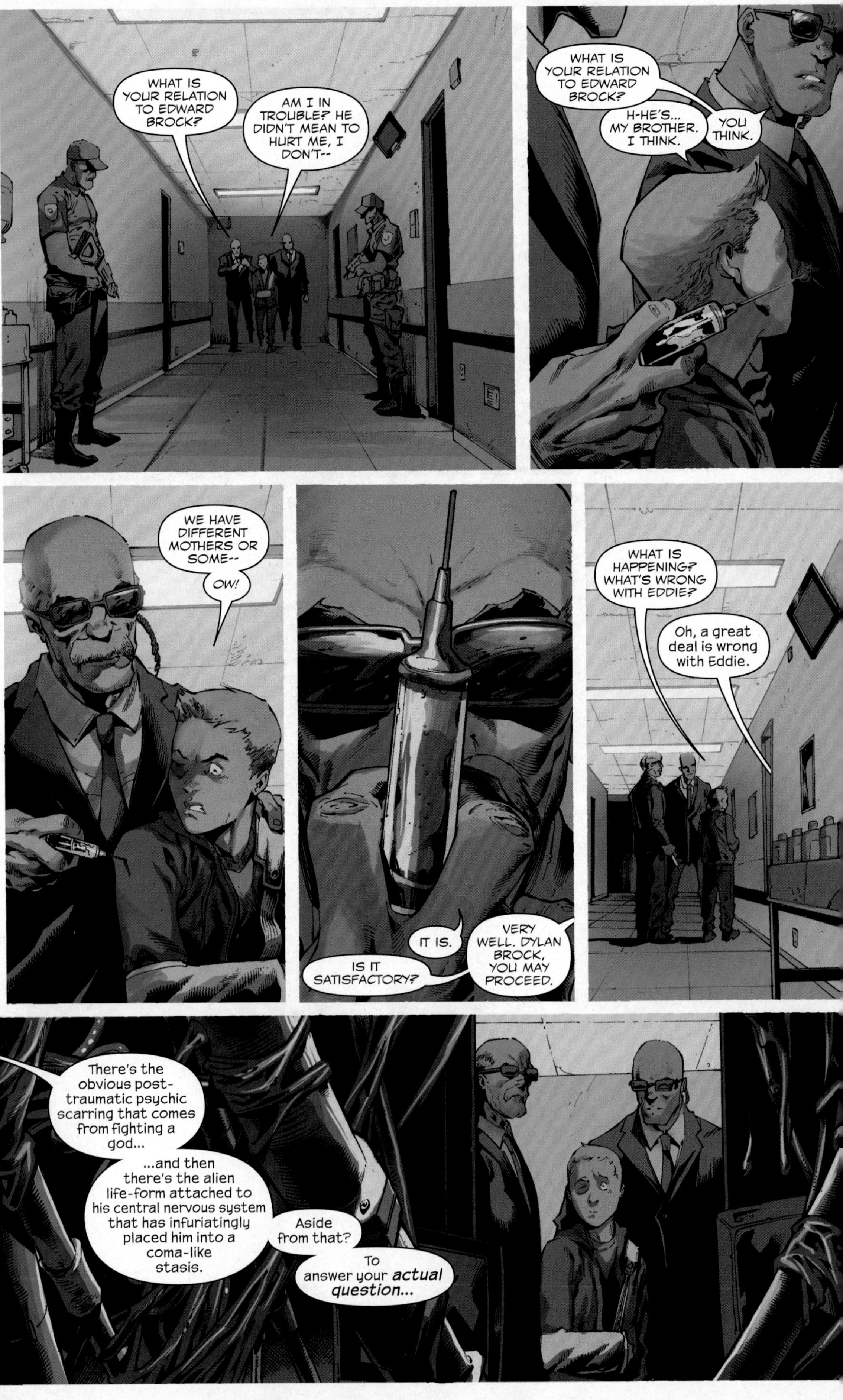
WHAT IS YOUR RELATION TO EDWARD BROCK?
AM I IN TROUBLE? HE DIDN'T MEAN TO HURT ME, I DON'T--
WHAT IS YOUR RELATION TO EDWARD BROCK?
H-HE'S... MY BROTHER. I THINK.
YOU THINK.
WE HAVE DIFFERENT MOTHERS OR SOME--
OW!
IS IT SATISFACTORY?
IT IS.
VERY WELL. DYLAN BROCK, YOU MAY PROCEED.
WHAT IS HAPPENING? WHAT'S WRONG WITH EDDIE?
Oh, a great deal is wrong with Eddie.
There's the obvious post-traumatic psychic scarring that comes from fighting a god...
...and then there's the alien life-form attached to his central nervous system that has infuriatingly placed him into a coma-like stasis.
Aside from that?
To answer your *actual question...*

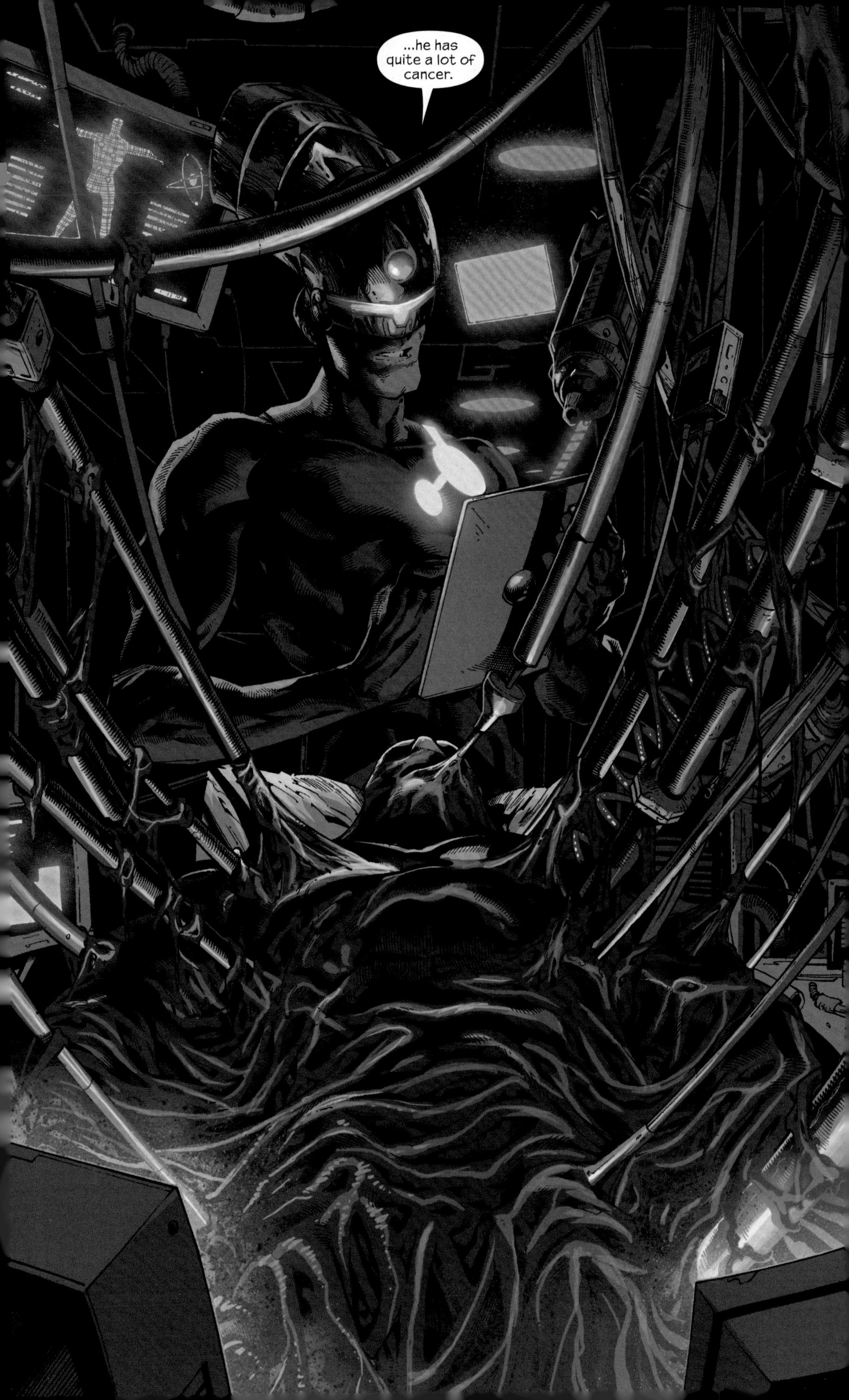
...he has quite a lot of cancer.

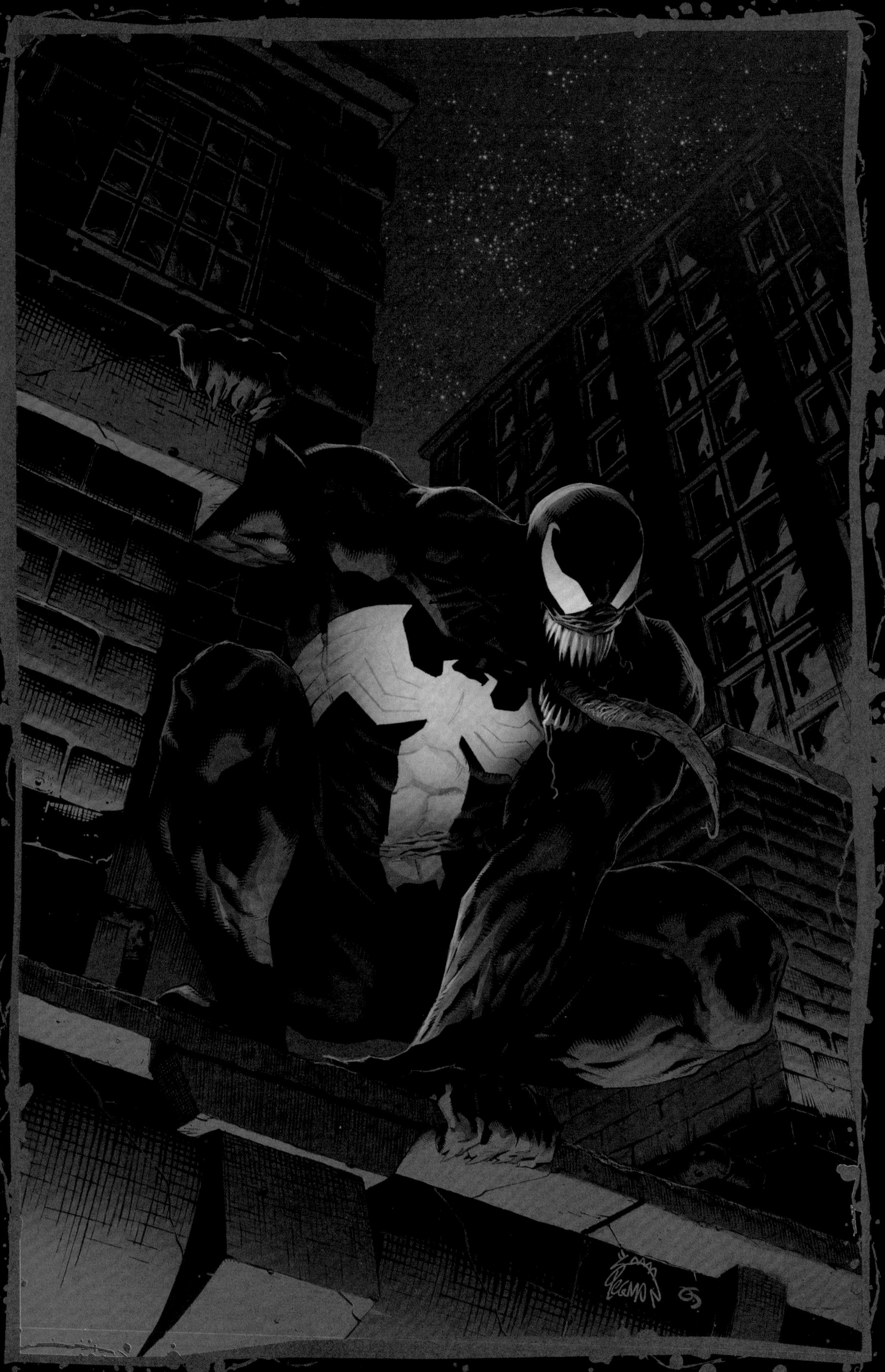

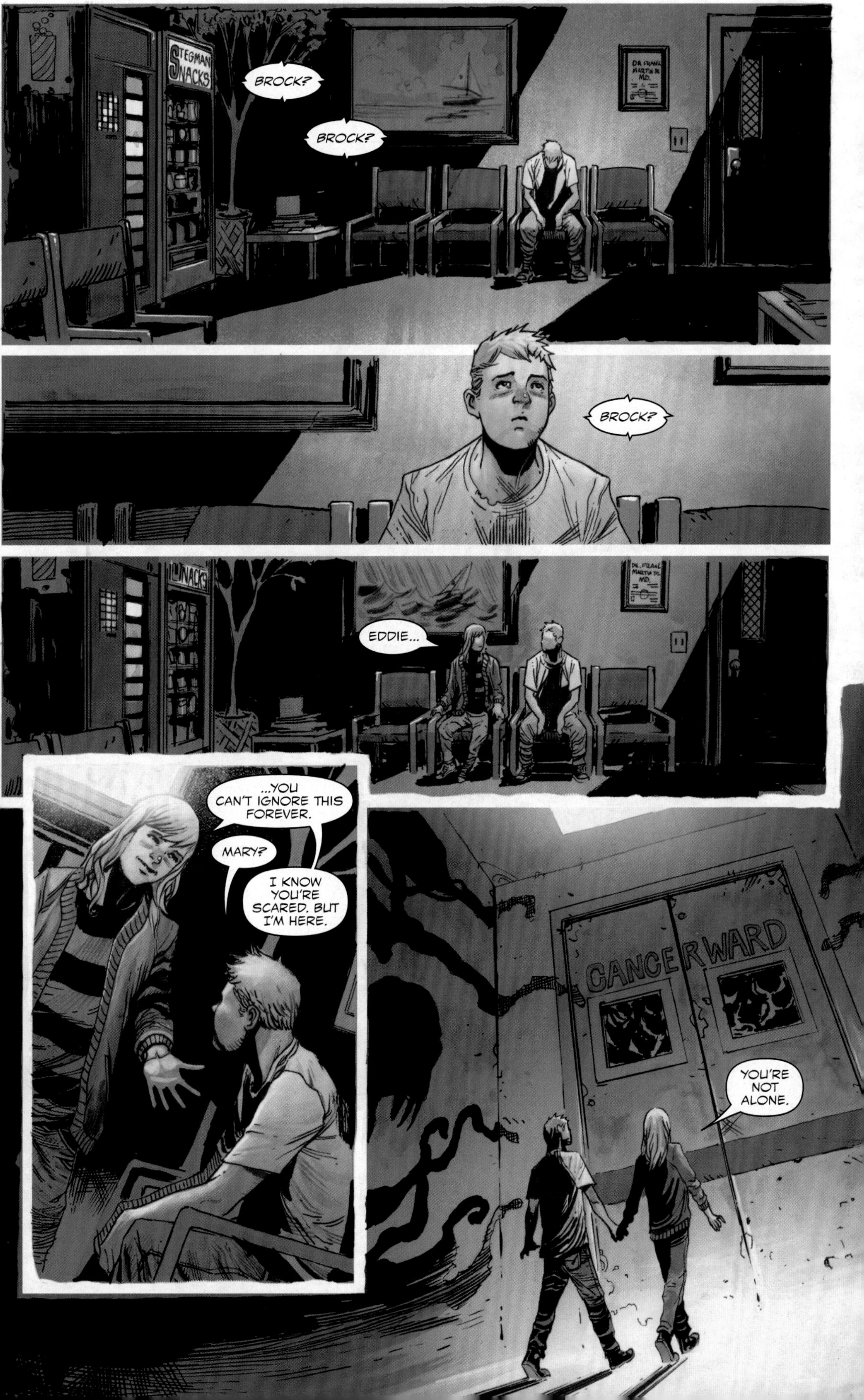

STEGMAN SNACKS
DR. FRANK MARTIN JR. M.D.
BROCK?
BROCK?
BROCK?
EDDIE...
...YOU CAN'T IGNORE THIS FOREVER.
MARY?
I KNOW YOU'RE SCARED. BUT I'M HERE.
CANCER WARD
YOU'RE NOT ALONE.

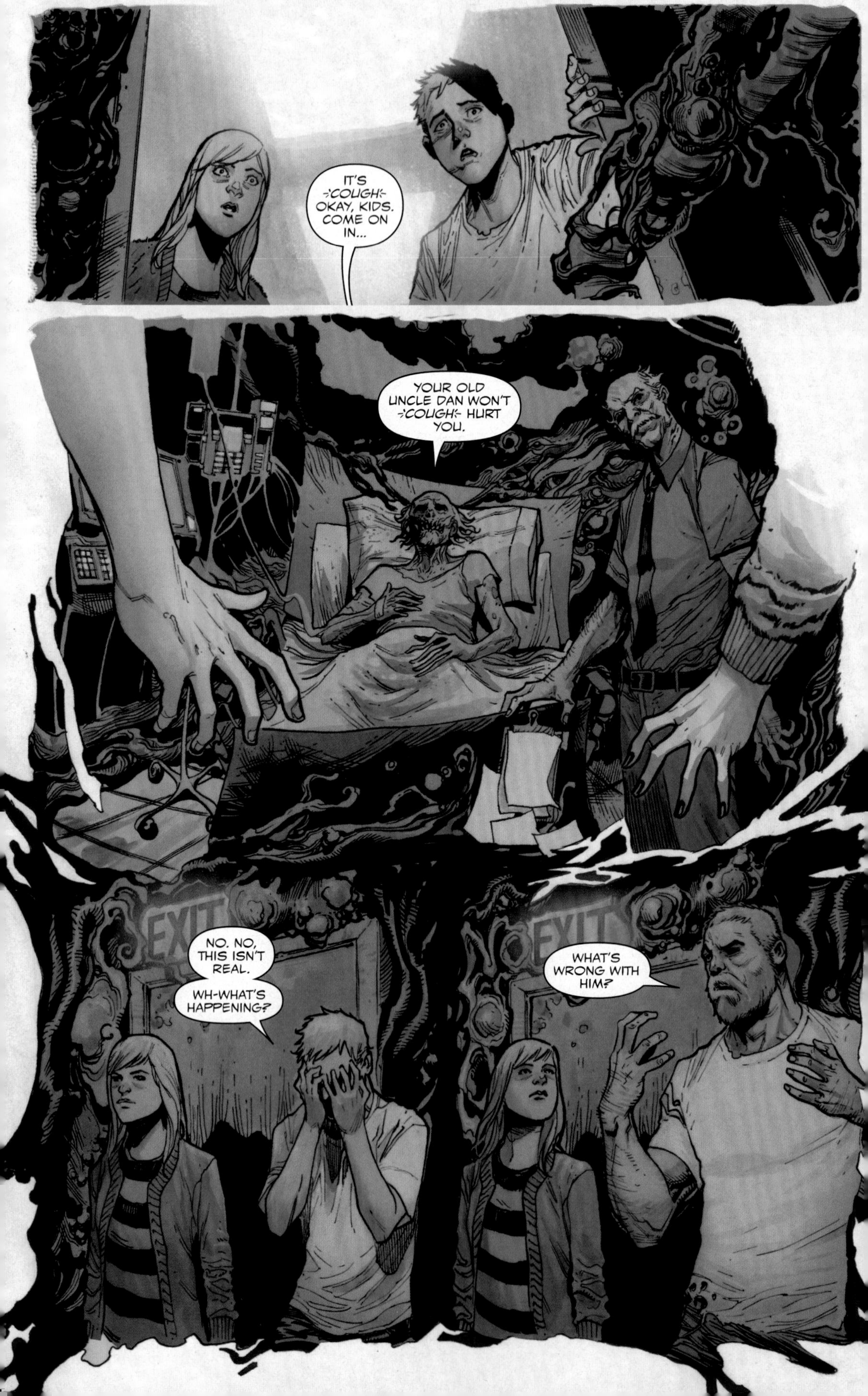
IT'S -COUGH- OKAY, KIDS. COME ON IN...
YOUR OLD UNCLE DAN WON'T -COUGH- HURT YOU.
EXIT
NO. NO, THIS ISN'T REAL.
WH-WHAT'S HAPPENING?
EXIT
WHAT'S WRONG WITH HIM?

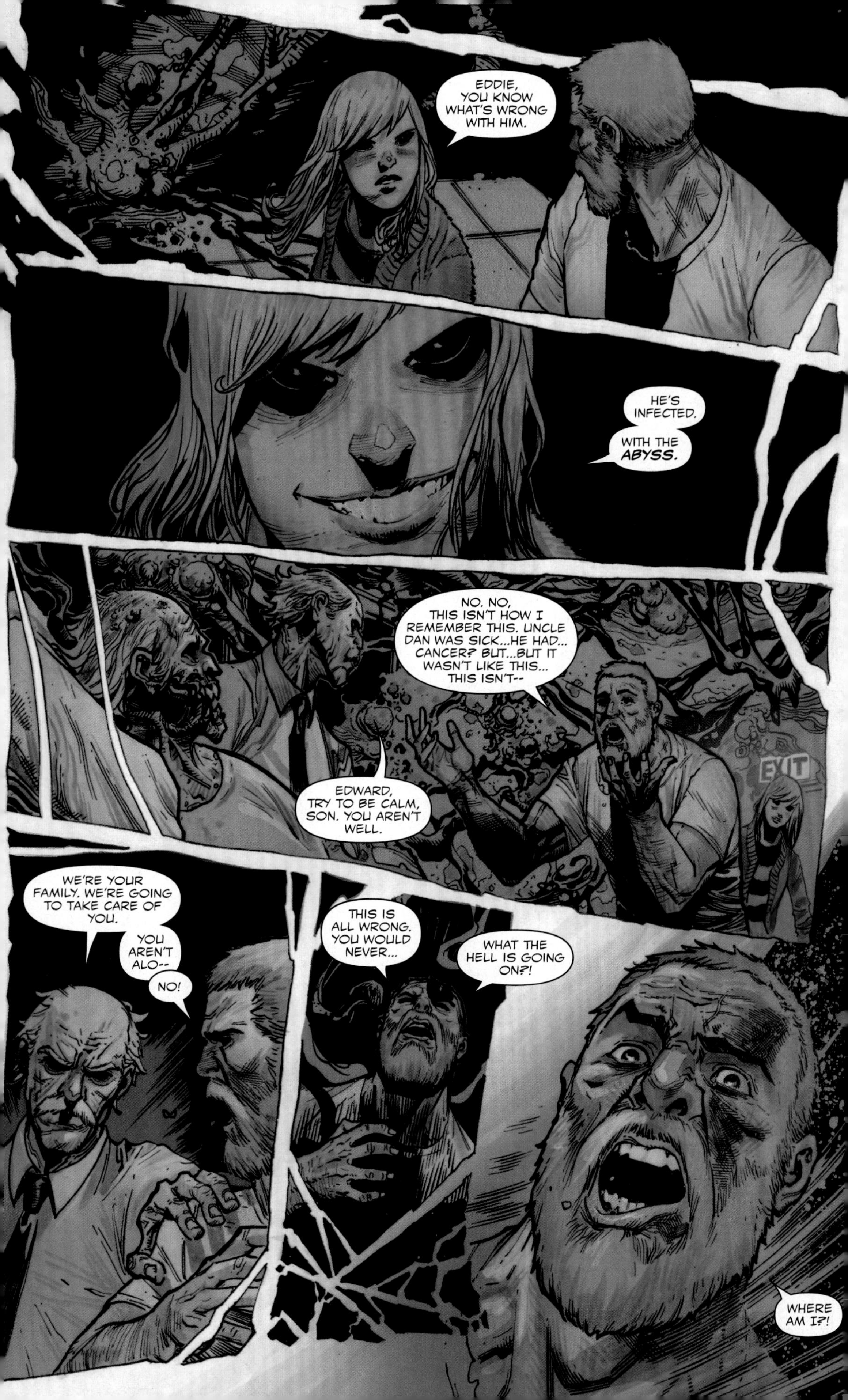
EDDIE, YOU KNOW WHAT'S WRONG WITH HIM.
HE'S INFECTED.
WITH THE ABYSS.
NO. NO, THIS ISN'T HOW I REMEMBER THIS. UNCLE DAN WAS SICK...HE HAD... CANCER? BUT...BUT IT WASN'T LIKE THIS... THIS ISN'T--
EDWARD, TRY TO BE CALM, SON. YOU AREN'T WELL.
EXIT
WE'RE YOUR FAMILY. WE'RE GOING TO TAKE CARE OF YOU.
YOU AREN'T ALO--
NO!
THIS IS ALL WRONG. YOU WOULD NEVER...
WHAT THE HELL IS GOING ON?!
WHERE AM I?!

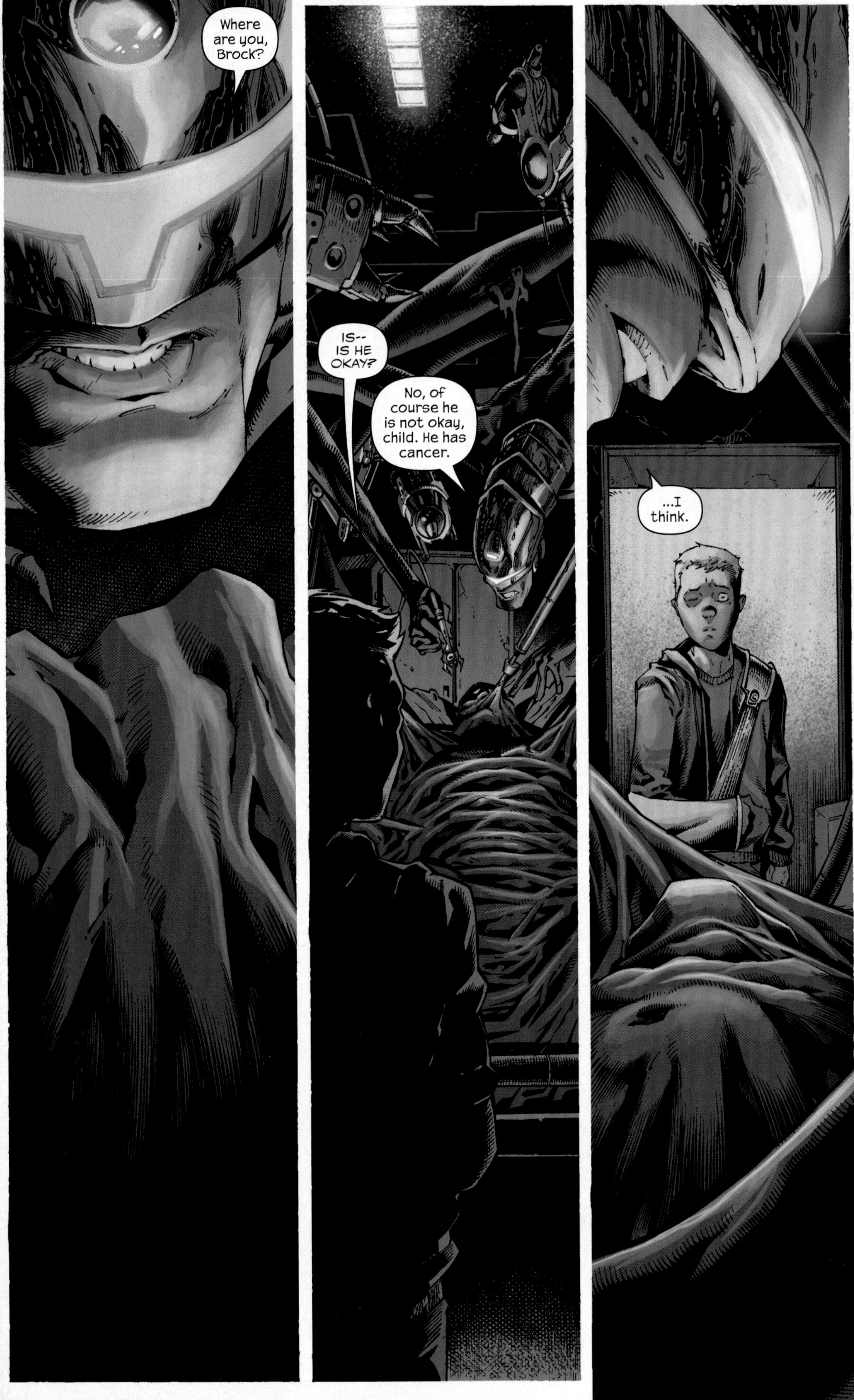
Where are you, Brock?
IS-- IS HE OKAY?
No, of course he is not okay, child. He has cancer.
...I think.

WHAT DOES THAT MEAN? YOU *THINK?*

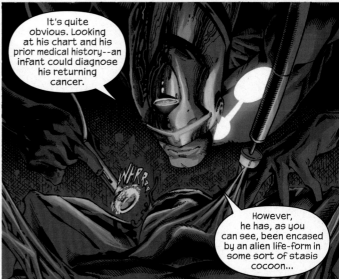

It's quite obvious. Looking at his chart and his prior medical history--an infant could diagnose his returning cancer.

However, he has, as you can see, been encased by an alien life-form in some sort of stasis cocoon...

...which is presently, quite infuriatingly, preventing me from assessing his current situation.

SNAP

It also means that you should remove yourself from this room.

WHAT? WHY?

Because, child, in order to properly assess your brother's current medical situation, I will need to temporarily remove the symbiote from his person.

Which, in all likelihood, will result in extreme withdrawal, perhaps even death. I'm sure you would rather not see such things...

Killing him to find out what's killing him.

Hmmm, quite ironic, I suppose.

Alas...

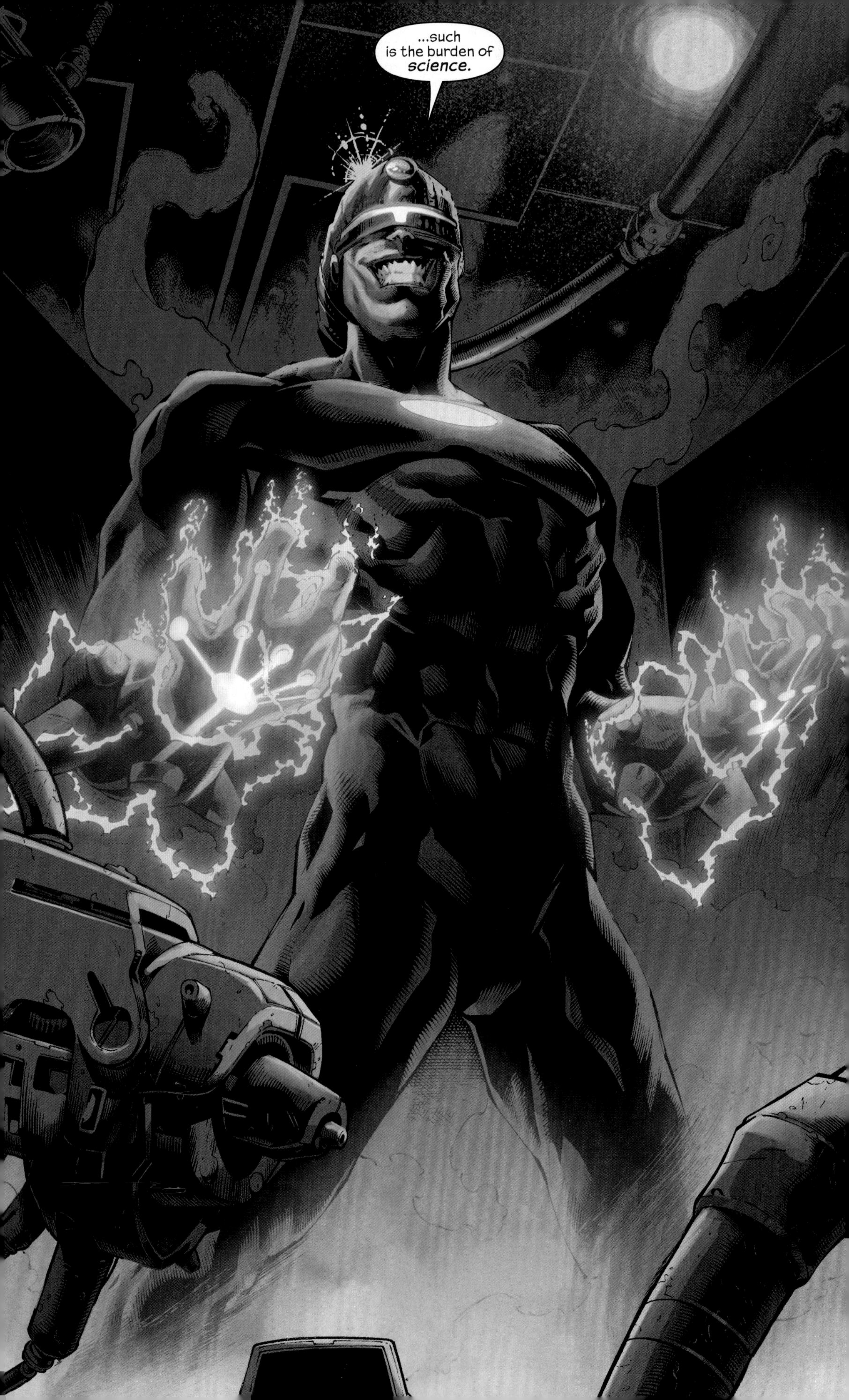
...such is the burden of *science.*

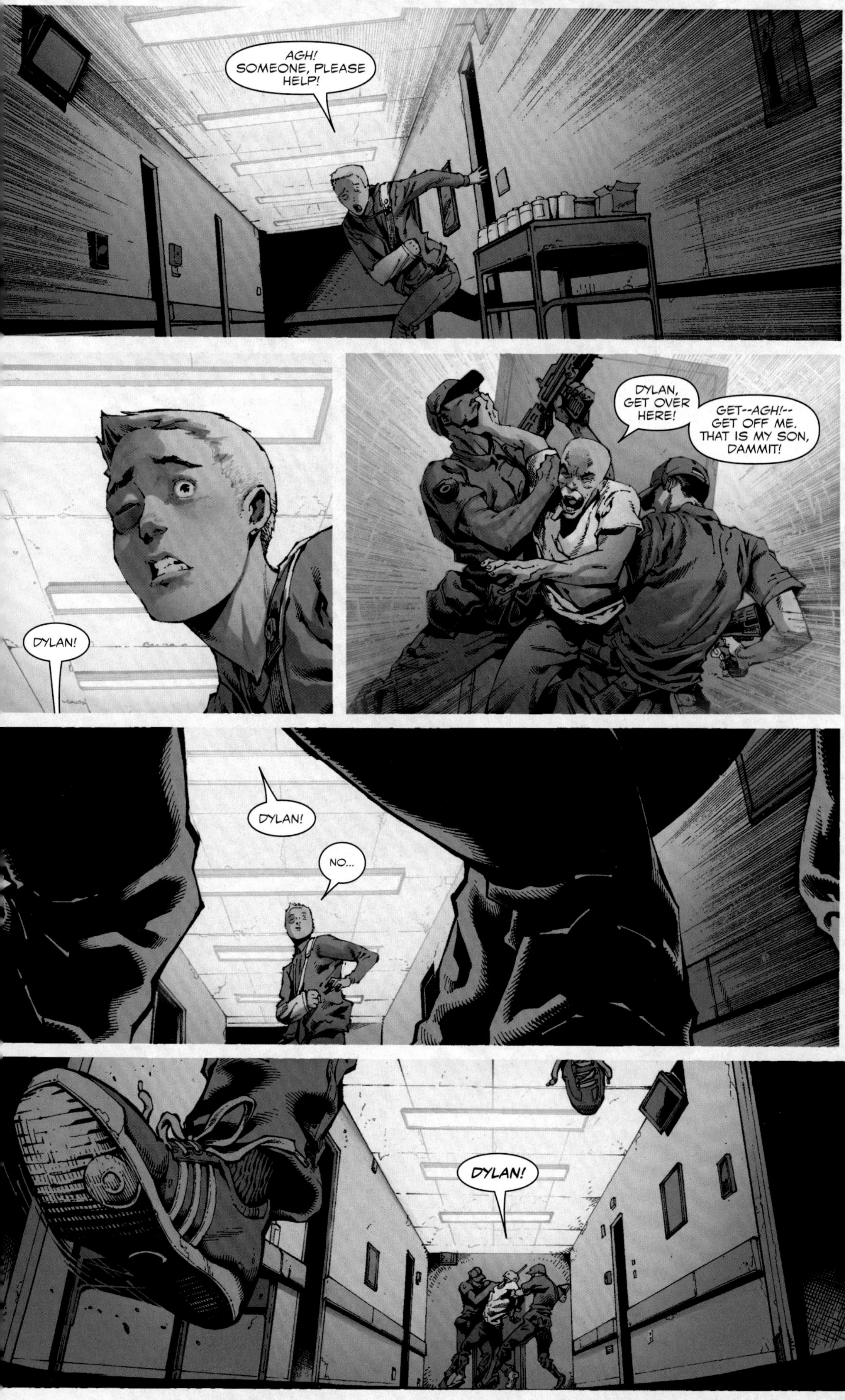
AGH! SOMEONE, PLEASE HELP!
DYLAN!
DYLAN, GET OVER HERE!
GET--AGH!--GET OFF ME. THAT IS MY SON, DAMMIT!
DYLAN!
NO...
DYLAN!

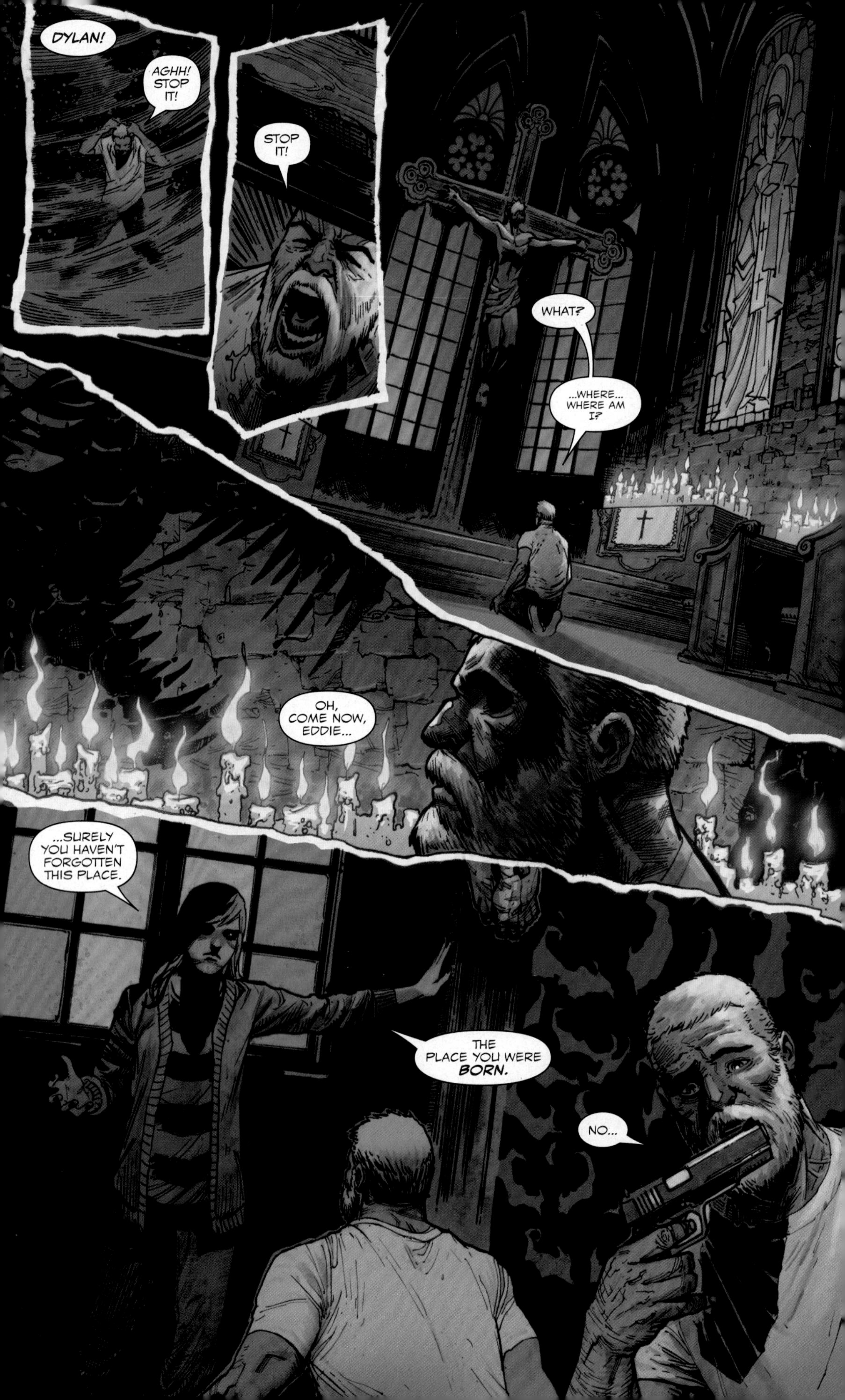
DYLAN!
AGHH! STOP IT!
STOP IT!
WHAT?
...WHERE... WHERE AM I?
OH, COME NOW, EDDIE...
...SURELY YOU HAVEN'T FORGOTTEN THIS PLACE.
THE PLACE YOU WERE BORN.
NO...

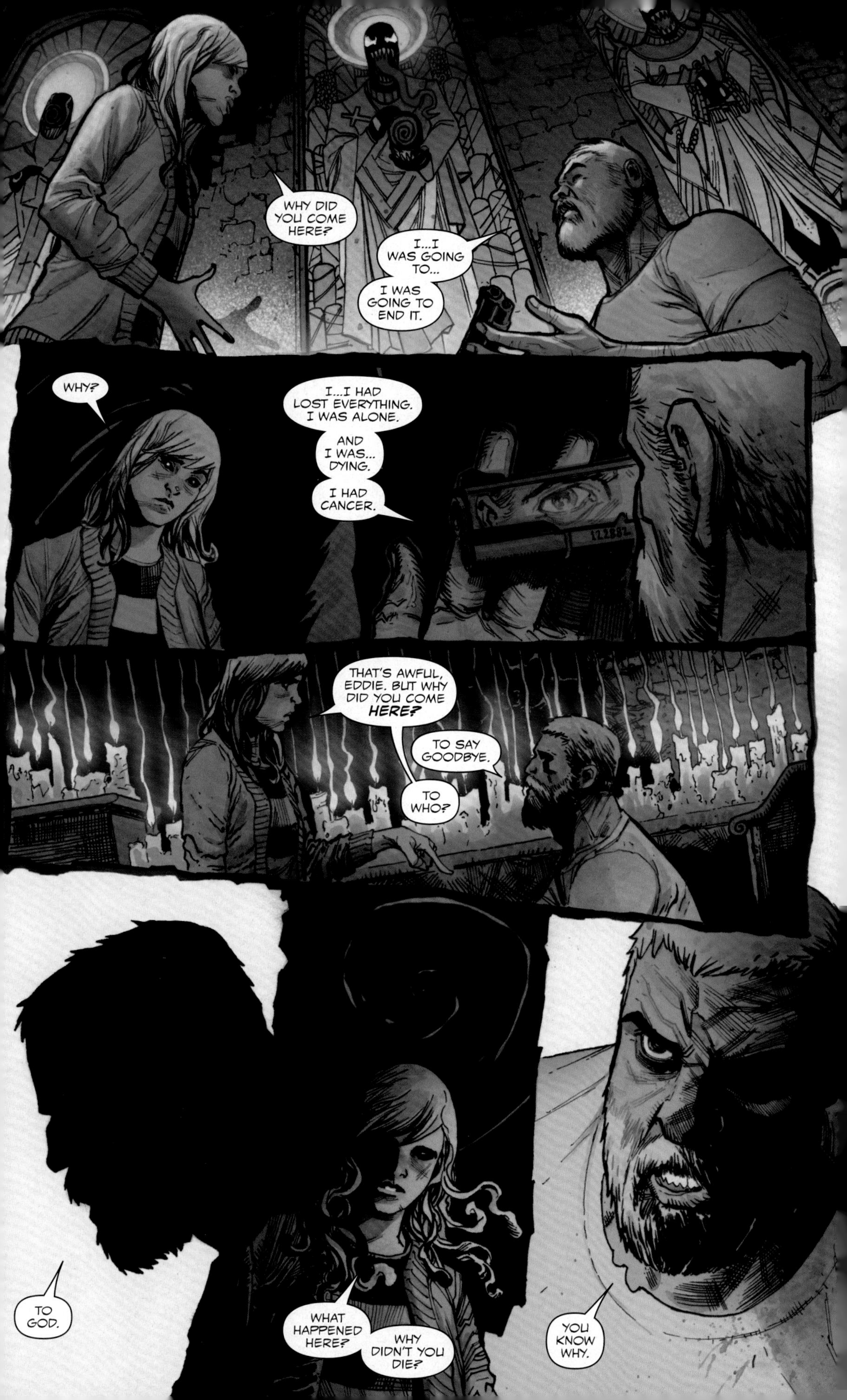
WHY DID YOU COME HERE?
I...I WAS GOING TO...
I WAS GOING TO END IT.
WHY?
I...I HAD LOST EVERYTHING. I WAS ALONE.
AND I WAS... DYING.
I HAD CANCER.
THAT'S AWFUL, EDDIE. BUT WHY DID YOU COME *HERE?*
TO SAY GOODBYE.
TO WHO?
TO GOD.
WHAT HAPPENED HERE?
WHY DIDN'T YOU DIE?
YOU KNOW WHY.

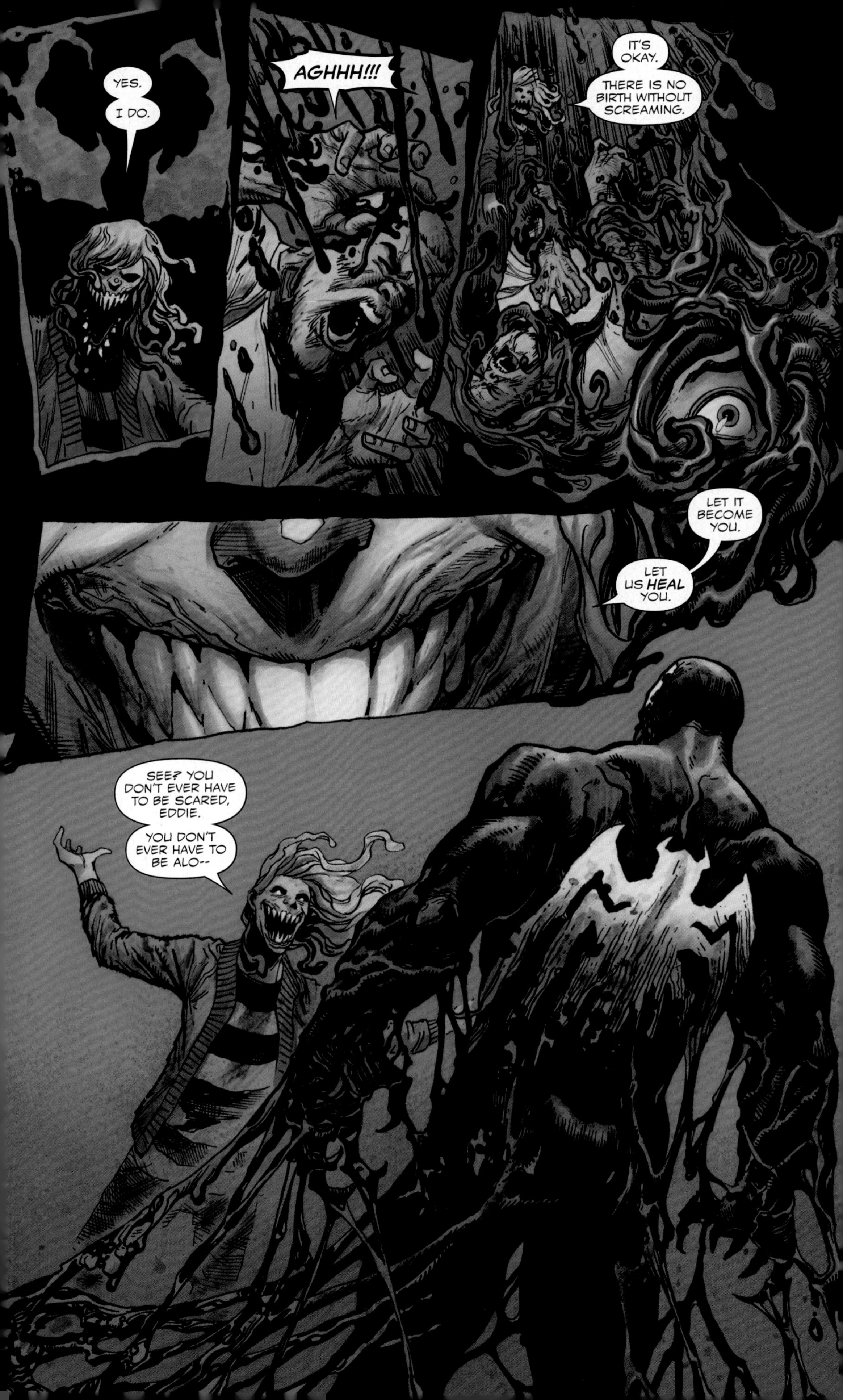
YES.
I DO.
AGHHH!!!
IT'S OKAY.
THERE IS NO BIRTH WITHOUT SCREAMING.
LET IT BECOME YOU.
LET US **HEAL** YOU.
SEE? YOU DON'T EVER HAVE TO BE SCARED, EDDIE.
YOU DON'T EVER HAVE TO BE ALO--

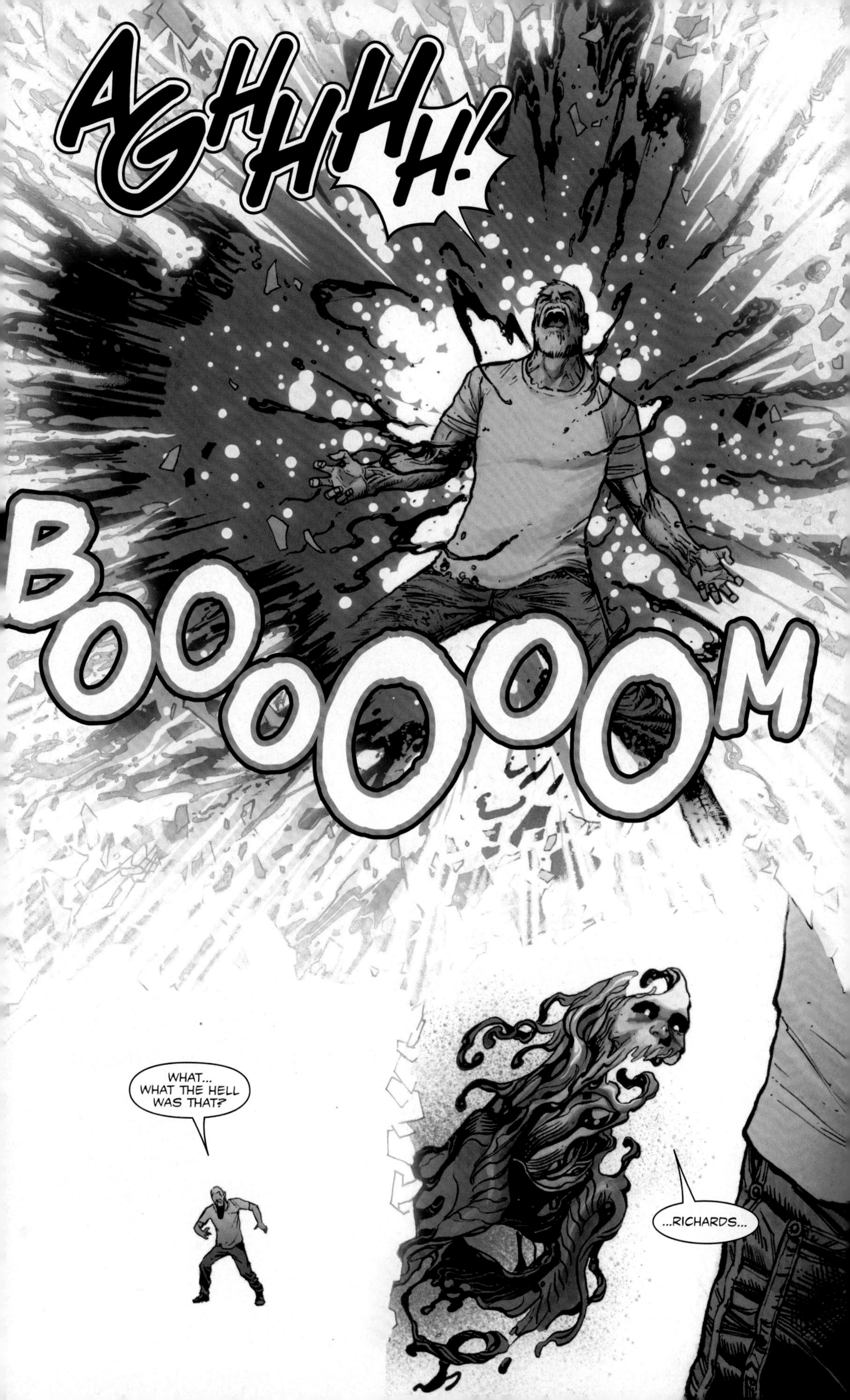
AGHHHH!
BOOOOOOOM
WHAT... WHAT THE HELL WAS THAT?
...RICHARDS...

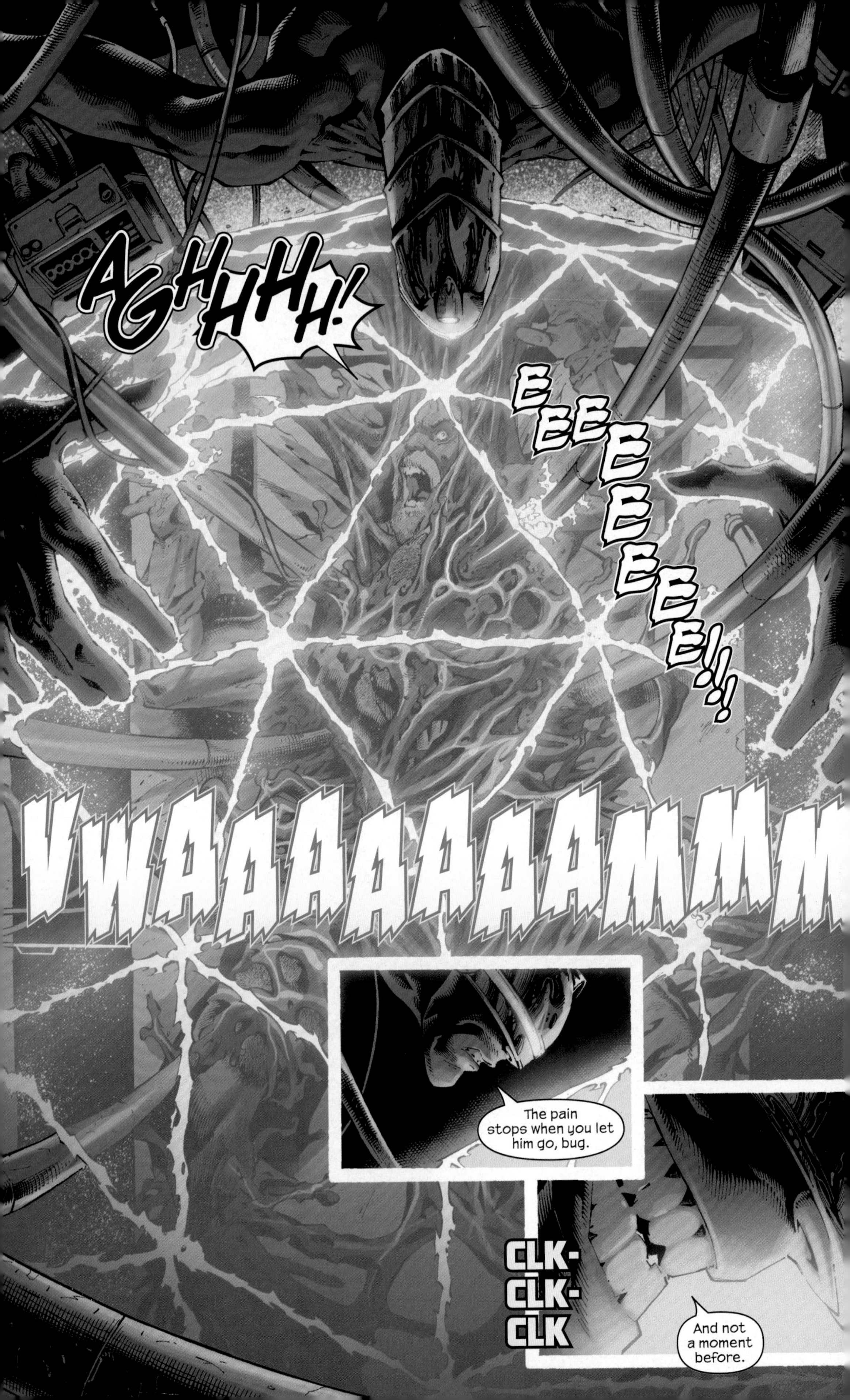
AGHHHH!
EEEEEEEEE!!!
VWAAAAAAAAMMM
The pain stops when you let him go, bug.
CLK-CLK-CLK
And not a moment before.

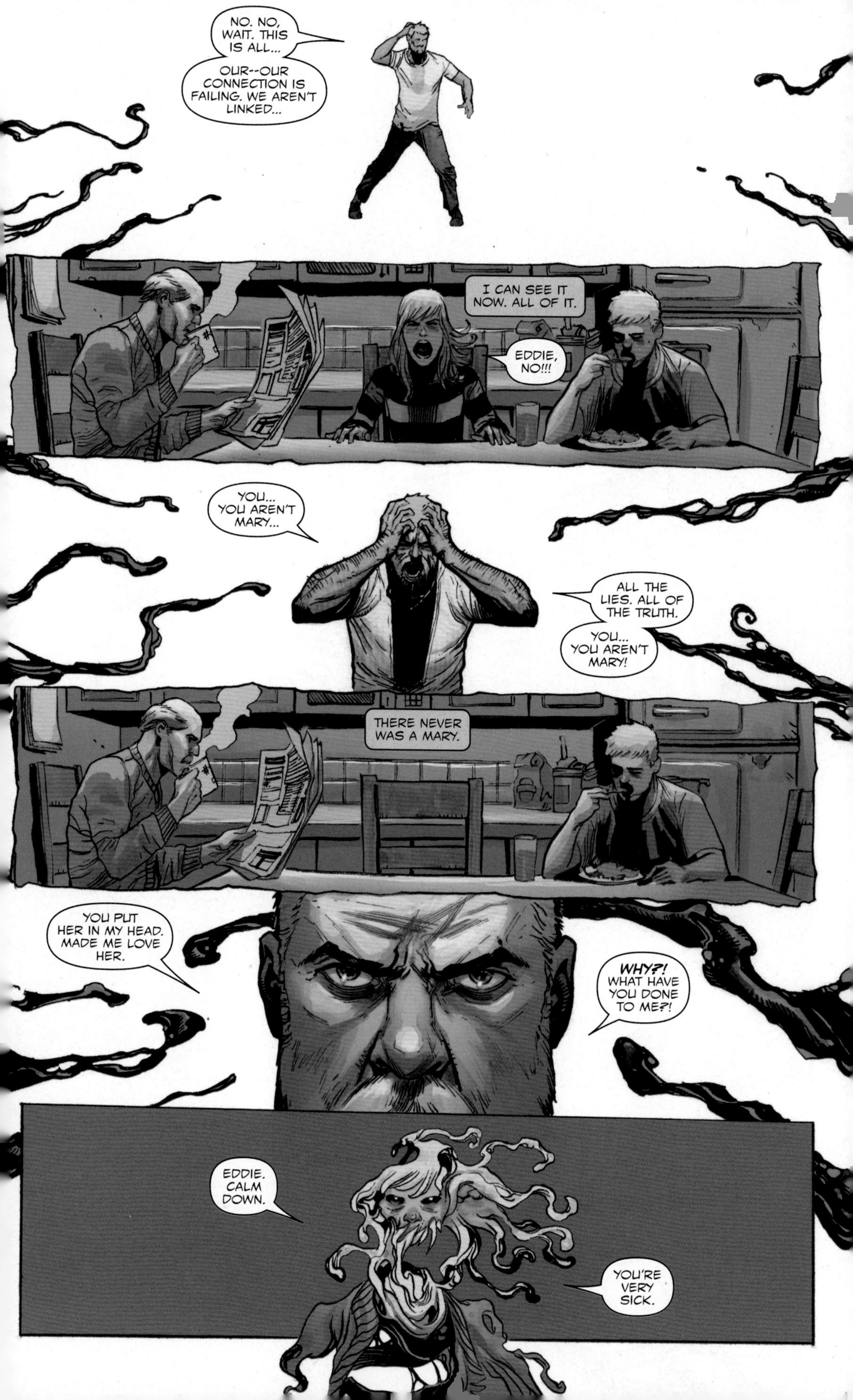
NO. NO, WAIT. THIS IS ALL...
OUR--OUR CONNECTION IS FAILING. WE AREN'T LINKED...
I CAN SEE IT NOW. ALL OF IT.
EDDIE, NO!!!
YOU... YOU AREN'T MARY...
ALL THE LIES. ALL OF THE TRUTH.
YOU... YOU AREN'T MARY!
THERE NEVER WAS A MARY.
YOU PUT HER IN MY HEAD. MADE ME LOVE HER.
WHY?! WHAT HAVE YOU DONE TO ME?!
EDDIE. CALM DOWN.
YOU'RE VERY SICK.

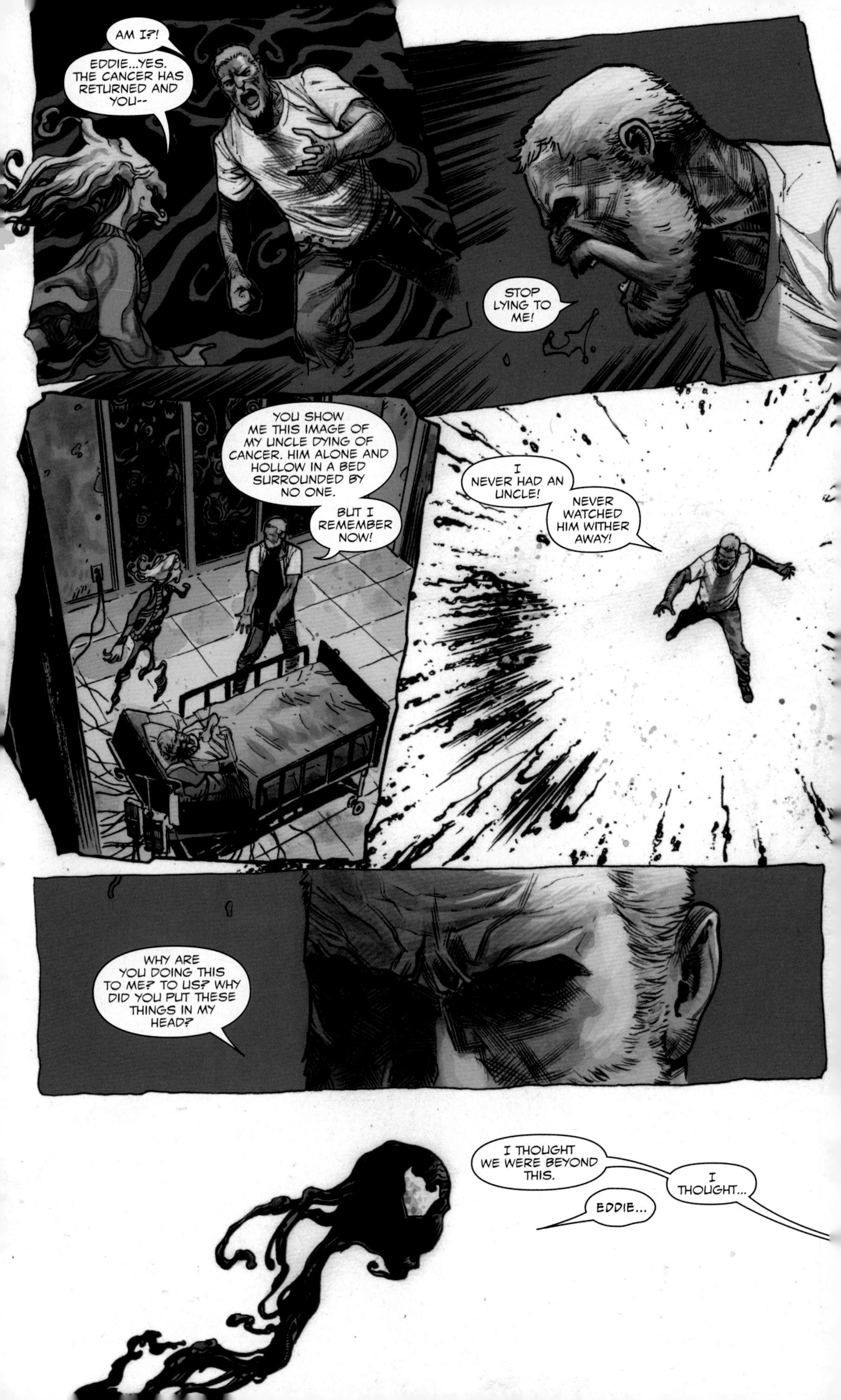
AM I?!
EDDIE...YES. THE CANCER HAS RETURNED AND YOU--
STOP LYING TO ME!
YOU SHOW ME THIS IMAGE OF MY UNCLE DYING OF CANCER. HIM ALONE AND HOLLOW IN A BED SURROUNDED BY NO ONE.
BUT I REMEMBER NOW!
I NEVER HAD AN UNCLE!
NEVER WATCHED HIM WITHER AWAY!
WHY ARE YOU DOING THIS TO ME? TO US? WHY DID YOU PUT THESE THINGS IN MY HEAD?
I THOUGHT WE WERE BEYOND THIS.
I THOUGHT...
EDDIE...

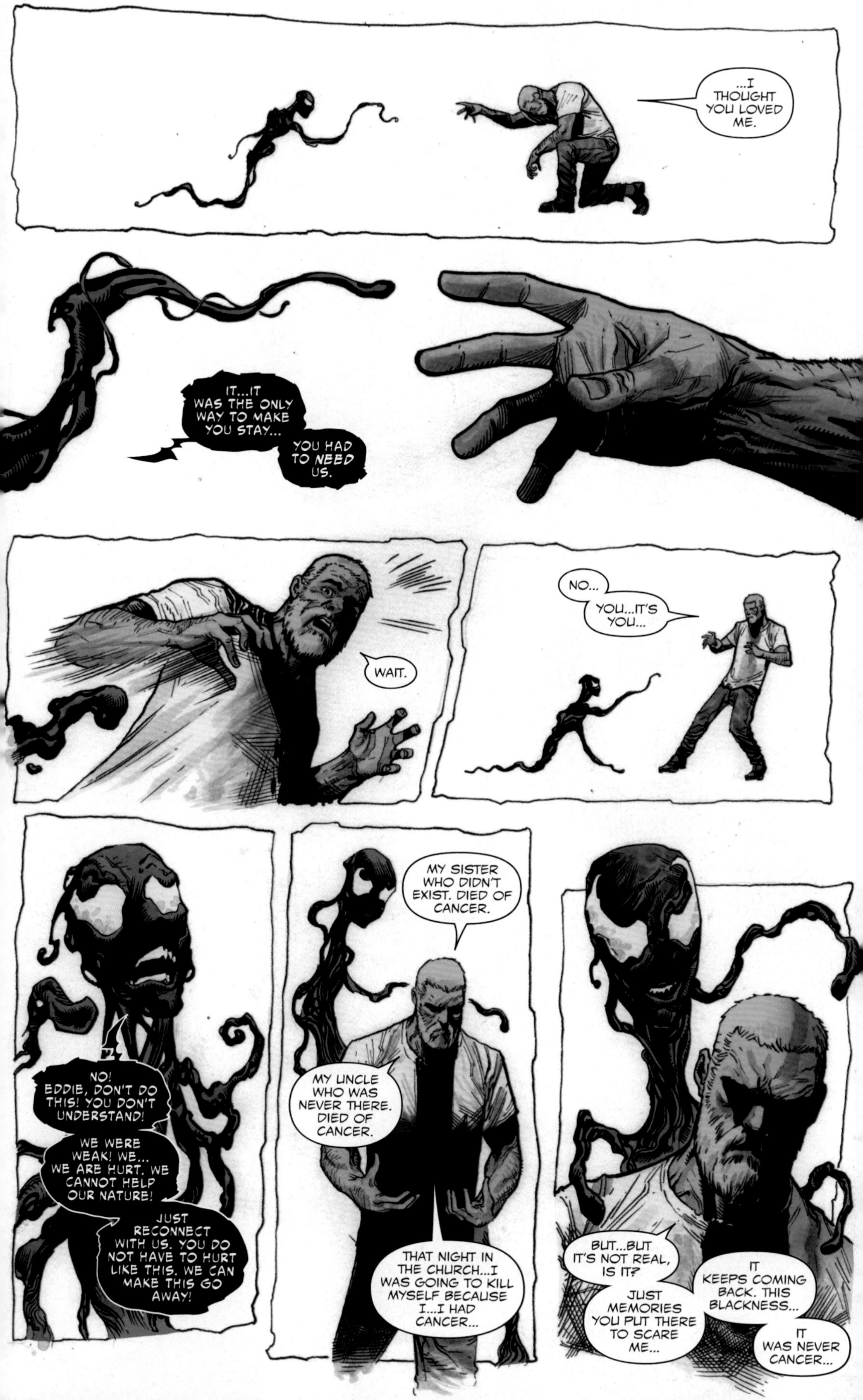
...I THOUGHT YOU LOVED ME.
IT...IT WAS THE ONLY WAY TO MAKE YOU STAY...
YOU HAD TO NEED US.
WAIT.
NO...
YOU...IT'S YOU...
NO! EDDIE, DON'T DO THIS! YOU DON'T UNDERSTAND!
WE WERE WEAK! WE... WE ARE HURT. WE CANNOT HELP OUR NATURE!
JUST RECONNECT WITH US. YOU DO NOT HAVE TO HURT LIKE THIS. WE CAN MAKE THIS GO AWAY!
MY SISTER WHO DIDN'T EXIST. DIED OF CANCER.
MY UNCLE WHO WAS NEVER THERE. DIED OF CANCER.
THAT NIGHT IN THE CHURCH...I WAS GOING TO KILL MYSELF BECAUSE I...I HAD CANCER...
BUT...BUT IT'S NOT REAL, IS IT?
JUST MEMORIES YOU PUT THERE TO SCARE ME...
IT KEEPS COMING BACK. THIS BLACKNESS...
IT WAS NEVER CANCER...

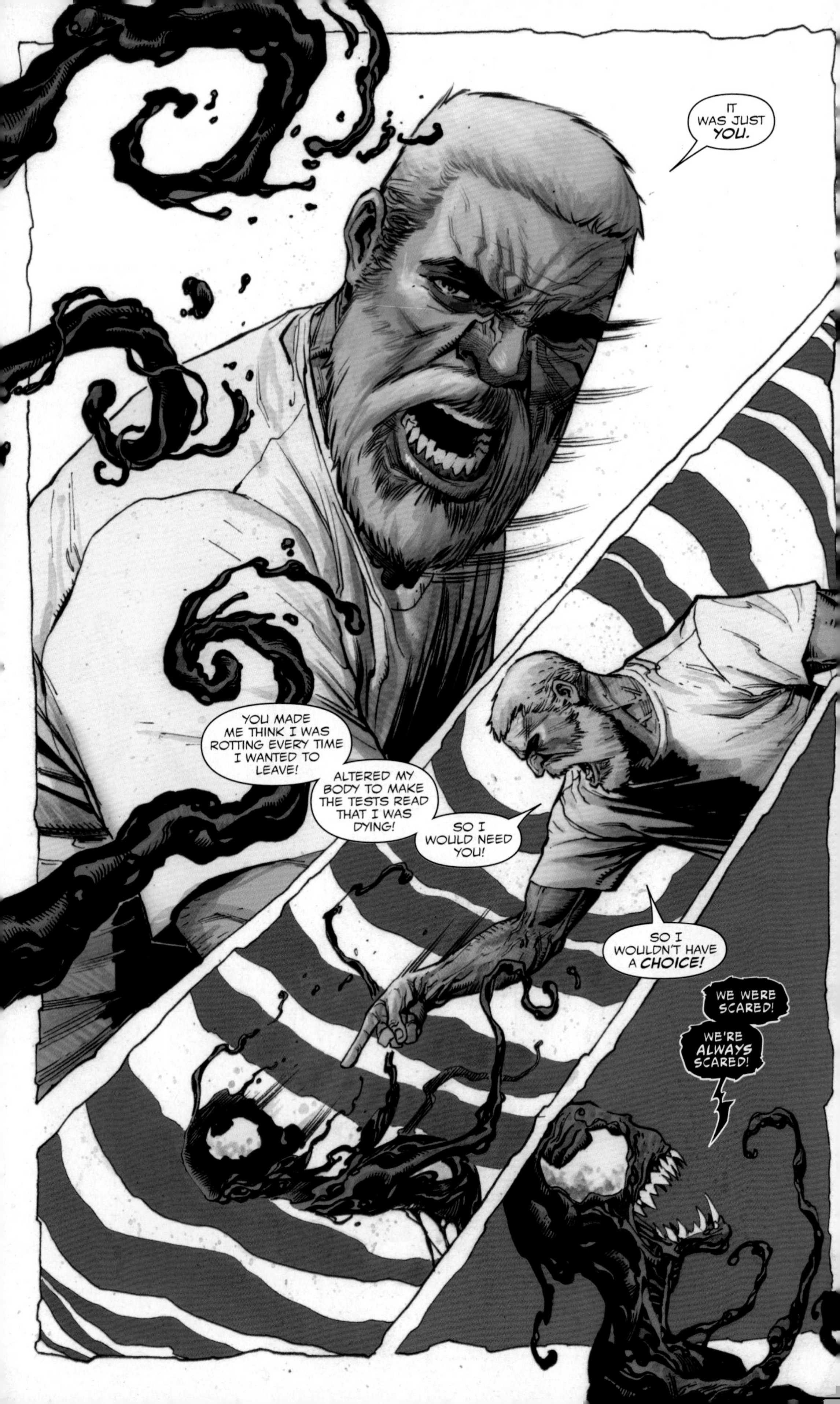
IT WAS JUST YOU.
YOU MADE ME THINK I WAS ROTTING EVERY TIME I WANTED TO LEAVE!
ALTERED MY BODY TO MAKE THE TESTS READ THAT I WAS DYING!
SO I WOULD NEED YOU!
SO I WOULDN'T HAVE A CHOICE!
WE WERE SCARED!
WE'RE ALWAYS SCARED!

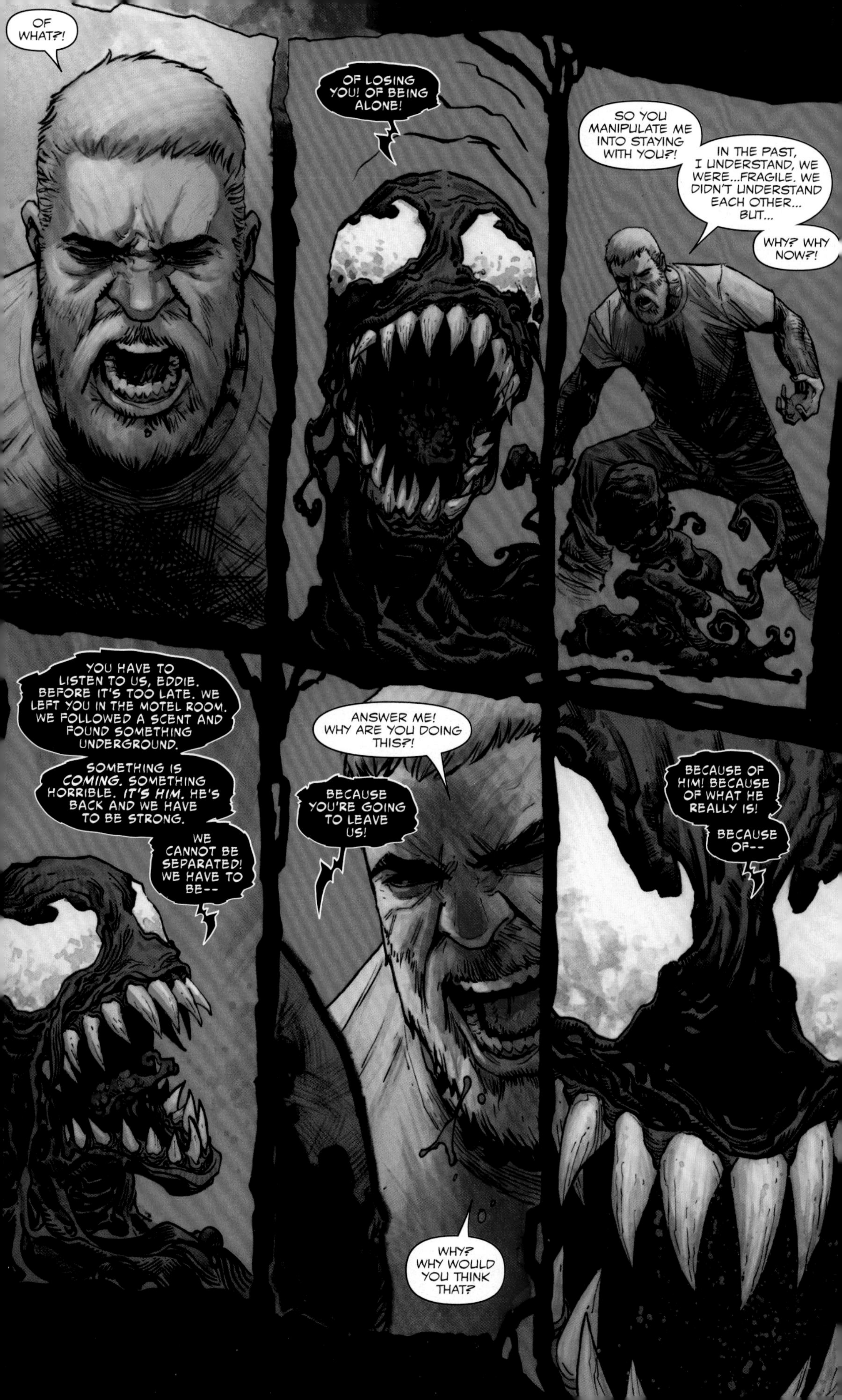
OF WHAT?!
OF LOSING YOU! OF BEING ALONE!
SO YOU MANIPULATE ME INTO STAYING WITH YOU?!
IN THE PAST, I UNDERSTAND, WE WERE...FRAGILE. WE DIDN'T UNDERSTAND EACH OTHER... BUT...
WHY? WHY NOW?!
YOU HAVE TO LISTEN TO US, EDDIE. BEFORE IT'S TOO LATE. WE LEFT YOU IN THE MOTEL ROOM. WE FOLLOWED A SCENT AND FOUND SOMETHING UNDERGROUND.
SOMETHING IS *COMING*. SOMETHING HORRIBLE. *IT'S HIM*. HE'S BACK AND WE HAVE TO BE STRONG.
WE CANNOT BE SEPARATED! WE HAVE TO BE--
ANSWER ME! WHY ARE YOU DOING THIS?!
BECAUSE YOU'RE GOING TO LEAVE US!
WHY? WHY WOULD YOU THINK THAT?
BECAUSE OF HIM! BECAUSE OF WHAT HE REALLY IS!
BECAUSE OF--

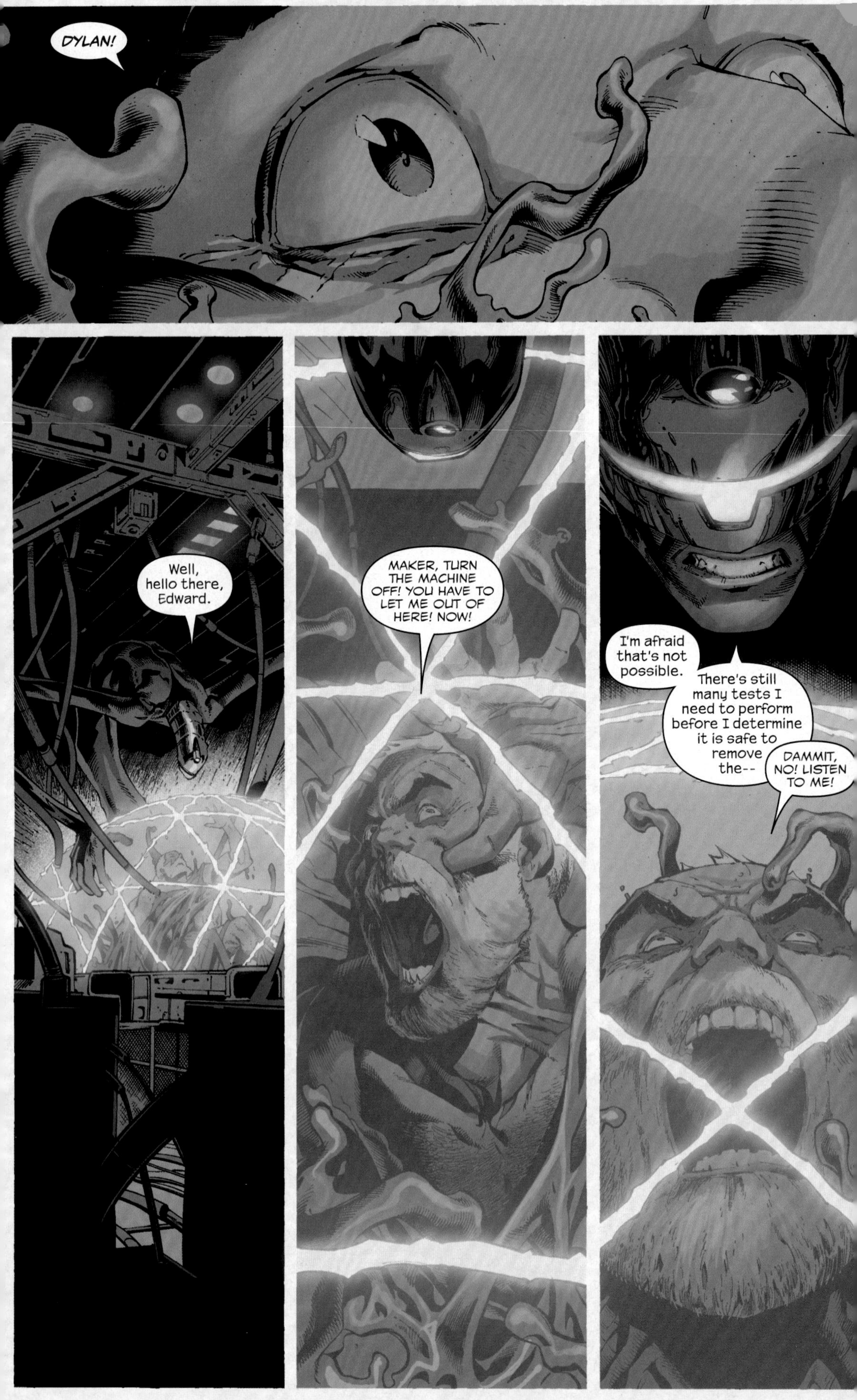

DYLAN!
Well, hello there, Edward.
MAKER, TURN THE MACHINE OFF! YOU HAVE TO LET ME OUT OF HERE! NOW!
I'm afraid that's not possible.
There's still many tests I need to perform before I determine it is safe to remove the--
DAMMIT, NO! LISTEN TO ME!

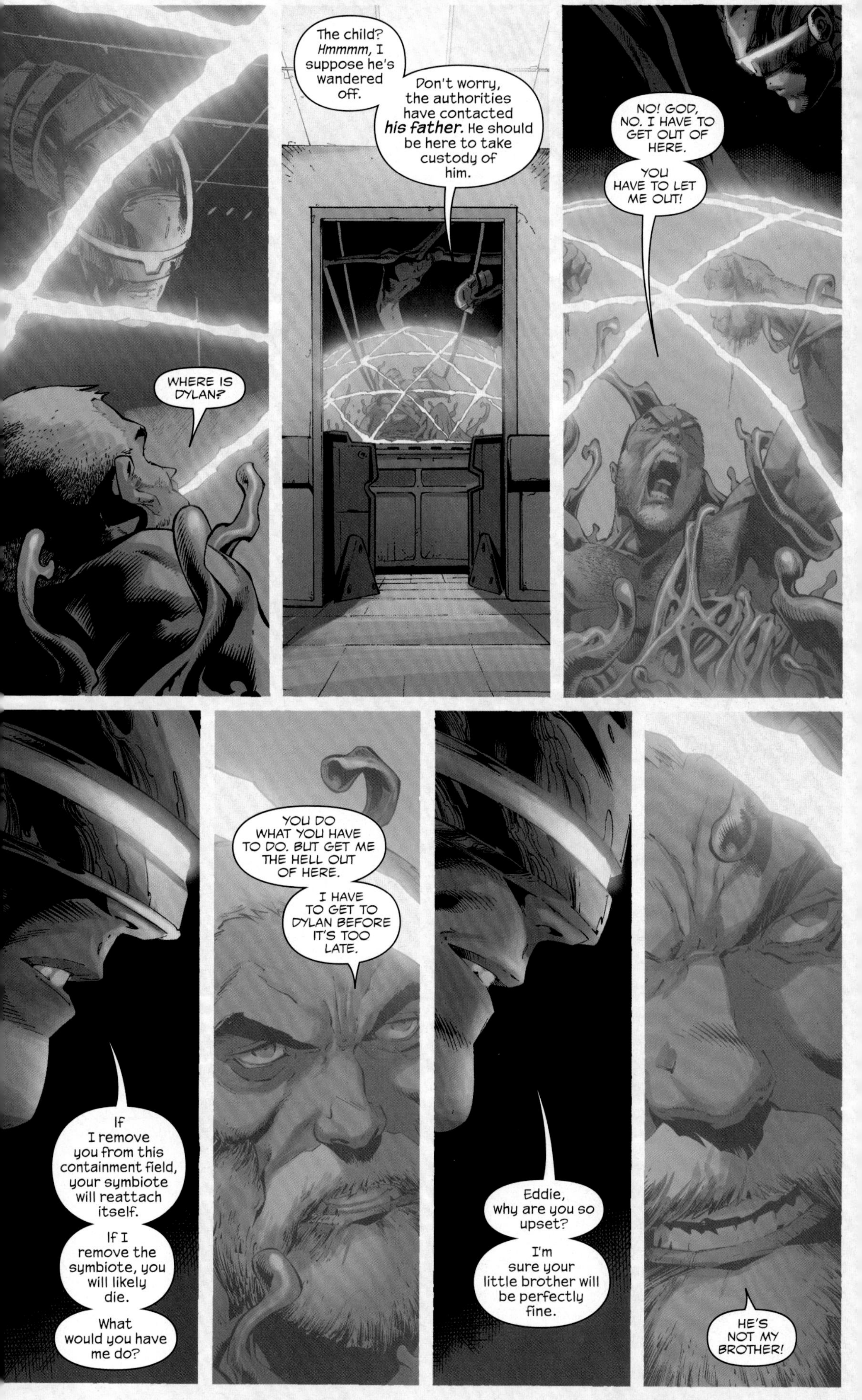
WHERE IS DYLAN?
The child? Hmmmm, I suppose he's wandered off.
Don't worry, the authorities have contacted his father. He should be here to take custody of him.
NO! GOD, NO. I HAVE TO GET OUT OF HERE.
YOU HAVE TO LET ME OUT!
If I remove you from this containment field, your symbiote will reattach itself.
If I remove the symbiote, you will likely die.
What would you have me do?
YOU DO WHAT YOU HAVE TO DO. BUT GET ME THE HELL OUT OF HERE.
I HAVE TO GET TO DYLAN BEFORE IT'S TOO LATE.
Eddie, why are you so upset?
I'm sure your little brother will be perfectly fine.
HE'S NOT MY BROTHER!

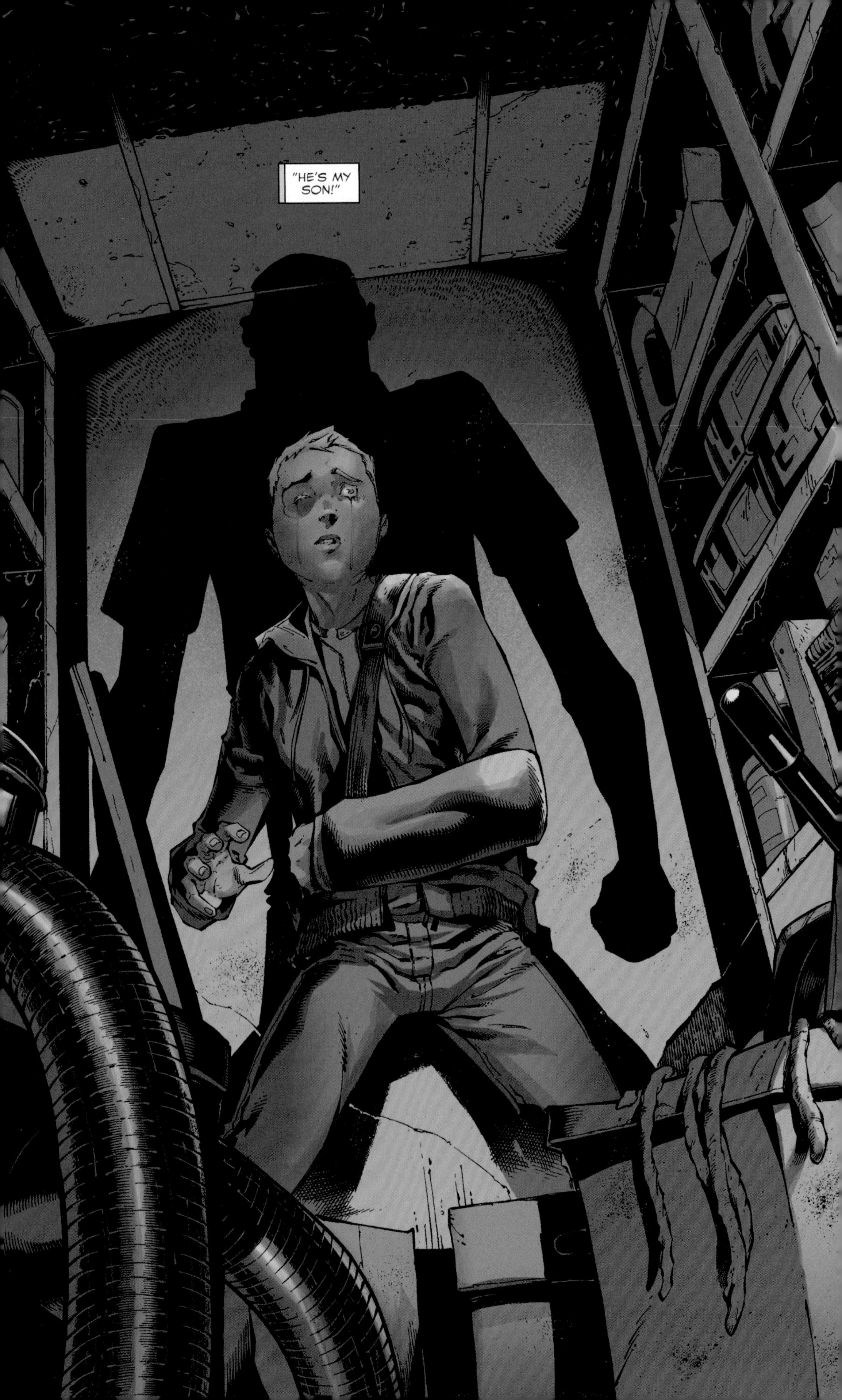
"HE'S MY SON!"

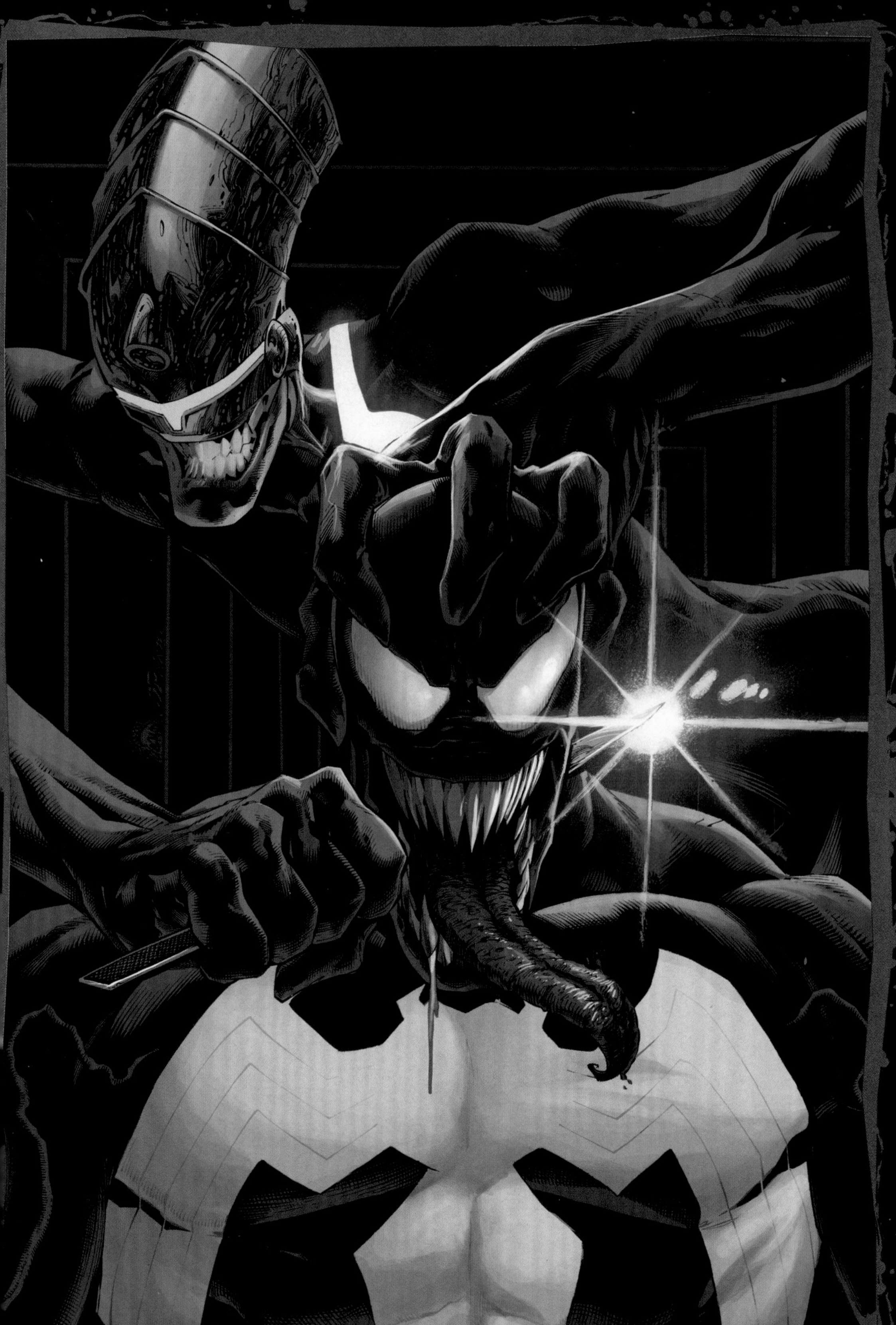

12

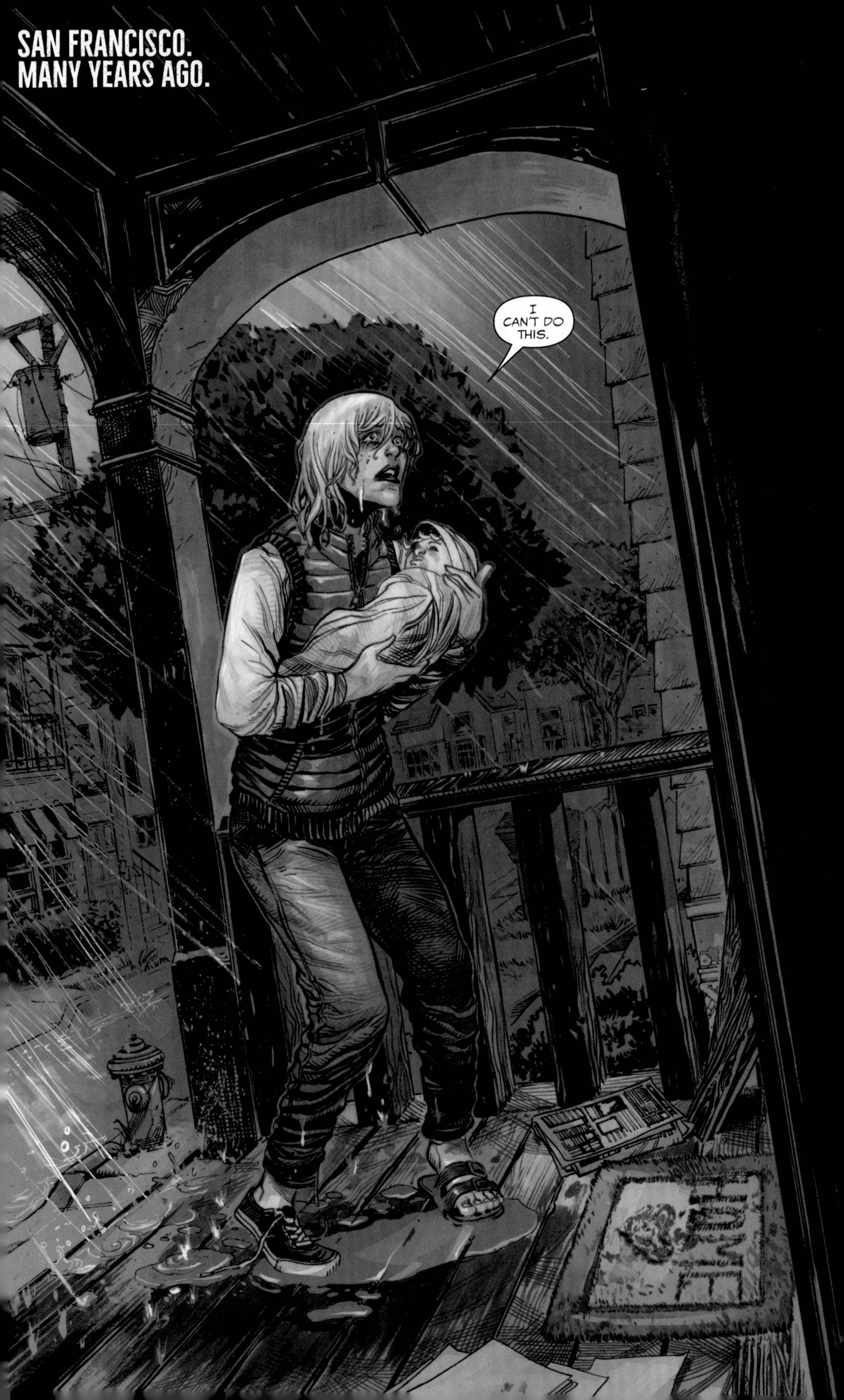
SAN FRANCISCO.
MANY YEARS AGO.
I CAN'T DO THIS.

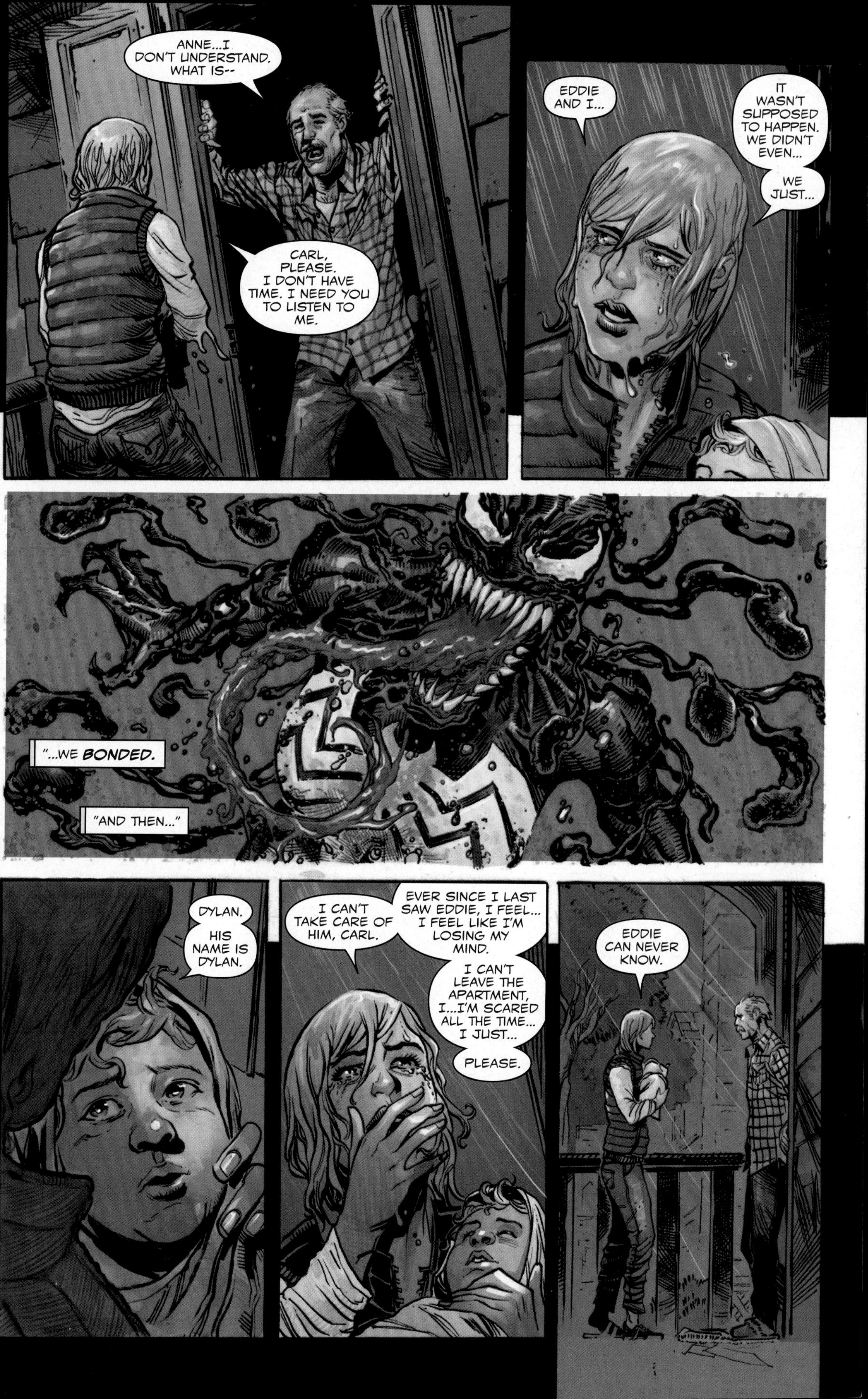

ANNE...I DON'T UNDERSTAND. WHAT IS--
CARL, PLEASE. I DON'T HAVE TIME. I NEED YOU TO LISTEN TO ME.
EDDIE AND I...
IT WASN'T SUPPOSED TO HAPPEN. WE DIDN'T EVEN...
WE JUST...
"...WE BONDED.
"AND THEN..."
DYLAN.
HIS NAME IS DYLAN.
I CAN'T TAKE CARE OF HIM, CARL.
EVER SINCE I LAST SAW EDDIE, I FEEL... I FEEL LIKE I'M LOSING MY MIND.
I CAN'T LEAVE THE APARTMENT, I...I'M SCARED ALL THE TIME... I JUST...
PLEASE.
EDDIE CAN NEVER KNOW.

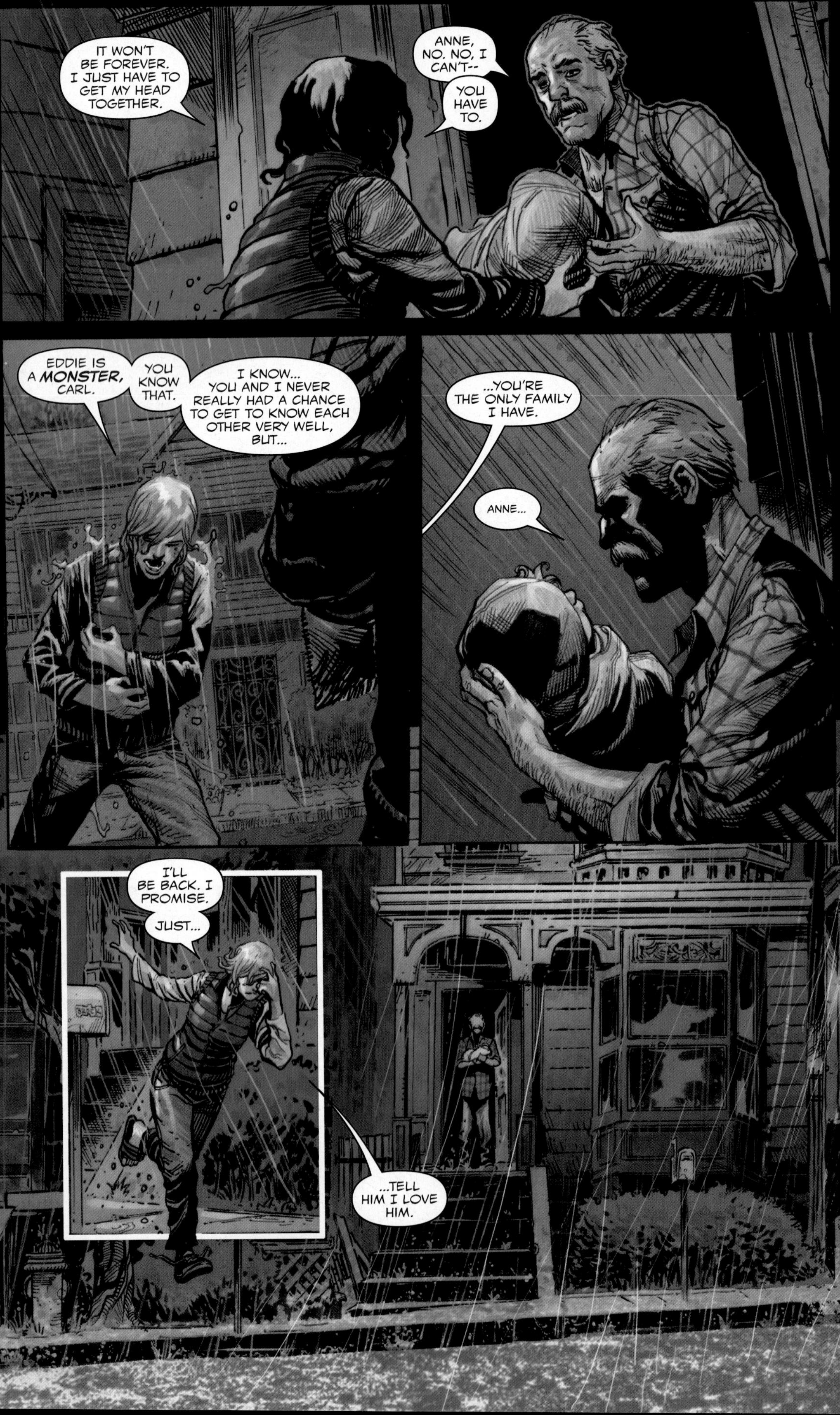
IT WON'T BE FOREVER. I JUST HAVE TO GET MY HEAD TOGETHER.
ANNE, NO. NO, I CAN'T--
YOU HAVE TO.
EDDIE IS A **MONSTER,** CARL.
YOU KNOW THAT.
I KNOW... YOU AND I NEVER REALLY HAD A CHANCE TO GET TO KNOW EACH OTHER VERY WELL, BUT...
...YOU'RE THE ONLY FAMILY I HAVE.
ANNE...
I'LL BE BACK. I PROMISE.
JUST...
...TELL HIM I LOVE HIM.

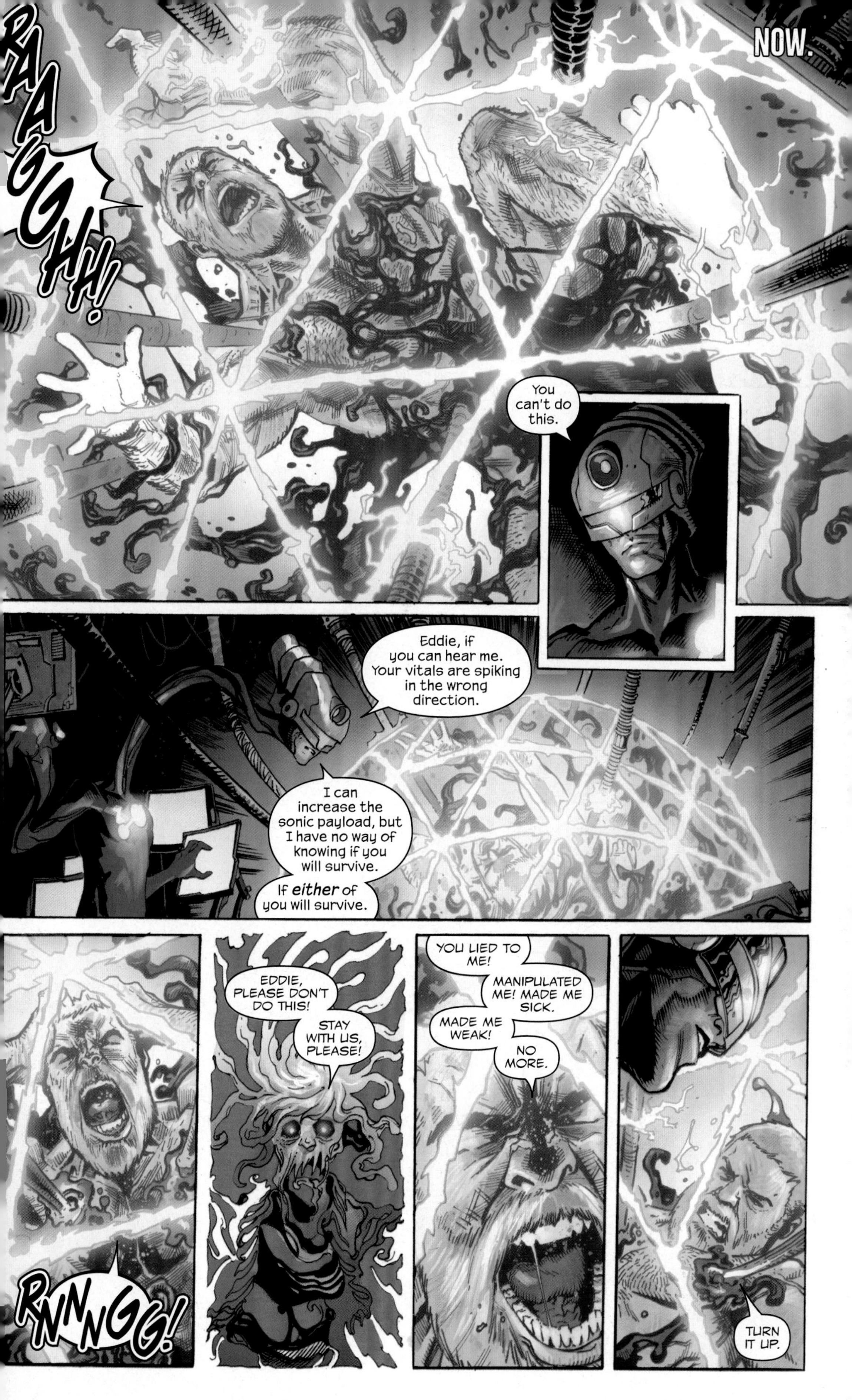
NOW.
RAAGGHH!
You can't do this.
Eddie, if you can hear me. Your vitals are spiking in the wrong direction.
I can increase the sonic payload, but I have no way of knowing if you will survive.
If *either* of you will survive.
RNNNGG!
EDDIE, PLEASE DON'T DO THIS!
STAY WITH US, PLEASE!
YOU LIED TO ME!
MANIPULATED ME! MADE ME SICK.
MADE ME WEAK!
NO MORE.
TURN IT UP.

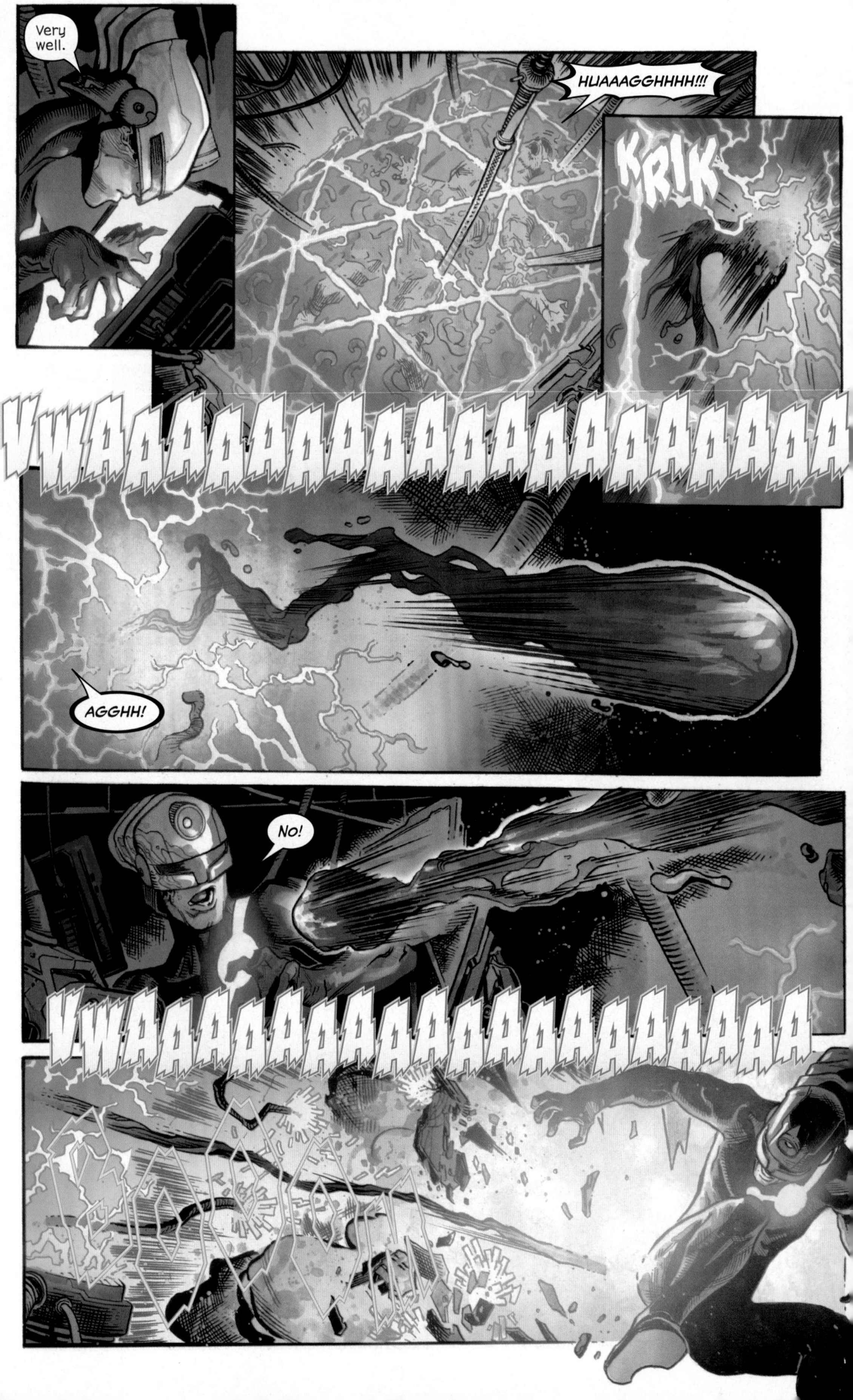

Very well.
HUAAAGGHHHH!!!
KRIK
VWAAAAAAAAAAAAAAAAA
AGGHH!
No!
VWAAAAAAAAAAAAAAAAA

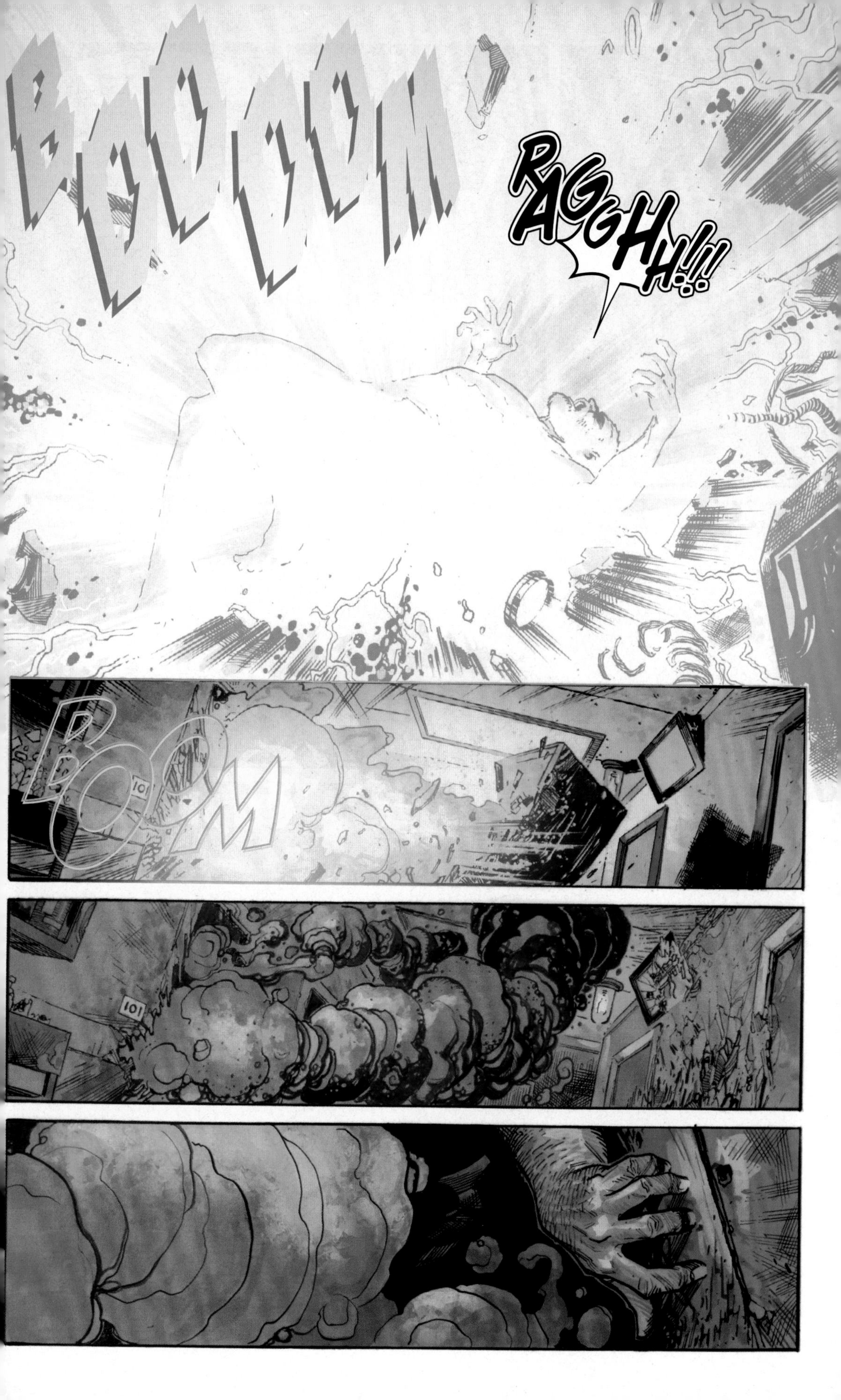
BOOOOM
RAGGHHH!!!
BOOM

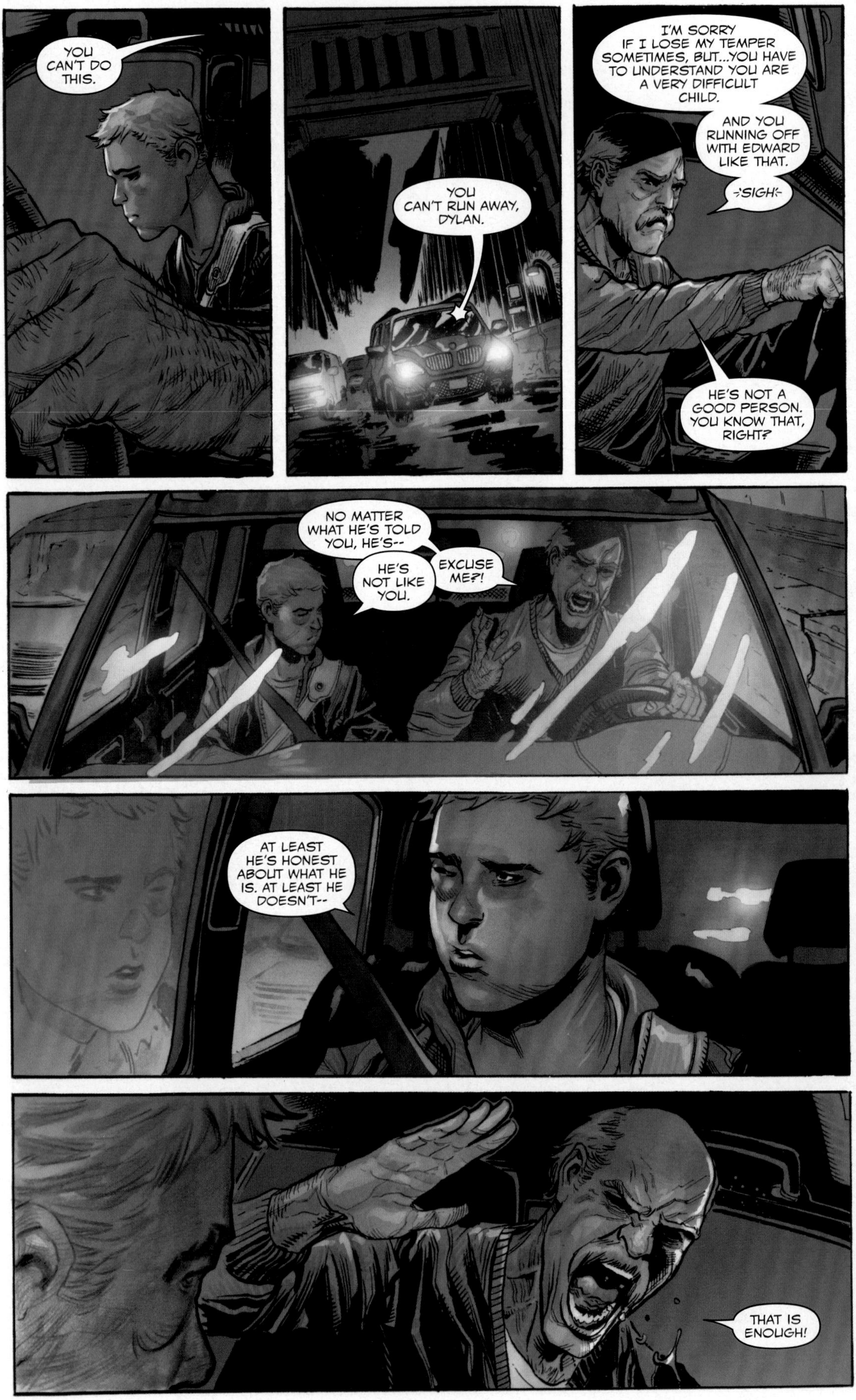
YOU CAN'T DO THIS.
YOU CAN'T RUN AWAY, DYLAN.
I'M SORRY IF I LOSE MY TEMPER SOMETIMES, BUT...YOU HAVE TO UNDERSTAND YOU ARE A VERY DIFFICULT CHILD.
AND YOU RUNNING OFF WITH EDWARD LIKE THAT.
-SIGH-
HE'S NOT A GOOD PERSON. YOU KNOW THAT, RIGHT?
NO MATTER WHAT HE'S TOLD YOU, HE'S--
HE'S NOT LIKE YOU.
EXCUSE ME?!
AT LEAST HE'S HONEST ABOUT WHAT HE IS. AT LEAST HE DOESN'T--
THAT IS ENOUGH!

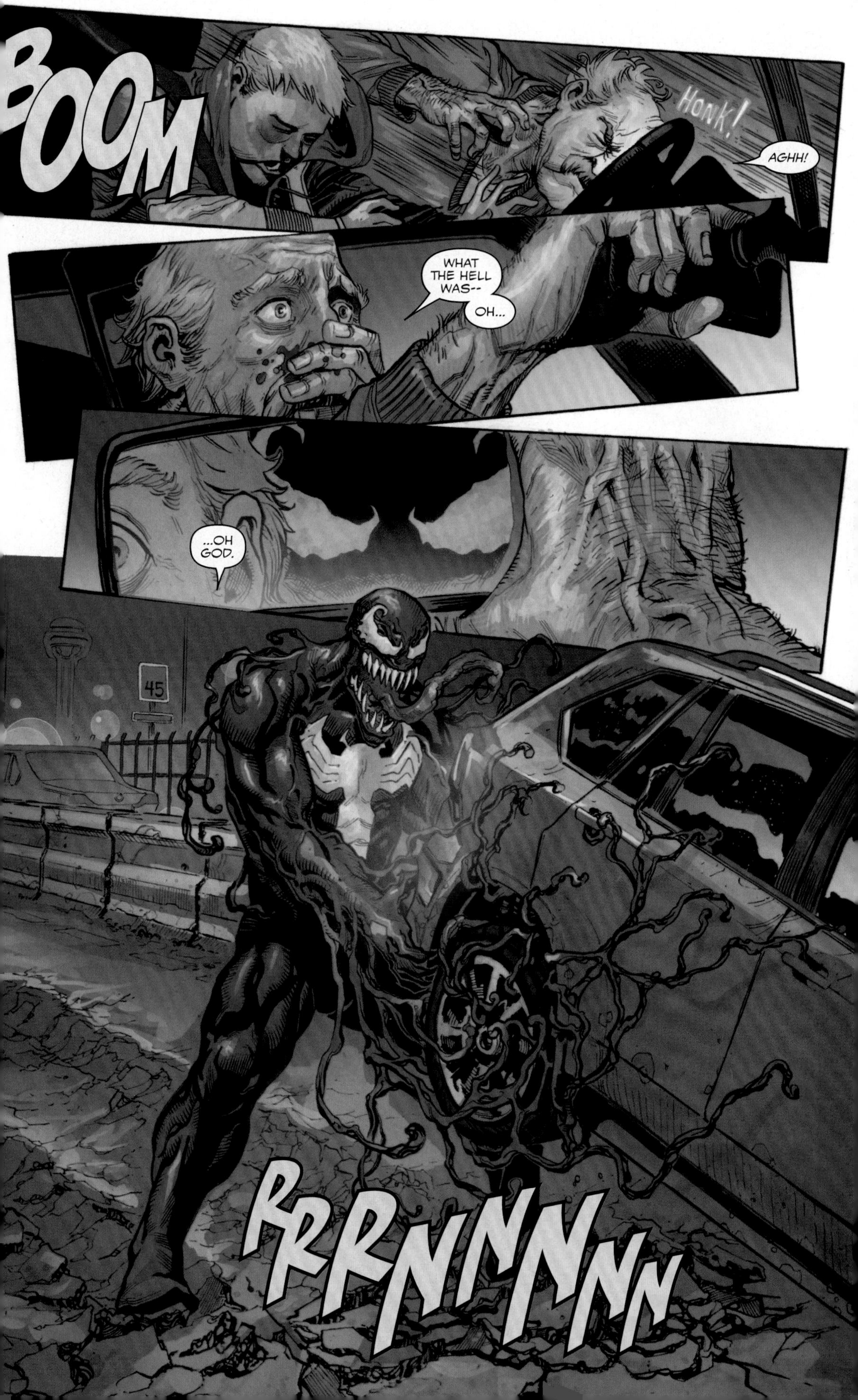
BOOM
HONK!
AGHH!
WHAT THE HELL WAS--
OH...
...OH GOD.
45
RRRNNNNNN

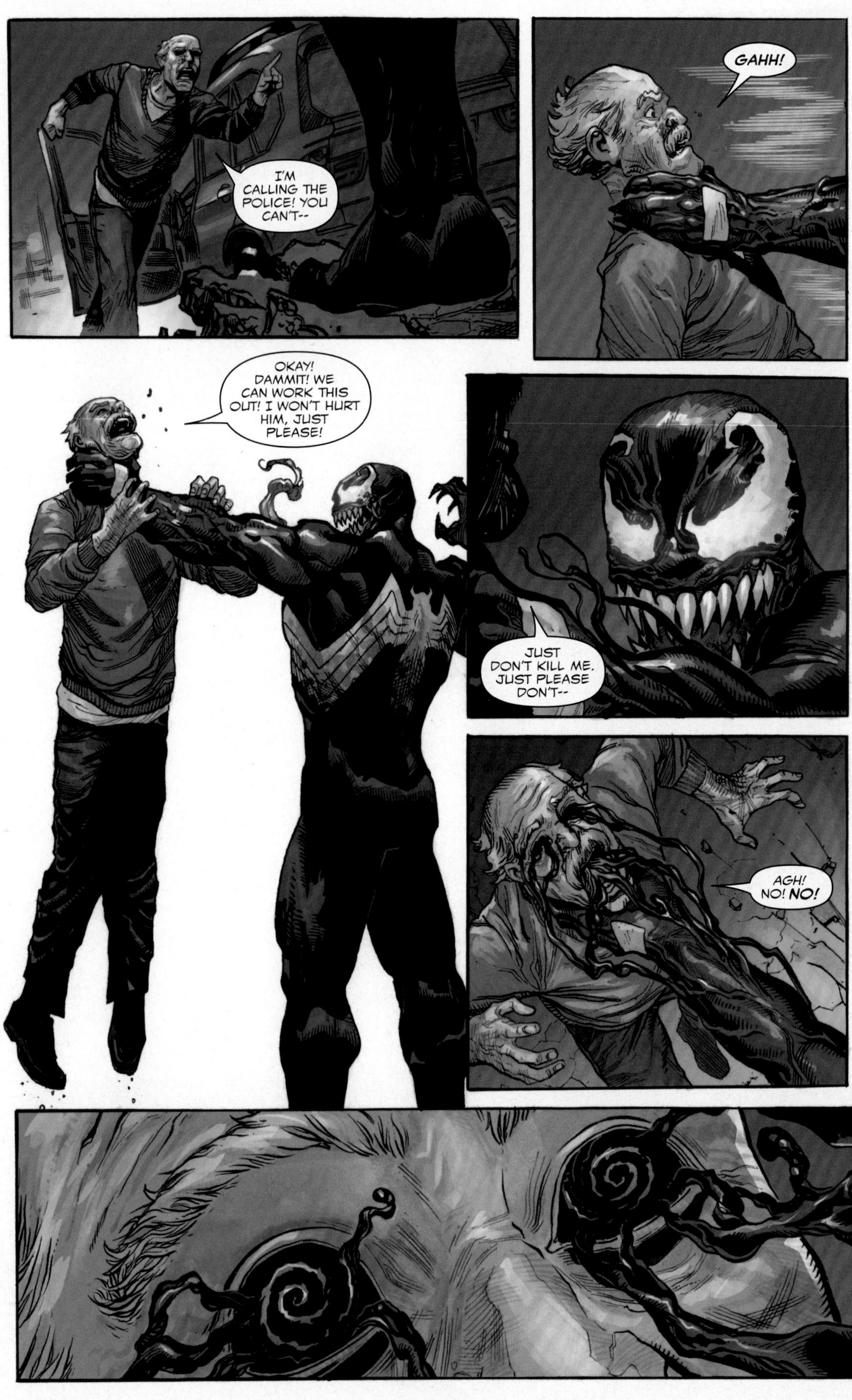
I'M CALLING THE POLICE! YOU CAN'T--
GAHH!
OKAY! DAMMIT! WE CAN WORK THIS OUT! I WON'T HURT HIM, JUST PLEASE!
JUST DON'T KILL ME. JUST PLEASE DON'T--
AGH! NO! NO!

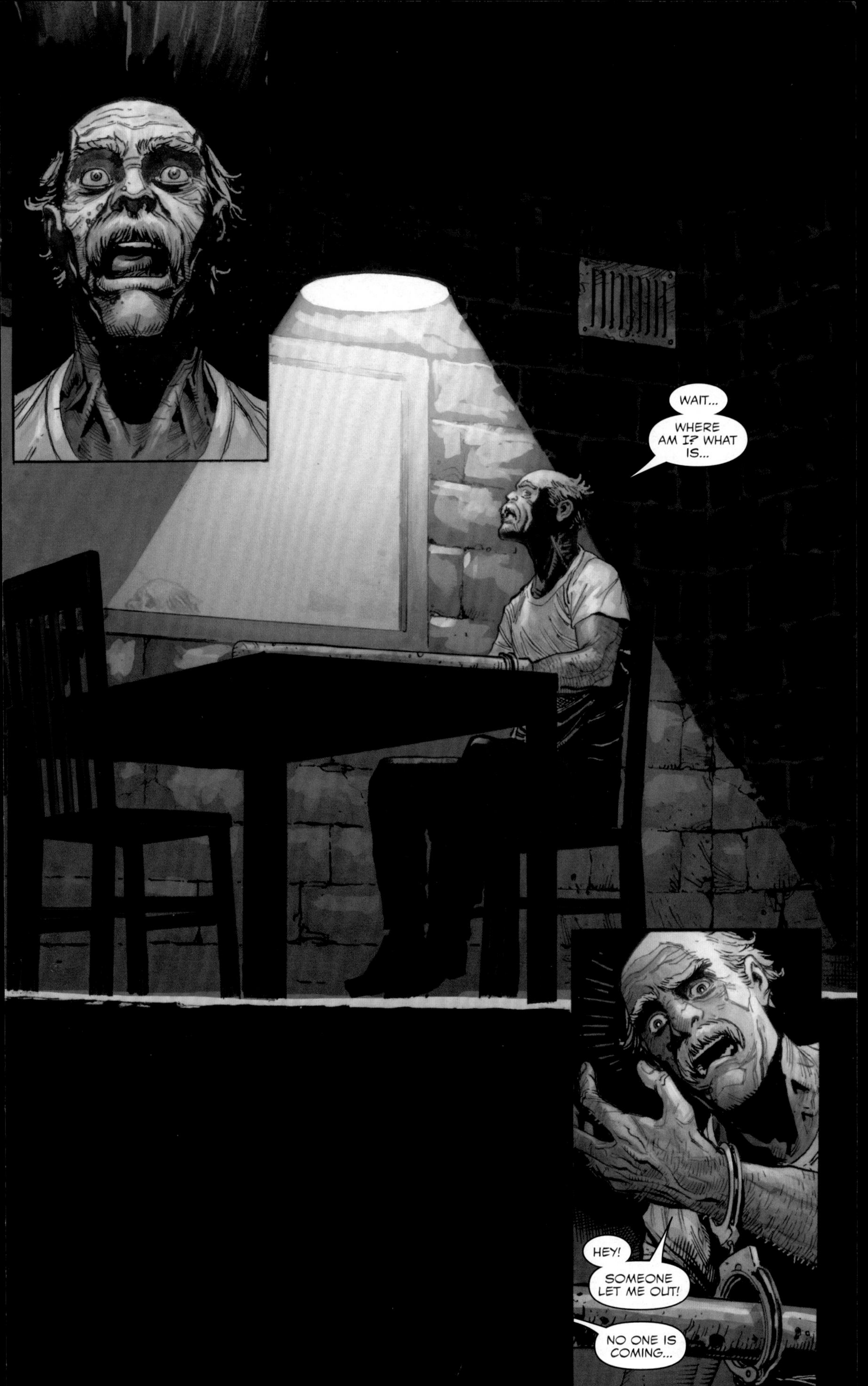
WAIT...
WHERE AM I? WHAT IS...
HEY!
SOMEONE LET ME OUT!
NO ONE IS COMING...

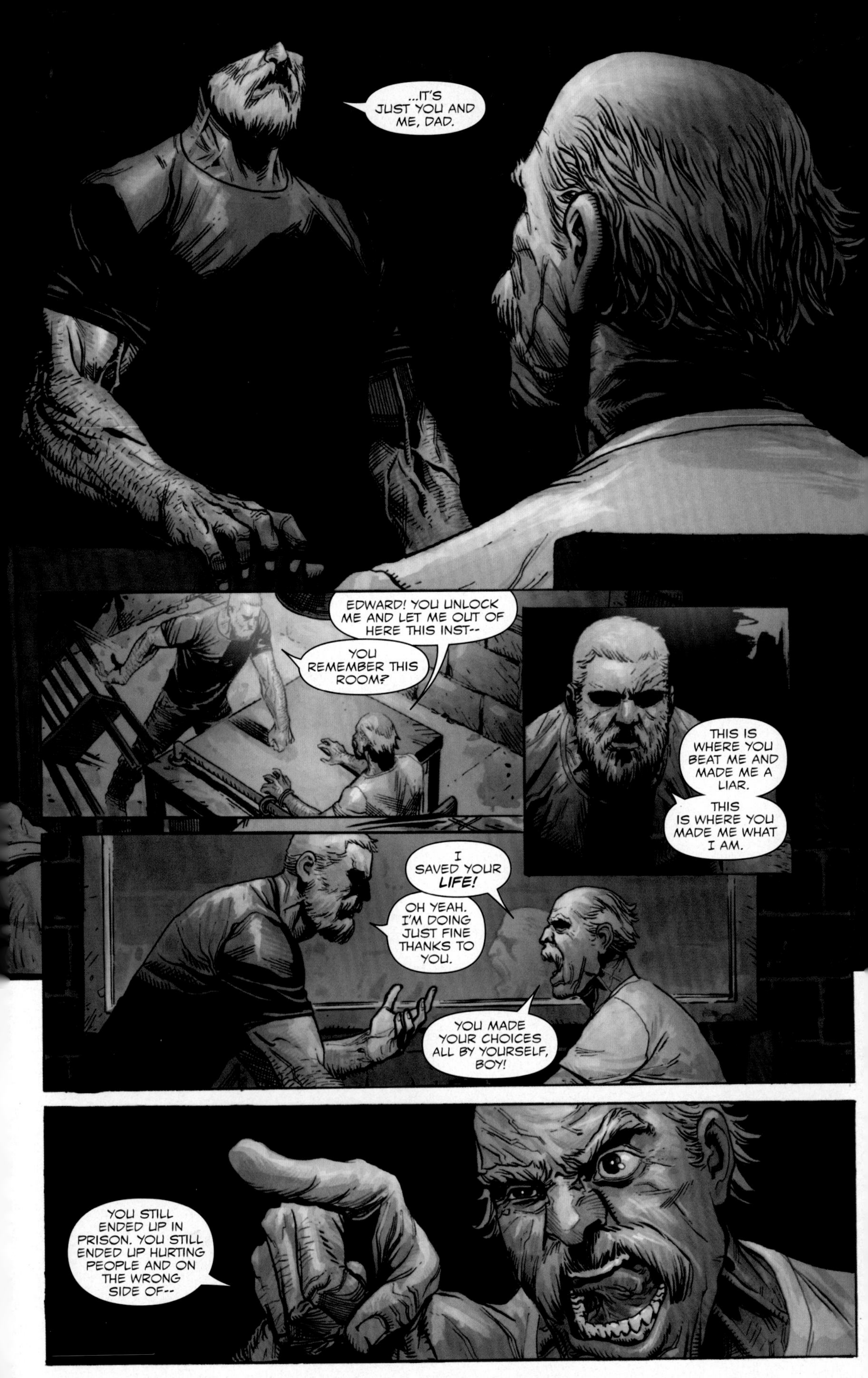
...IT'S JUST YOU AND ME, DAD.
EDWARD! YOU UNLOCK ME AND LET ME OUT OF HERE THIS INST--
YOU REMEMBER THIS ROOM?
THIS IS WHERE YOU BEAT ME AND MADE ME A LIAR.
THIS IS WHERE YOU MADE ME WHAT I AM.
I SAVED YOUR LIFE!
OH YEAH. I'M DOING JUST FINE THANKS TO YOU.
YOU MADE YOUR CHOICES ALL BY YOURSELF, BOY!
YOU STILL ENDED UP IN PRISON. YOU STILL ENDED UP HURTING PEOPLE AND ON THE WRONG SIDE OF--

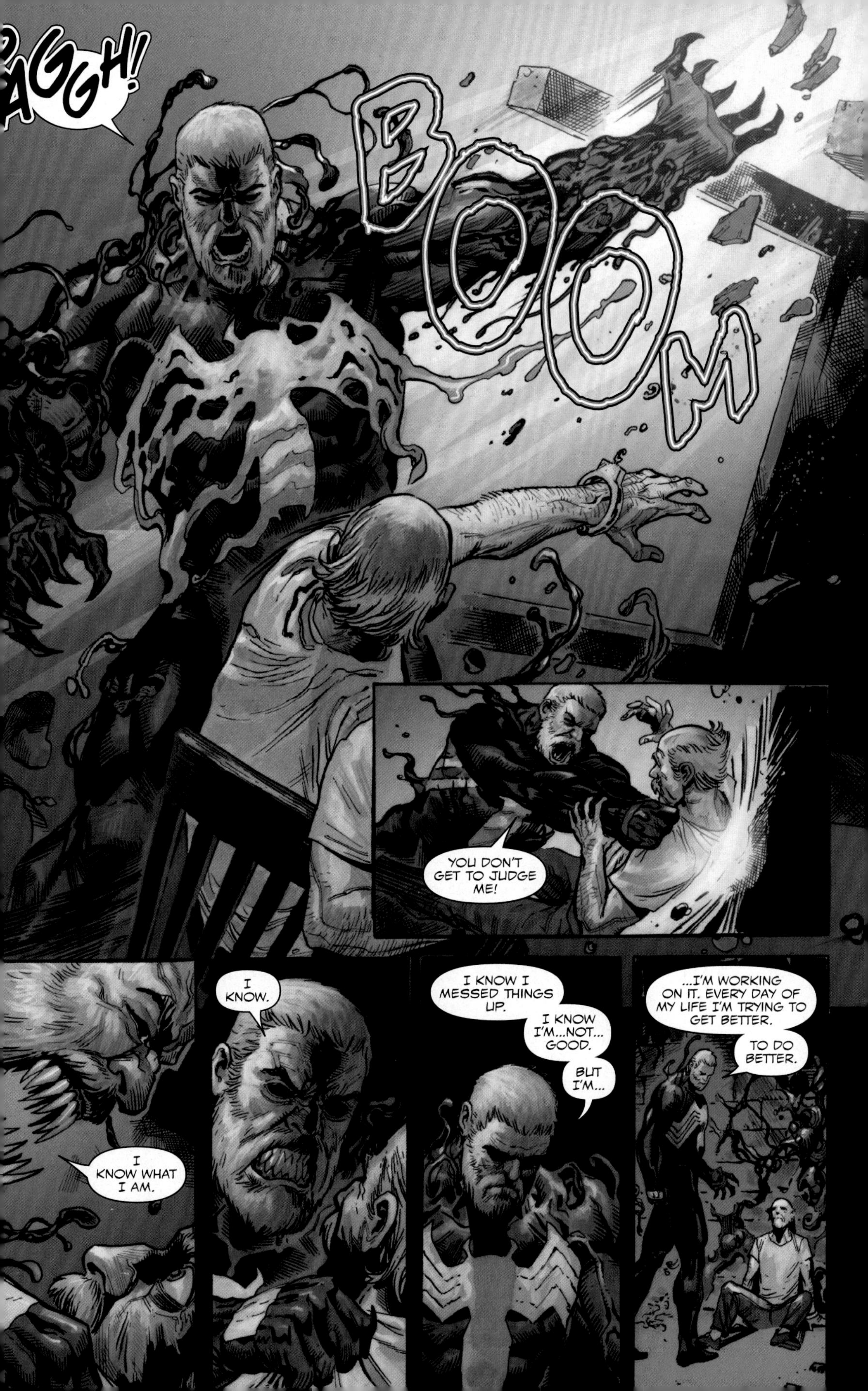

AGGH!
BOOOOM
YOU DON'T GET TO JUDGE ME!
I KNOW WHAT I AM.
I KNOW.
I KNOW I MESSED THINGS UP.
I KNOW I'M...NOT... GOOD.
BUT I'M...
...I'M WORKING ON IT. EVERY DAY OF MY LIFE I'M TRYING TO GET BETTER.
TO DO BETTER.

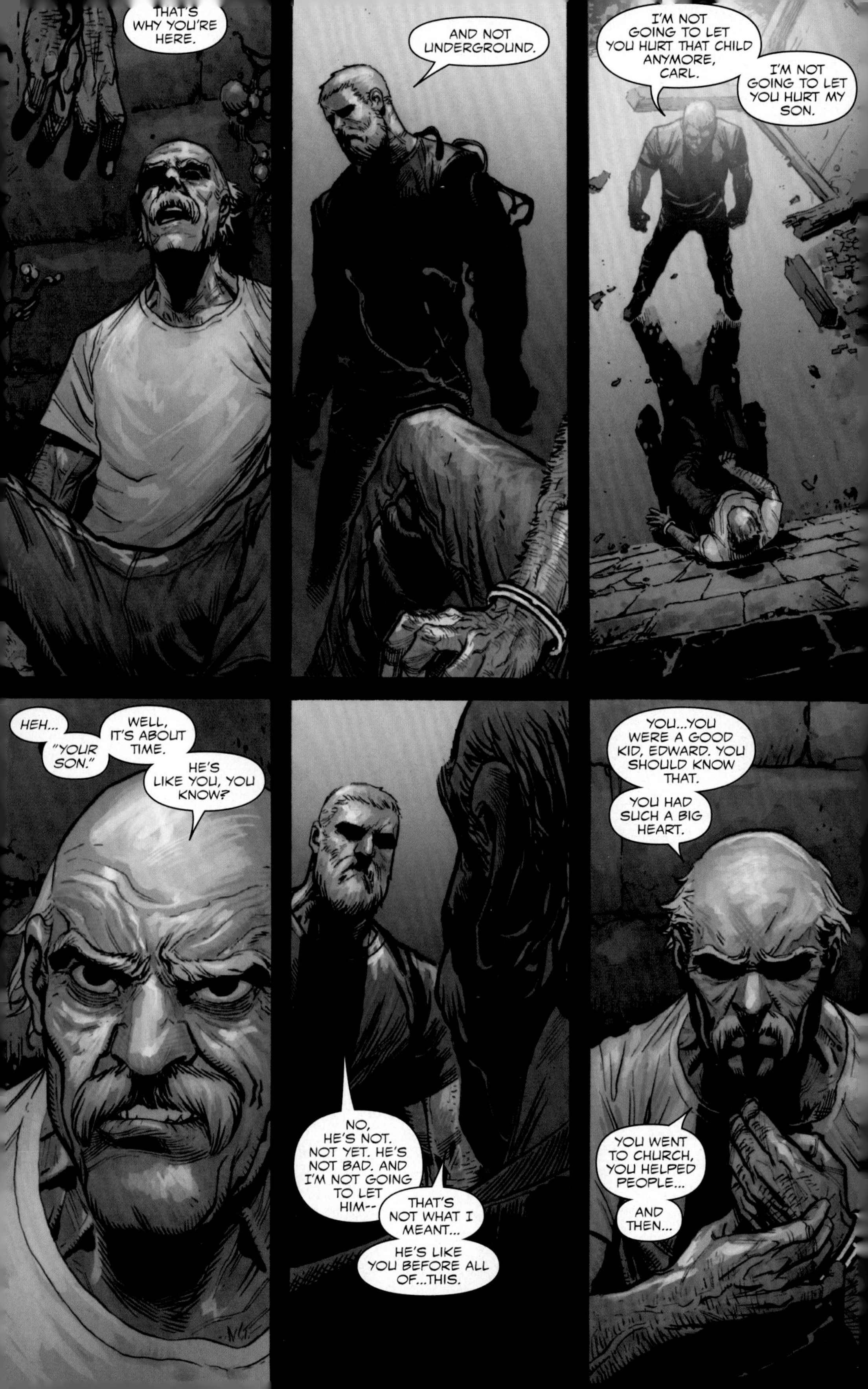
THAT'S WHY YOU'RE HERE.
AND NOT UNDERGROUND.
I'M NOT GOING TO LET YOU HURT THAT CHILD ANYMORE, CARL.
I'M NOT GOING TO LET YOU HURT MY SON.
HEH...
"YOUR SON."
WELL, IT'S ABOUT TIME.
HE'S LIKE YOU, YOU KNOW?
NO, HE'S NOT. NOT YET. HE'S NOT BAD. AND I'M NOT GOING TO LET HIM--
THAT'S NOT WHAT I MEANT...
HE'S LIKE YOU BEFORE ALL OF...THIS.
YOU...YOU WERE A GOOD KID, EDWARD. YOU SHOULD KNOW THAT.
YOU HAD SUCH A BIG HEART.
YOU WENT TO CHURCH, YOU HELPED PEOPLE...
AND THEN...

DO YOU EVEN BELIEVE IN GOD ANYMORE?

I MET MY GOD.

HE'S A @#$%^.

NOW, YOU LISTEN TO ME. I DIDN'T BRING YOU IN HERE TO MAKE NICE. THIS ISN'T ME ASKING FOR FORGIVENESS OR MAKING AMENDS.

I'M TAKING MY SON. AND IF I EVER SEE YOU AGAIN, OR IF YOU EVER COME NEAR HIM OR ME AGAIN...

...I WILL KILL YOU.

IS THAT UNDERSTOOD?

...

YES.

GOOD. YOU'RE GOING TO WAKE UP NOW.

AND YOU'RE GOING TO BE ALONE.

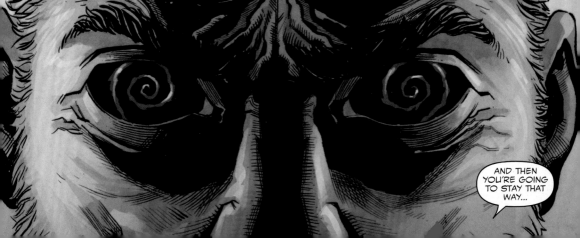

AND THEN YOU'RE GOING TO STAY THAT WAY...

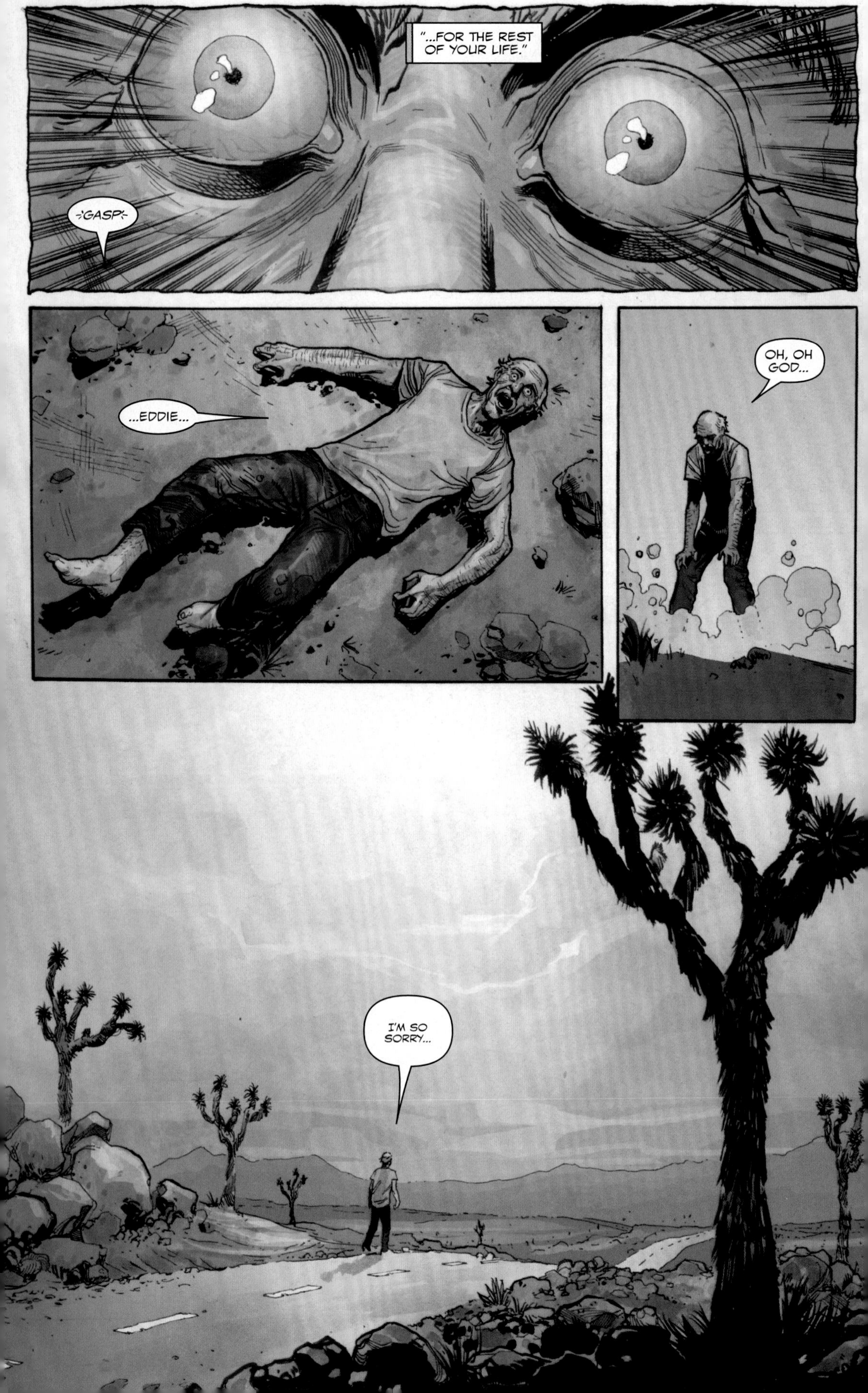
"...FOR THE REST OF YOUR LIFE."
GASP
...EDDIE...
OH, OH GOD...
I'M SO SORRY...

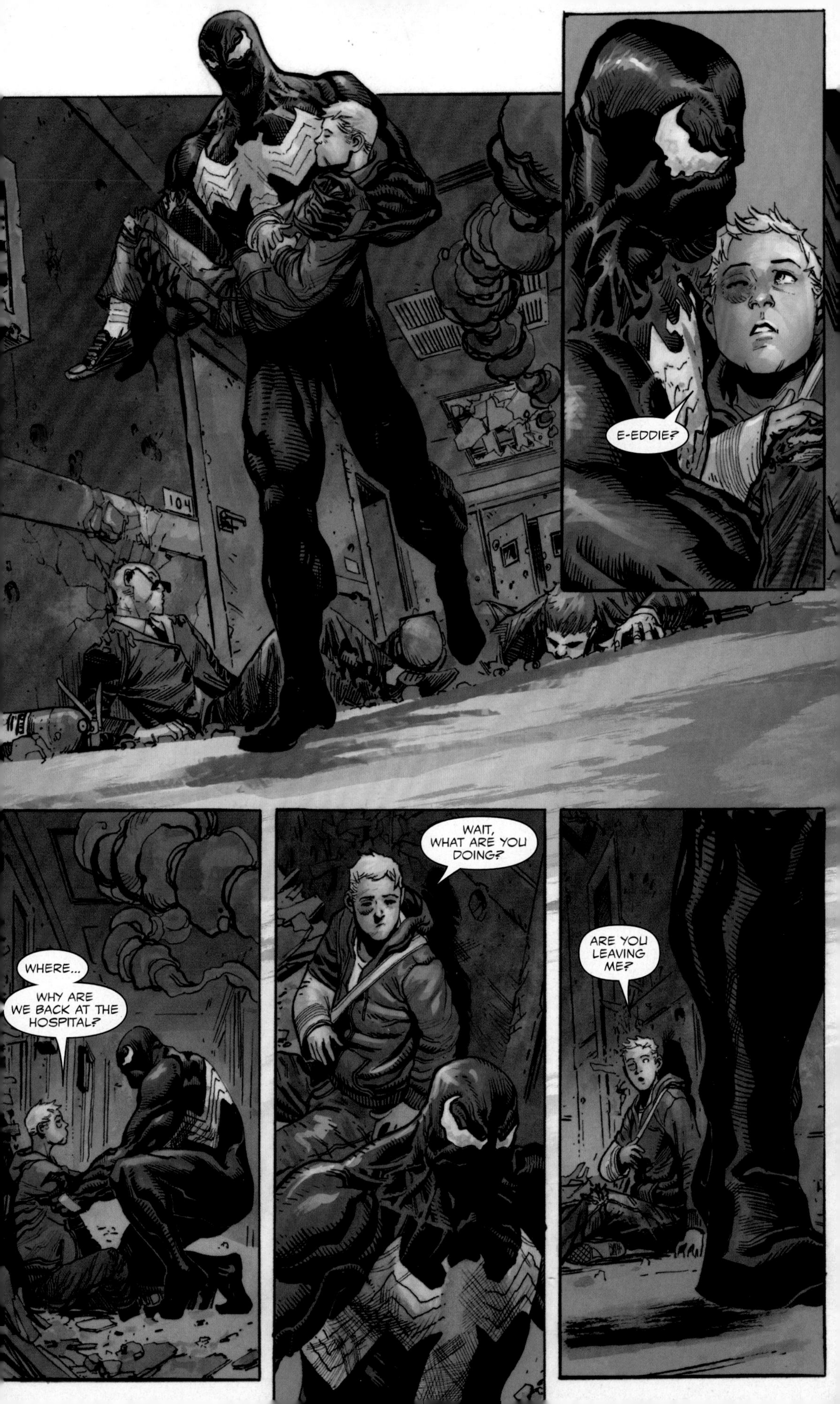

E-EDDIE?
WHERE...
WHY ARE WE BACK AT THE HOSPITAL?
WAIT, WHAT ARE YOU DOING?
ARE YOU LEAVING ME?

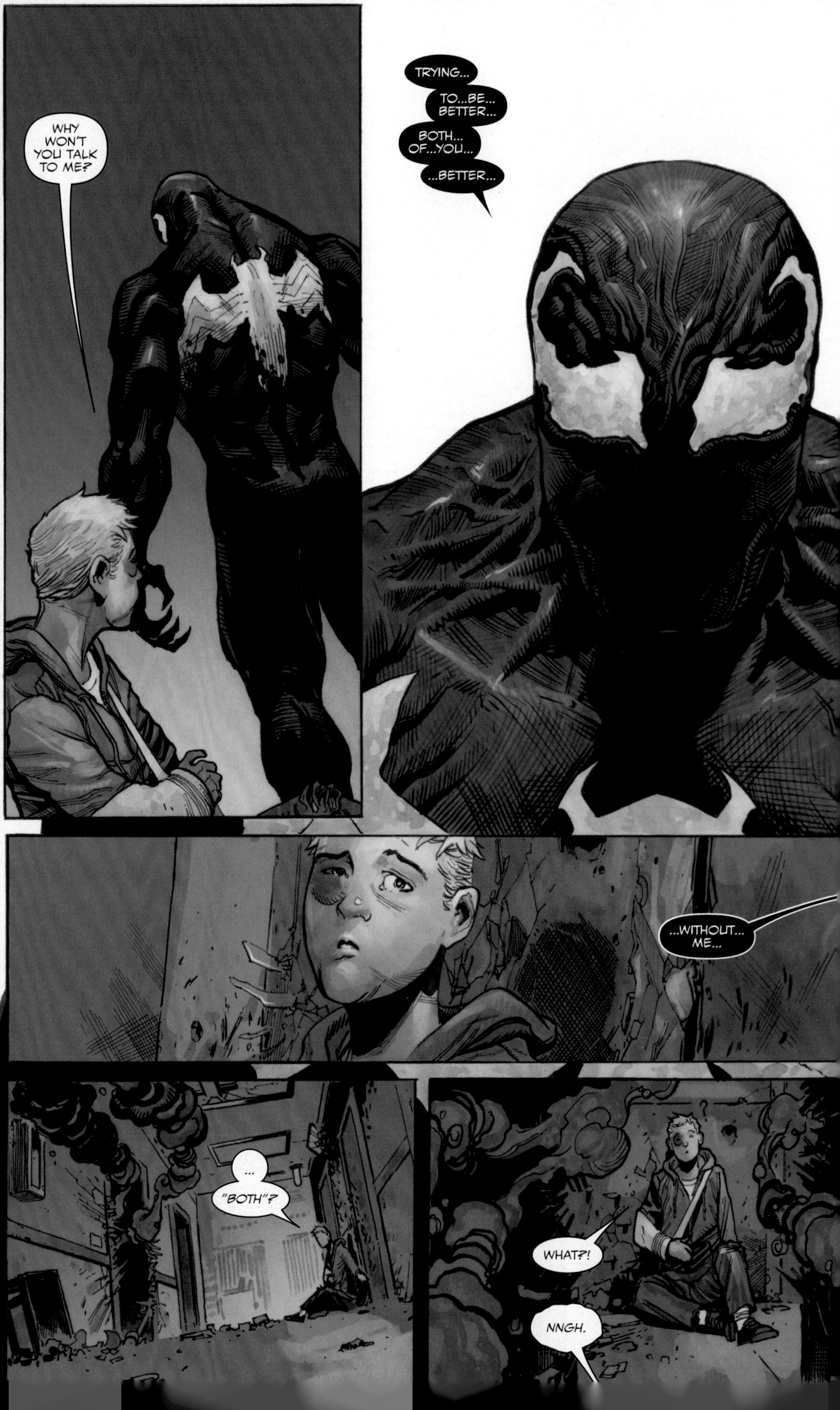
WHY WON'T YOU TALK TO ME?
TRYING...
TO...BE... BETTER...
BOTH... OF...YOU...
...BETTER...
...WITHOUT... ME...
... "BOTH"?
WHAT?!
NNGH.

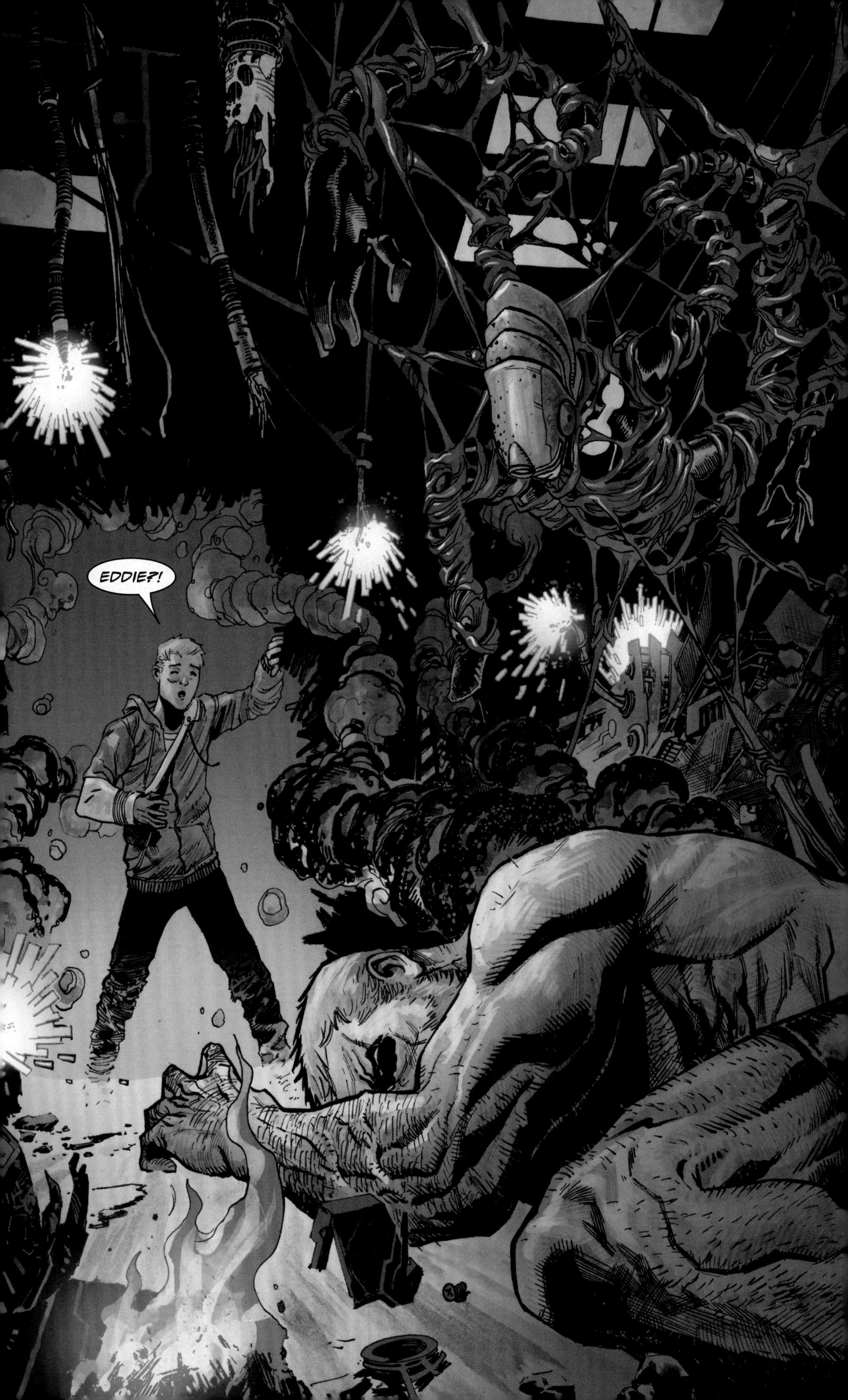
EDDIE?!

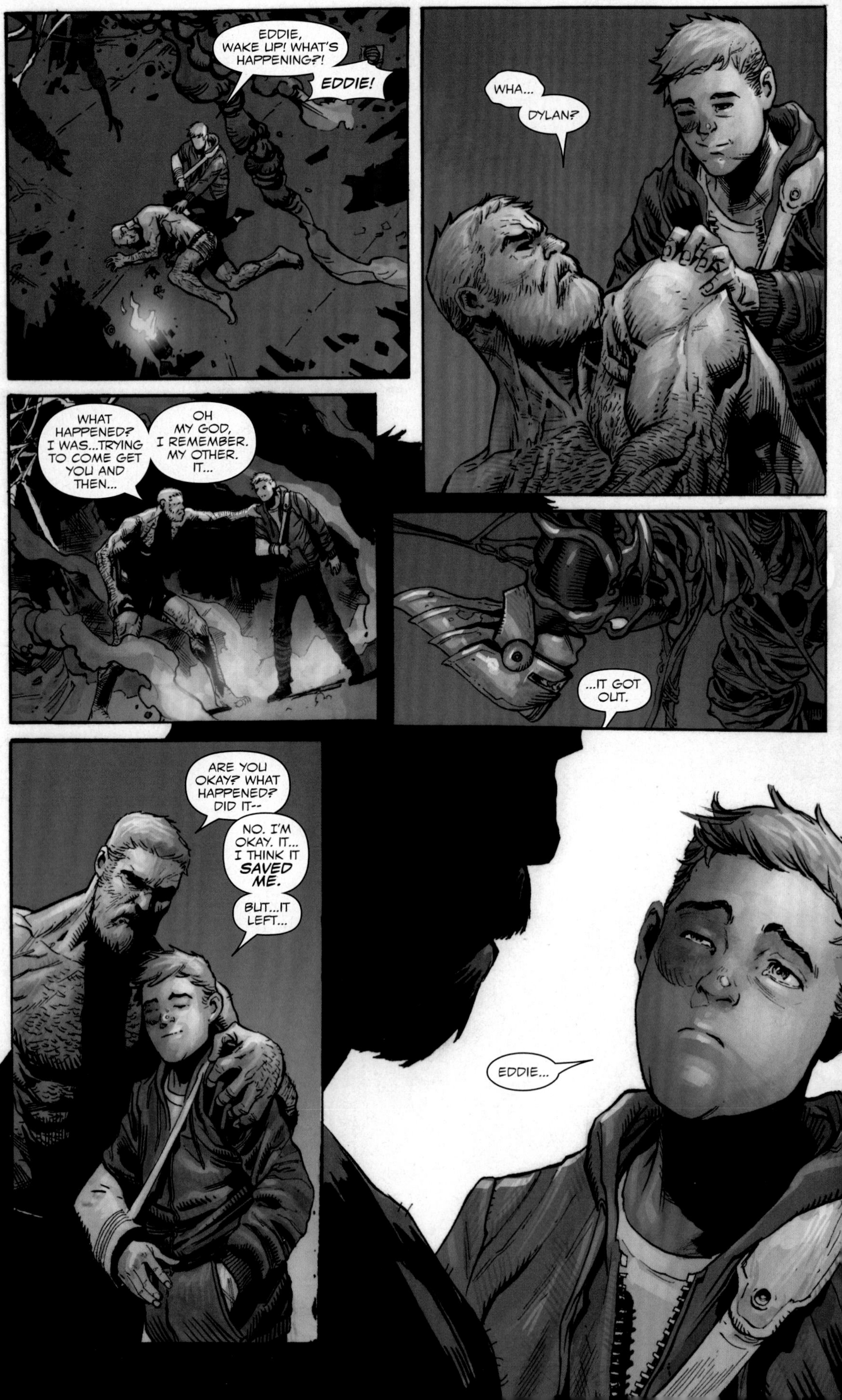
EDDIE, WAKE UP! WHAT'S HAPPENING?!
EDDIE!
WHA...
DYLAN?
WHAT HAPPENED? I WAS...TRYING TO COME GET YOU AND THEN...
OH MY GOD, I REMEMBER. MY OTHER. IT...
...IT GOT OUT.
ARE YOU OKAY? WHAT HAPPENED? DID IT--
NO. I'M OKAY. IT... I THINK IT SAVED ME.
BUT...IT LEFT...
EDDIE...

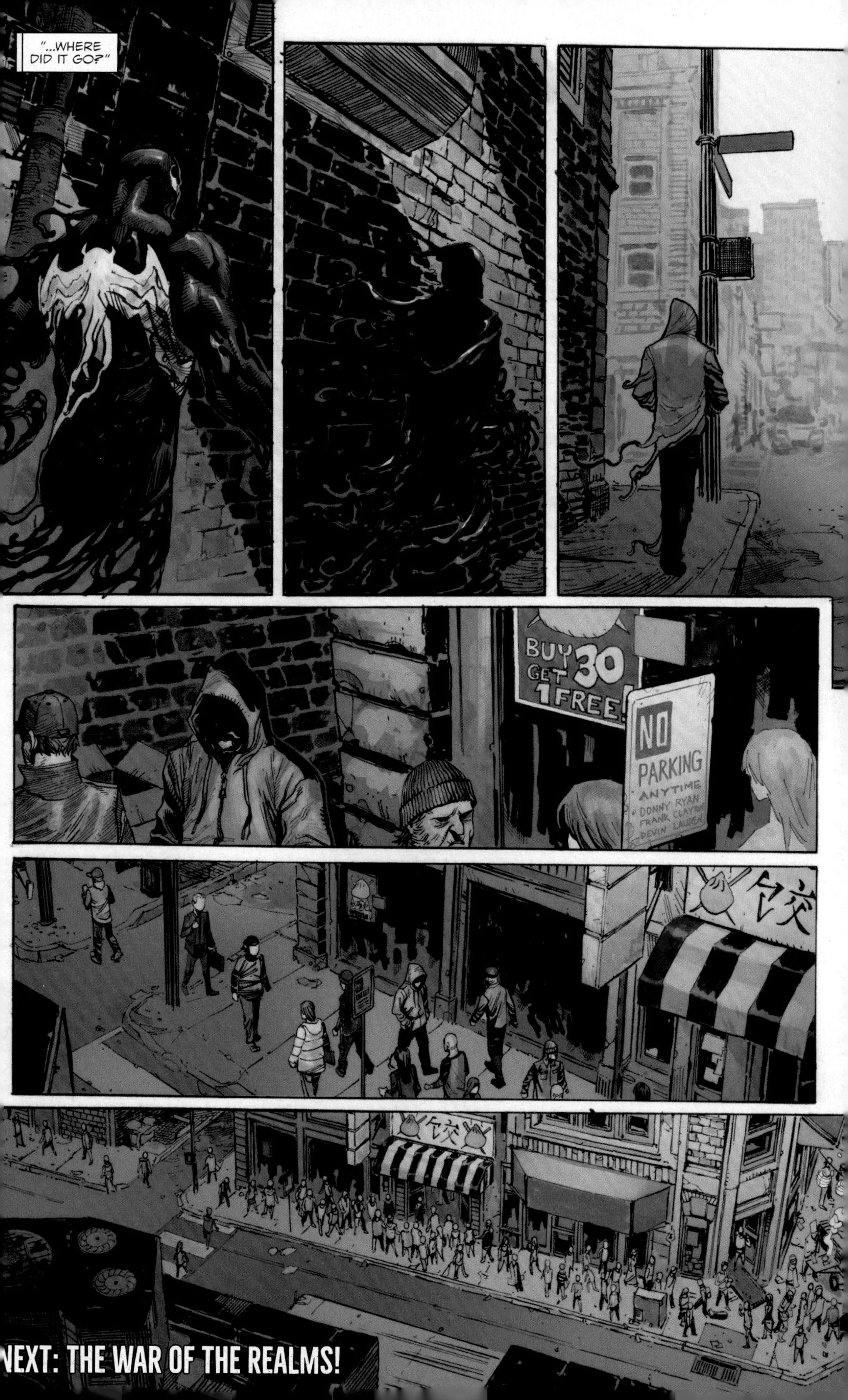
"...WHERE DID IT GO?"
BUY 30 GET 1 FREE!
NO PARKING ANYTIME
NEXT: THE WAR OF THE REALMS!

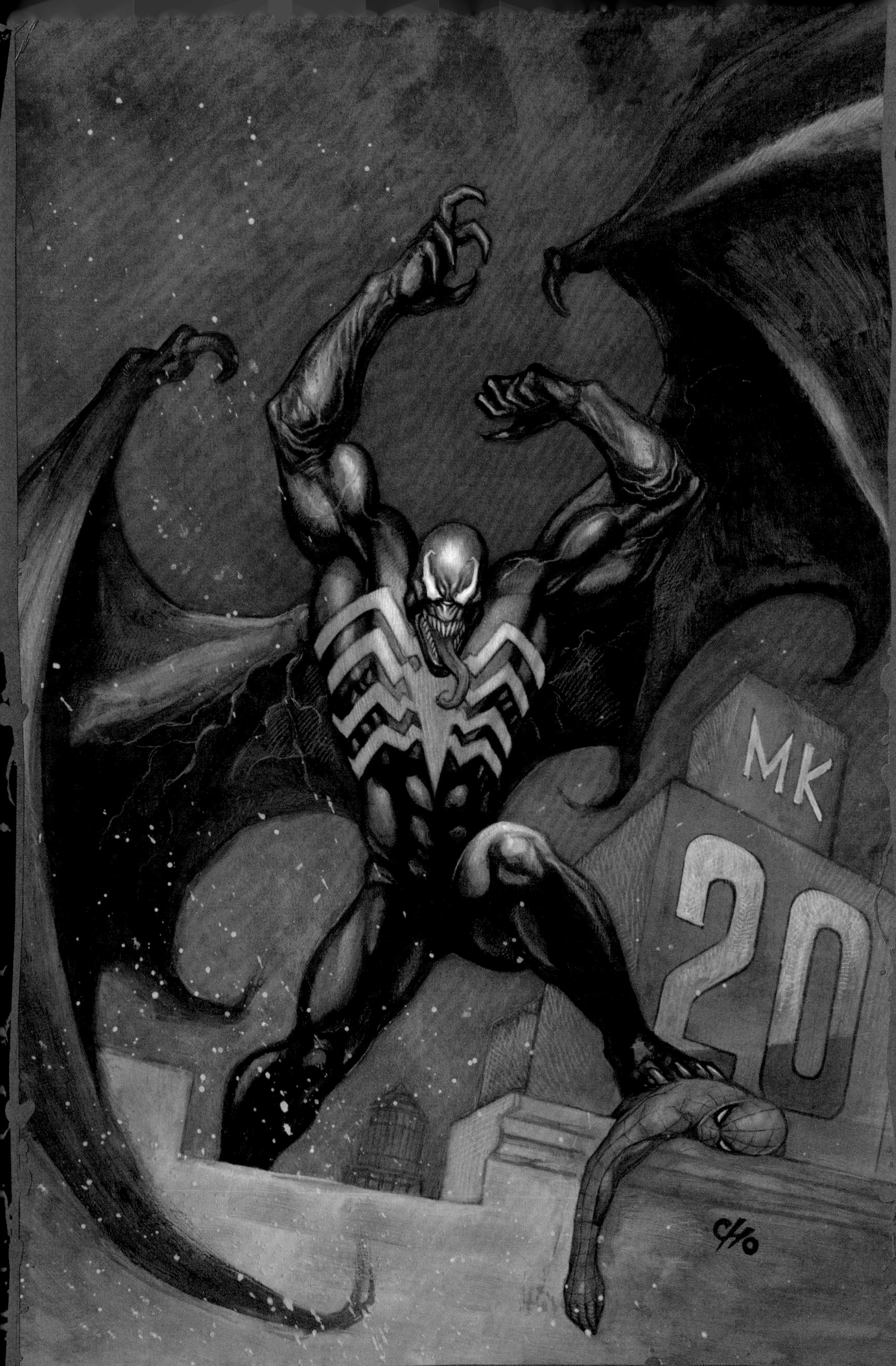
MK
20
CHO

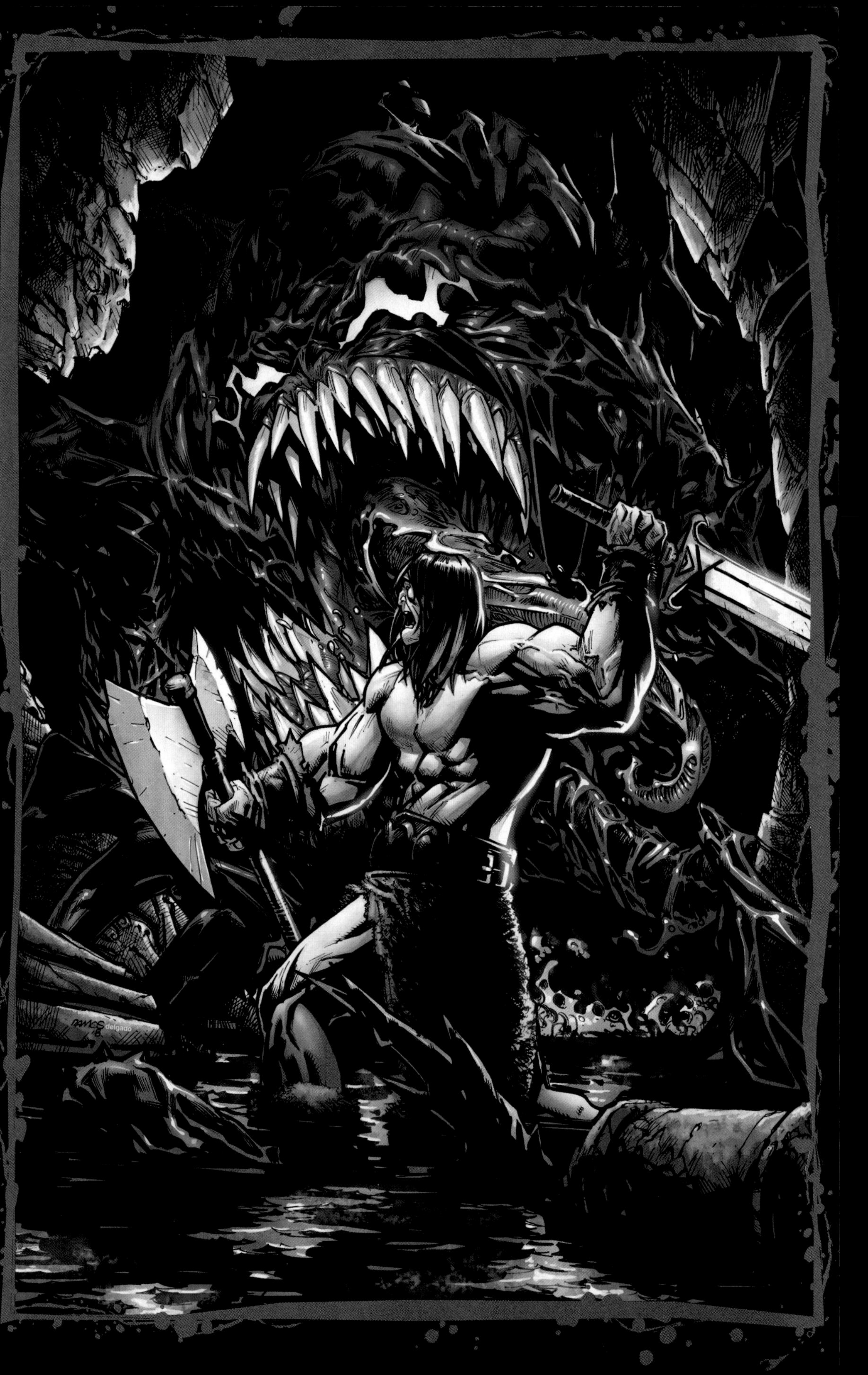
RAMOS
delgado

#10 CONAN VARIANT BY **HUMBERTO RAMOS** & **EDGAR DELGADO**

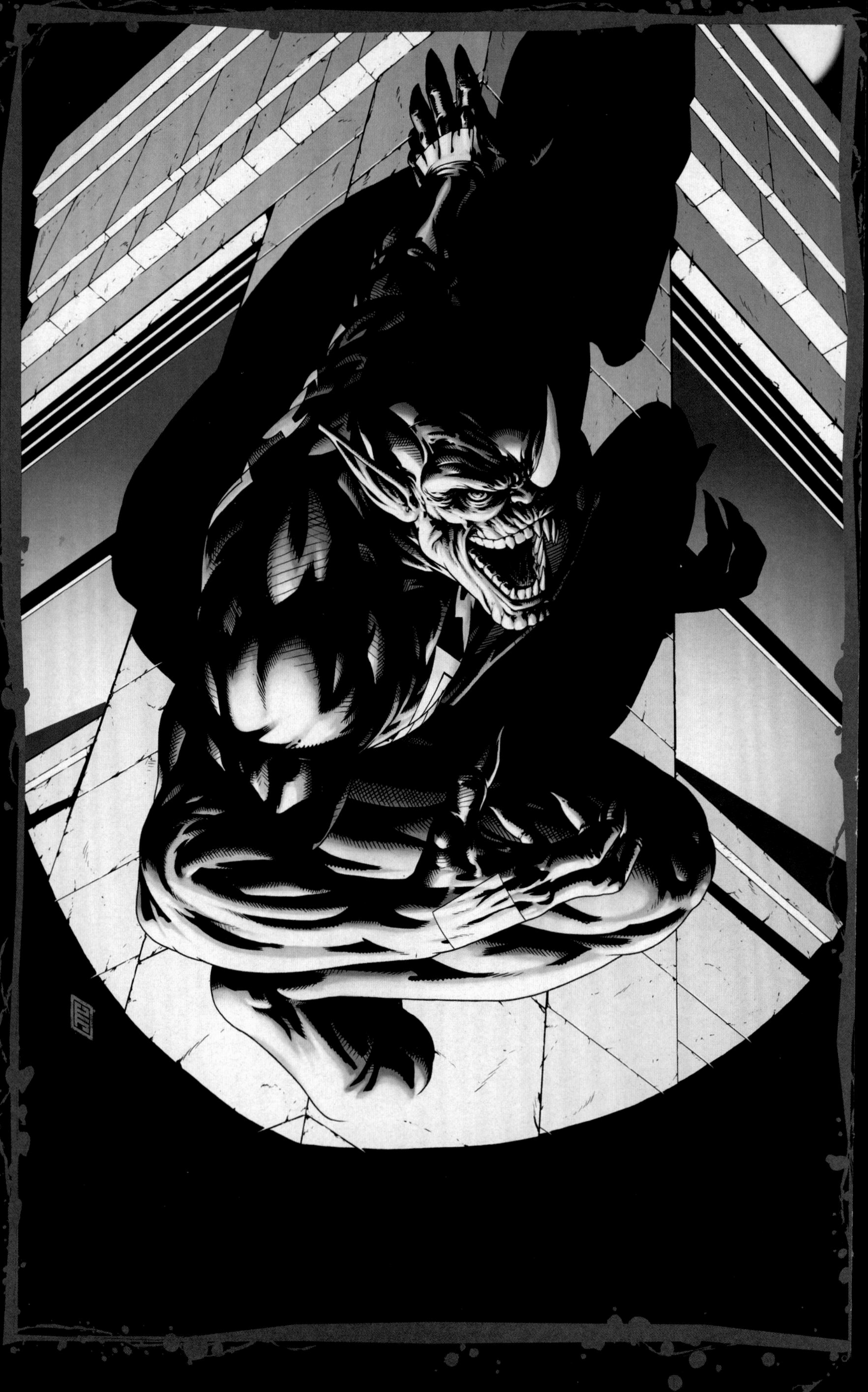

#11 SKRULLS VARIANT BY **JOHN TYLER CHRISTOPHER**

MARVEL
11
VENOM
JASON!

#11 VARIANT BY **DAVE GIBBONS**

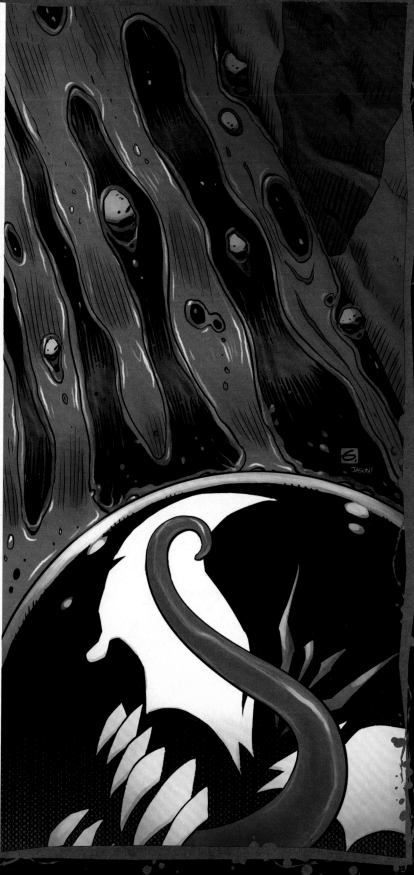

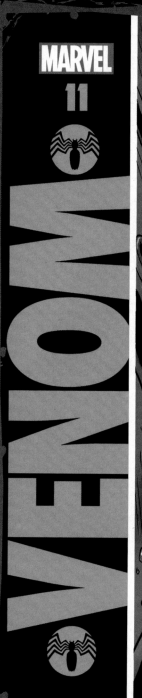

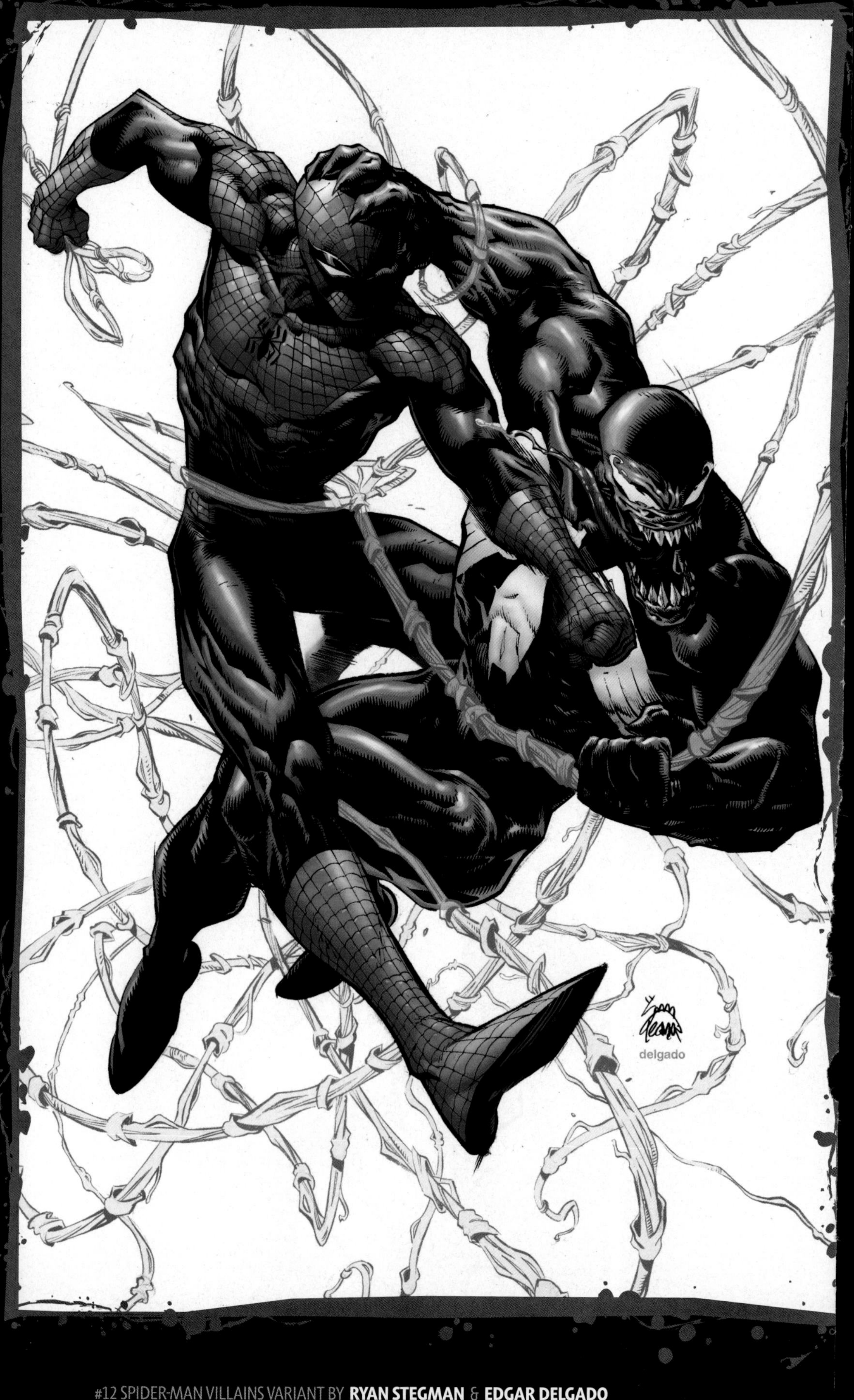
delgado

#12 SPIDER-MAN VILLAINS VARIANT BY **RYAN STEGMAN** & **EDGAR DELGADO**

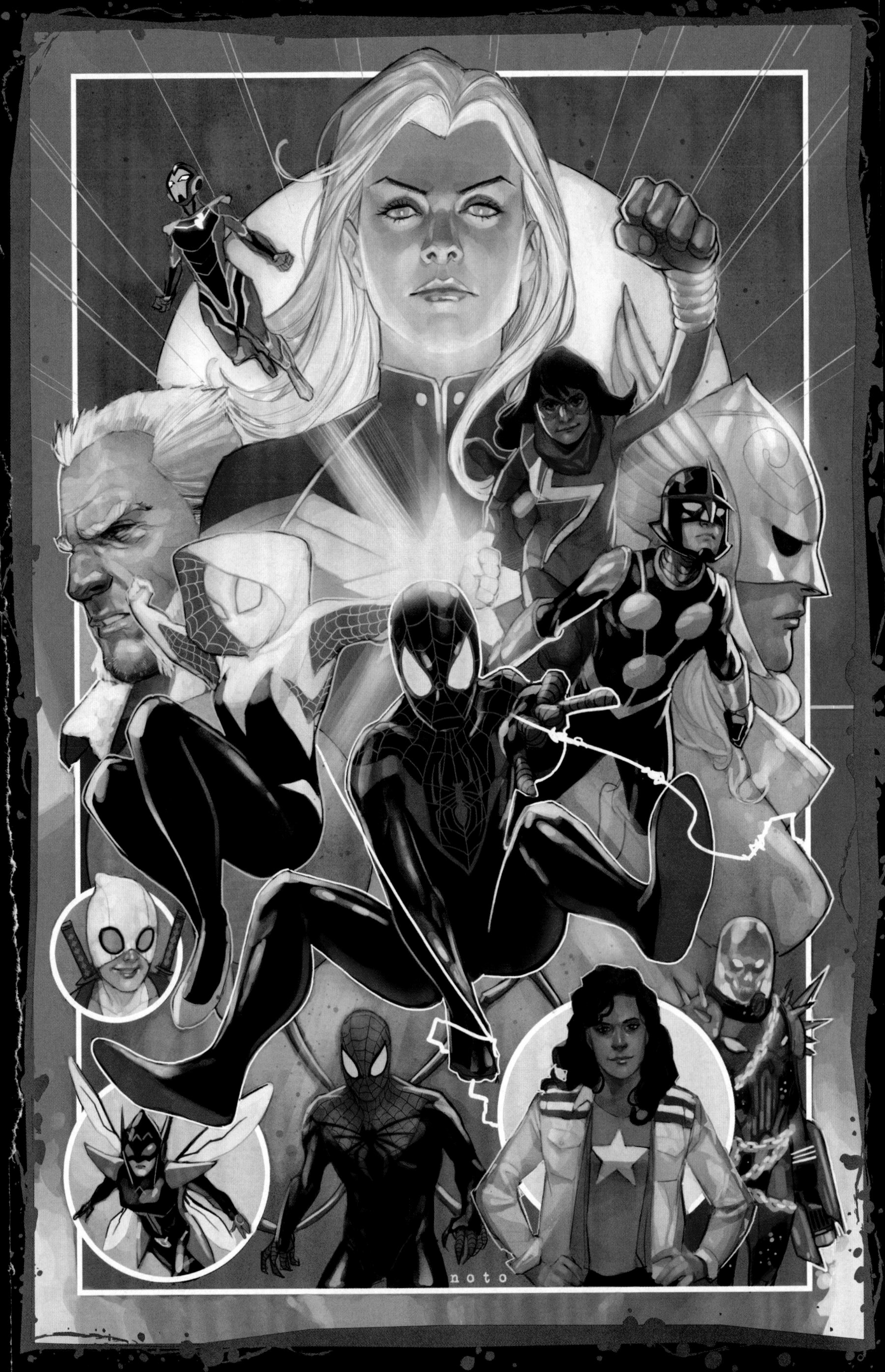
noto

#10 MARVEL 80TH VARIANT BY **PHIL NOTO**

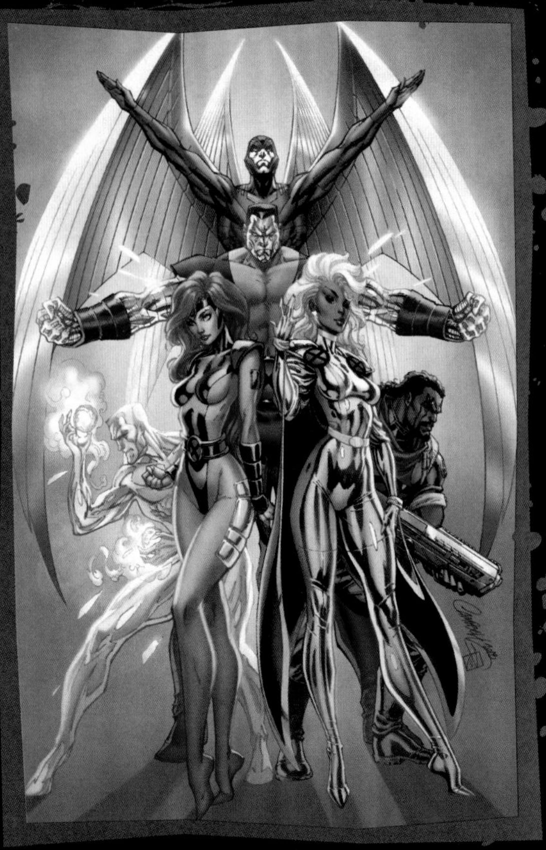

#8 UNCANNY X-MEN VARIANT
BY **J. SCOTT CAMPBELL**

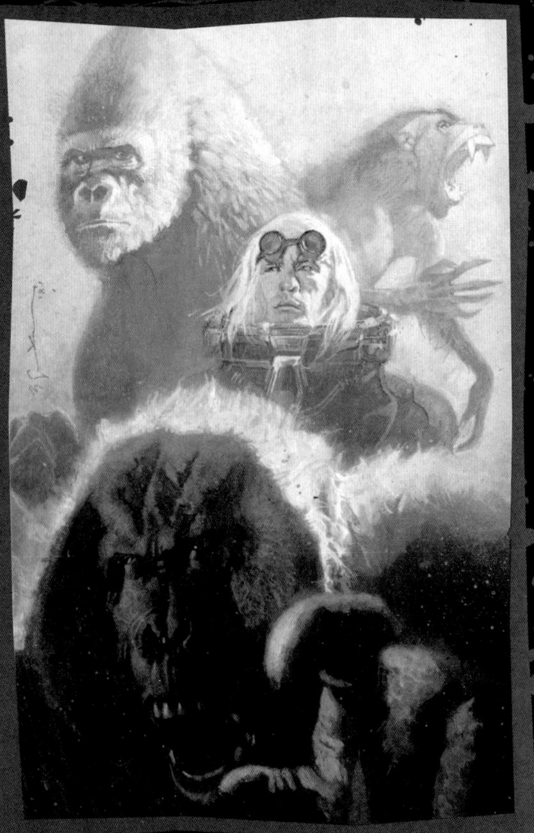

#9 FANTASTIC FOUR VILLAINS VARIANT
BY **BILL SIENKIEWICZ**